AGAINST FASHION

The MIT Press Cambridge, Massachusetts London, England

AGAINST FASHION

FASHION

Clothing as Art, 1850–1930   **Radu Stern**

Originally published as *A Contre-Courant/Gegen den Strich*, © 1992 Radu Stern

© 2004 Massachusetts Institute of Technology

This book was set in Syntax and Memphis by Graphic Composition, Inc.

Printed and bound in the United States of America.
Library of Congress Cataloging-in-Publication Data

Stern, Radu, 1951–
  [A contre-courant. English]
  Against fashion : clothing as art, 1850–1930 / Radu Stern.
      p. cm.
  Includes bibliographical references and index.
   ISBN 0-262-19493-7 (hc. : alk. paper)
   1. Fashion and art—History—20th century. 2. Fashion and art—History—19th century. 3. Costume design—History—20th century. 4. Costume design—History—19th century.
I. Title.

GT523 .S7413 2004
391—dc21

                              2003042000

10 9 8 7 6 5 4 3 2 1

Illustration credits are found on page 189.

CONTENTS

Acknowledgments **viii**

AGAINST FASHION: THE AVANT-GARDE AND CLOTHING

Fashion and Modernity **2**

Romanticism: From Eccentricity to Artistic Dress **4**

Rational, Artistic, and Aesthetic Dress in England **5**

Henry van de Velde and Germany **11**

Klimt and the Wiener Werkstätte **23**

Futurism and Dress **29**

The Russian Avant-Garde and Dress **45**

Sonia Delaunay **63**

Notes **69**

TEXTS

Elizabeth Cady Stanton The New Dress **80**

Amelia Bloomer Dress Reform **82**

E. W. Godwin A Lecture on Dress (1868) **83**

George H. Darwin Development in Dress **96**

Walter Crane Of the Progress of Taste in Dress in Relation to Art Education **105**

Oscar Wilde Slaves of Fashion **111**

Oscar Wilde Woman's Dress **113**

Oscar Wilde More Radical Ideas upon Dress Reform **115**

Oscar Wilde The Relation of Dress to Art: A Note in Black and White on Mr Whistler's Lecture **120**

Josef Hoffmann The Individual Dress **122**

Henry van de Velde The Artistic Improvement of Women's Clothing **125**

Henry van de Velde A New Art Principle in Modern Women's Clothing **137**

Friedrich Deneken Artistic Dress and Personalized Dress **143**

Eduard Josef Wimmer-Wisgrill On the Becoming of Fashion **148**

Lilly Reich Questions of Fashion **151**

Giacomo Balla Male Futurist Dress: A Manifesto   155

Giacomo Balla The Antineutral Dress: A Manifesto   157

Volt (Vincenzo Fani) Futurist Manifesto of Women's Fashion   160

F. T. Marinetti, Francesco Monarchi, Enrico Frampolini, and Mino Somenzi The
    Futurist Manifesto of the Italian Hat   162

Ernesto Thayaht The Aesthetics of Dress: Sunny Fashion, Futurist Fashion   164

Ernesto Thayaht and Ruggero Michahelles Manifesto for the Transformation of
    Male Clothing   167

Renato di Bosso and Ignazio Scurto The Futurist Manifesto of the Italian Tie   170

Varst (Varvara Stepanova) Present-Day Dress—Production Clothing   172

Nadezhda Lamanova Concerning Contemporary Dress   174

Nadezhda Lamanova The Russian Fashion   177

Aleksandra Exter The Constructivist Dress   178

Guillaume Apollinaire The Fortnight Review: The Reformers of Dress   181

Blaise Cendrars On Her Dress She Has a Body   182

Sonia Delaunay The Influence of Painting on Fashion   183

Sonia Delaunay Artists and the Future of Fashion   186

Illustration Credits   189

Selected Bibliography   198

Index   202

ACKNOWLEDGMENTS

I would like to thank Professor Patricia Cunningham, Professor Bettina Friedl, and Professor Dan Simovici, who supplied valuable information.

I was greatly assisted by Kerrith McKenzie in preparing the manuscript. Alice Falk did terrific work on its editing.

Special thanks are due to Rosmarie Lippuner, who was the first person who developed an interest in this project.

Finally, I owe a great debt of gratitude to my publisher, Roger Conover, who made many pertinent suggestions as to style and content.

AGAINST FASHION

THE AVANT-GARDE AND CLOTHING

FASHION AND MODERNITY

Under the banner of the battle against Eurocentrism, some cultural critics have recently tried to argue that fashion is not a purely Western phenomenon.[1] Though one can emphasize that cultures in other parts of the world have also experienced an evolution in clothing, it is Procrustean to define fashion as simply any type of change in dress style.[2] As an offspring of emerging European capitalism, from which it cannot be separated,[3] fashion, strictly speaking, did not exist before the second half of the fourteenth century. Gilles Lipovetsky, the author of an influential cultural study of the topic, describes fashion history as being divided into two periods: one from the second half of the fourteenth century until, roughly, 1850, and another from 1850 on. According to him, the second period in the history of fashion is, without doubt, essentially different from all previous developments: "Fashion as we understand it today emerged during the latter half of the nineteenth century." This "one hundred years' fashion" is described by Lipovetsky as "more than a fashion, it is a metaphor for the advent of modern, bureaucratic societies."[4]

From Lipovetsky's perspective, Thorstein Veblen's classical assumption of "dress as an expression of pecuniary culture" or the neo-Marxist "distinction" theory of Pierre Bourdieu cannot be accepted.[5] Lipovetsky squarely rejects the notion that "fashion's fickleness has its place and its ultimate truth in the existence of class rivalries, in the competitive struggles for prestige that occur among the various layers and factions of the social body." From the moment one keeps one's distance from and resists the spell of Bourdiean "distinction" as an intellectual model of thought, one realizes that such statements not only fail to explain much but also become "an obstacle to a historical understanding of the phenomenon."[6]

Instead of considering fashion as a simple "sign of class ambition," Lipovetsky sees it as one of the signals that announce "the end of the traditional world." Indeed, the removal of "the heavy artillery of social class, of the dialectics of social distinction and class pretensions," enables one to realize that "modern cultural meanings and values, in particular those that elevate newness and the expression of human individuality to a position of dignity, have played a preponderant role."[7] Instead of believing that fashion was invented by the textile industry to artificially create markets in an attempt to exploit its new capacities of production, one might wonder whether the industrial growth was not just a response to the demand generated by the new valorization of modernity. Fashion, therefore, is not merely any kind of change in dress style: it is a particular type of change indissolubly linked to modernity and the pursuit of the New. In this light, fashion appears to be not just a consequence of capitalism but one of the factors that contributed to its rise. Thus, according to one follower of Lipovetsky, "we must greatly expand our conception of Fashion as the major force for shaping the forms of contemporary social experience[.]"[8]

It is precisely in the field of modernity that artists were confronted with fashion. It is not by chance that the Baudelairean conceptual construction of modernity, of "a rational and historical theory of Beauty as opposed to a theory of a unique and absolute Beauty," begins with an evocation of fashion prints. The poet of *Les fleurs du mal* had grasped the full importance that a theoretical analysis of fashion could have for the debate over the aesthetic doctrine of his time. For Baudelaire, the essential question is whether "fashion should be considered a symptom of the taste for an ideal lingering on in the human brain above all that is crude, mundane, and vile brought by the natural life, as a sublime deformation of nature, or *rather as a constant and repeated attempt to reform nature*" (italics mine).[9]

This excerpt from *Curiosités esthétiques* clearly shows Baudelaire's use of the historicity of fashion as arguing against historicism in art, as disproving the idea of an eternal and immutable Beauty. The historicity of fashion backed up the idea of Beauty as a historical variable, as an ever-evolving concept, which would necessarily make artists abandon historicism and develop an interest in modern life.

However, after Baudelaire, the debate over fashion only became more intense. It involved controversies over fundamental issues in the art theory and aesthetics of the second half of the nineteenth century, including the abolition of the traditional hierarchy between "major" and "minor" arts, a questioning of the difference in "status" of artists and craftsmen, and the artist's wish to go beyond the traditional boundaries of art. For many artists at the end of the nineteenth century and the first half of the twentieth, dress design was something far too important to be left to couturiers alone. The historical avant-gardes would appropriate dress design as a privileged field in which the artist could overstep the limits of "pure" art and act directly on daily life.

These artists' dress proposals are very diverse in terms of style, but they all proceed from a common will to reject "official" fashion, refusing its mercantile logic and striving to replace it by a utopian "antifashion."

ROMANTICISM: FROM ECCENTRICITY TO ARTISTIC DRESS

As one might expect, the first important reaction against an established fashion came from Romanticism. According to Théophile Gautier, the French dress scene around 1830 was divided between bourgeois *grisâtres* and Romantic *flamboyants*.[1] However, this Romantic quest for the unusual or the gaudy was more than just a way of distancing oneself from the bourgeois. The sartorial individualism of the Romantics made them conspicuous and put in question one basic principle of conventional fashion—namely, its uniformity. For Louis Magron, "the true Romantic, the *abracadabrant* individual, does not make any concession. He does not acquiesce to an accepted fashion, he creates his own. Instead of resembling everyone else, he aspires to be just himself."[2]

Consequently, in their quest for individuality Romantic artists and writers adopted eccentric outfits, such as the famous red waistcoat of Théophile Gautier or Eugène Devéria's hats *à la Rubens,* and began to be interested in dress. Quoted mostly for its defense of the crinoline, Gautier's text *De la mode* began by asking "why the art of clothing is abandoned entire with the whim of tailors and dressmakers, in a civilization where the dress is of great importance, since, in consequence of the ideals, morals and climate, the naked one never appears to with it?"[3] Too important to be left to the clothing trade, dress should become an artistic concern.

RATIONAL, ARTISTIC, AND AESTHETIC DRESS IN ENGLAND

The French Romantic refusal of fashion, based principally on individual eccentricity, could not have a widespread or significant social impact. While the first attempts at dress reform emerged on the other side of the Atlantic, the American phenomenon of Bloomerism was also limited to a relatively small circle.[1] In 1857, Amelia Bloomer herself gave up her revolutionary bloomers for the fashionable crinoline.

The first systematic offensive against fashion, however, took place in England around 1870. There, clothing was a major subject of interest; books such as Mary Merrifield's *Dress as a Fine Art* (1854), Margaret Oliphant's *Dress* (1878), and Mary Eliza Haweis's *The Art of Dress* (1879) were very successful and many magazines and newspapers published regular dress columns.

Militants came from various, and even opposite, ranks: the escapism of the Arts and Crafts movement or of the Pre-Raphaelites was the antithesis of the practicality of feminists and hygienists, and the moral condemnation of fashion by conservatives was diametrically opposed to the amoral stand of Aestheticism.

The attempt by members of the Arts and Crafts movement to reform society through the decorative arts necessarily included clothes. In William Morris's eyes, "the lesser arts" had the power to change people's lives. In advocating the "simplicity of life, begetting simplicity of taste," Morris was in complete agreement with John Ruskin, who, several years later, would ask Miss Bintog "never to increase the *labour* of dressmaking unnecessarily" and "not to use costly garnitures," which "usually . . . are in bad taste, as well as expensive."[2] In the 1890s, Godfrey and Ethel Blount tried to apply Ruskin's and Morris's ideas as they began to produce simple cheap and "unusually comfortable" clothes with the Haslemere Peasant Industries. This British tradition of simplicity in dress would be continued by the Fabian socialist Edward Carpenter, who would militate for a simple and "natural" life consisting of swimming in lakes and sunbathing, wearing simple clothes, and making sandals.

In order to put his theories into practice, Morris probably designed around 1865 a number of loose-fitting dresses for his wife, Jane,[3] which strongly contrasted in their simplicity with the devilishly complicated decoration of contemporary fashion. Many other artists' wives were to imitate Jane Morris's example. In accordance with William Morris's famous golden rule, "Have nothing in your houses that you do not know to be useful or believe to be beautiful,"[4] clothes had to be both functional and beautiful at the same time. The constant changes imposed by fashion had to be rejected because they did not obey any functional logic; their resulting "absurdity" prevented them from being beautiful. Clothing, Morris argued, should be designed on the basis of an intimate relationship with the human body rather than being dictated by fashion's whims:

Garments should veil the human form, and neither caricature it, nor obliterate its lines: the body should be draped, and neither sewn up in a sack, nor stuck in the middle of a

box: drapery, properly managed, is not a dead thing, but a living one, expressive of the endless beauty of motion; and if this be lost, half the pleasure of the eyes in common life is lost.[5]

But the paramount reproach against fashion was its mercantile nature:

Indeed if it were but ridding ourselves, the well-to-do people, of this mountain of rubbish that would be something worth doing: things which everybody knows are of no use; the very capitalists know well that there is no genuine healthy demand for them, and they are compelled to foist them off on the public by stirring up a strange feverish desire for petty excitement, the outward token of which is known by the conventional name of fashion—a strange monster born of the vacancy of the lives of rich people, and the eagerness of competitive Commerce to make the most of the huge crowd of workmen whom it breeds as unregarded instruments for what is called the making of money.[6]

The essence of fashion was commercialism, and Morris deeply regretted that modern civilization prevented art from having anything to do with clothing.[7] Although he once wrote that he lacked the courage "even to suggest a rebellion against these sartorial laws,"[8] it is obvious that the eradication of fashion was necessarily on Morris's social agenda. A new way of approaching the design of clothing was essential in his endeavor to achieve a moral reform of society, and this line of thought greatly influenced artists of the following generation who were interested in dress, like Henry van de Velde.

Other British artists strongly held similar opinions. In 1868, well before William Morris, the architect and designer E. W. Godwin had already expressed his dissatisfaction with contemporary fashion:

There is no such thing now-a-days as contentment in dress, for is [sic] perchance a becoming hat, a graceful mantle or an artistic serviceable coat be approved by the world this season it must be given up next season. No amount of gracefulness or appropriateness being powerful enough to stay the restless hand of fickle fashion.[9]

Godwin identified three main reasons for this deplorable situation: the variability of modern fashion, the wide difference between the male and female costume, and the absence of color. One consequence of the difference between male and female clothing was that men "have been forced by fashion to give up all claim to the richer materials and to encase themselves in gloomy monotony of broad-cloth." The absence of color, he argued, made English crowds look dull and gray "owing to the preponderance of black and white." But Godwin's first reason was undoubtedly the most important: "The changeableness of 19th century fashion is perhaps not only the greatest evil, but the parent of all the other evils in modern costume with which we have to contend."[10] Needless to say, to contest change in fashion was to deny fashion's raison d'être. Sensible and beautiful clothing "would have no chance so long as there exists that passionate longing for mere novelty which is one of the great curses of modern society in each and all its phases."[11] Although dress had to be functional—that is, designed in accordance with the imperatives of health and the climate[12]—it should also be beautiful. In his *Ethics of Dust* (1865), Ruskin specifically asked his readers "to consider every ill-dressed woman or child as a personal disgrace."[13] For Godwin, the solution was to be found in transferring the responsibility for creating dress from milliners and dressmakers to poets, painters, sculptors, and architects, who alone were able "to labour for the good through the action of the Beautiful."[14] Illogical fashionable clothing had to be replaced by artistic dress. Godwin considered dress design to be as important as his architectural practice:

As Architecture is the art and science of building, so Dress is the art and science of clothing. To construct and decorate a covering for the human body that shall be beautiful and healthy is as important as to build a shelter for it when so covered that shall be beautiful and healthy. . . . Health can never be perfect so long as your eye is troubled with ugliness.[15]

The influence of Godwin's ideas was considerable; those affected included several major players in the field of aesthetic dress, such as Oscar Wilde. As Lionel Lambourne has noted, "many of Wilde's ideas on interior decoration and dress, which were advanced in his lecture towns, had been adapted from Godwin's own pronouncements."[16]

The fellow artists who were most interested in dress were the Pre-Raphaelites. The changeable nature of fashion was a problem for painters because, as one historian asks, "what would infuriate an artist more than that his picture might seem out of date, merely because the sitter's clothes had dated?"[17] In order to avoid such problems, Dante Gabriel Rossetti shifted from accurately reproducing medieval or early Renaissance costumes in his paintings to creating nonfashionable timeless clothes for his models.[18] Initially reserved for his sitters, this type of garment was soon worn outside Rossetti's studio by his wife, Elizabeth Siddal, the first muse of the Pre-Raphaelites, and by other women in their circle, such as Jane Morris and John Ruskin's wife, Effie.

Influenced by Rossetti, other painters and sculptors—including Thomas Armstrong, Henry Holiday, William Holman Hunt, and George Frederic Watts—became interested in dress. Holman Hunt, for example, designed the wedding dress of the actress Ellen Terry when she married G. F. Watts in 1864,[19] and Henry Holiday became the editor of *Aglaia,* the journal of the Healthy and Artistic Dress Society.

Concomitant with developments in artistic dress were fierce attacks on fashion by hygienists.[20] Partisans of both rational and artistic dress wanted to achieve a new harmonious resonance between clothing and the human body. Artificial, fashionable body constructions, such as the corset and the crinoline, were rejected in favor of a type of clothing that was more respectful of the "natural" body. But while the first group, which eventually founded the Rational Dress Society in June 1881 under the presidency of Viscountess Florence Harberton and the vice presidency of Mrs. Emily M. King, initially meant by this to protect the anatomy of the body from fashionable aggressive practices such as tight-lacing, the artistic group's idea of the "natural" body was based on classical Greek proportions. This artistically idealized approach finally influenced the hygienists, and dress reformers began "distinguishing between 'civilized' Greek views of the body and 'atavistic' Asiatic attitudes."[21] Since the classical Greek standard was accepted as "natural," strange comparisons between photographs of the deformed bodies of victims of the corset and of a "healthy" Venus de Milo followed and were often used in the Dress Reform literature.[22] Paradoxically, the medieval revival advocated by the Pre-Raphaelites and the Greek revival of the Aesthetes were taken as the basic approaches to redesigning the modern body.

Classical Greek clothing was thought by both G. F. Watts and E. W. Godwin to be the true model to follow. Similarly venerating Grecian attire, the dress arbiter Mary Eliza Haweis declared "the finest costume ever worn" to be that on the Greek clay figures in the British Museum.[23] Oscar Wilde, however, warned against the mere imitation of classical Greek models, although he believed that "Greek costume is perfectly applicable to our climate, our country and our century" and preferred high-waisted gowns in the Greek style.[24] What had to be done was to apply "the principles, the laws of Greek dress" to modern dress design. In practice, this meant that suspending garments from the hips should be abandoned in favor of suspension from the shoulders, because "it is from the shoulders, and from the shoulders only, that all garments should be hung." A synthesis between healthy and artistic principles was needed:

I am not proposing any antiquarian revival of an ancient costume, but trying merely to point out the right laws of dress, laws which are dictated by art and not by archaeology, by science and not by fashion; and just as the best work of art in our days is that which combines classic grace with absolute reality, so from a continuation of the Greek principles of beauty with the German principles of health will come, I feel certain, the costume of the future.[25]

Drawing heavily on Ruskin's, Godwin's, and Morris's writings, Wilde developed his own antifashion stand in his lectures and articles for the *Pall Mall Gazette* and the *Woman's World.* Frank Harris, his biographer, recalled that he had once said that dress reform is "a second and greater reformation" than that of Luther.[26] In a celebrated formula, Wilde defined fashion as "a form of ugliness so intolerable that we have to alter it every six months." In order to fight ugliness, "one should either be a work of art, or wear a work of art."[27] While each dress had to be artistic, it also had to be rationally designed. Nothing that was not rational could be beautiful. According to Wilde, "*The value of the dress is simply that every separate article of it expresses a law.*"[28] For dress to achieve this, fashion had to be abolished, since it was ugly, irrational, impractical, and uncomfortable: "Fashion's motto is: *Il faut souffrir pour être belle;* but the motto of art and of commonsense is: *Il faut être bête pour souffrir.*"[29]

Dressmakers were the "slaves of fashion"; consequently, they had to be replaced by more-educated persons who were truly qualified and able to create: "The ordinary milliner, with her lack of taste and lack of knowledge, her foolish fashions and her feeble inventions, will have to make way for the scientific and artistic dress designer.[30] Undoubtedly, Wilde believed himself to be such a person, as he designed the wedding dress of his wife, Constance. During his famous tour of the United States, his eccentric clothing created a scandal. His aesthetic poet's attire—dark-purple velvet coat, silk black or brown breeches, lace cuffs, and silk top hat—became a legend.[31]

It is obvious that Wilde attempted both to be a work of art and, at the same time, to wear works of art. Those people whose lives were not aesthetic enough to transform them into living works of art could nevertheless try to achieve the latter. Dress as a work of art was a central element in the Aesthetic Movement's attempt to introduce beauty into every aspect of life. Vaguely medieval and largely inspired by paintings, Aesthetic dresses escaped any influence from "official" Victorian fashion. Sometimes designed by artists, they were often made by women with artistic ambitions; they were thus the first examples of either artistic or individual and personalized clothing. These Aesthetic dresses were to be seen at the openings of art exhibitions, such as the celebrated *Private Views* at the newly opened Grosvenor Gallery, which was supposed to be a modern Aesthetic alternative to the traditional Royal Academy:

There were quaint, beautiful, extraordinary costumes walking about—ultra-aesthetics, artistic-aesthetics, aesthetics that made up their minds to be daring, and suddenly gave way in some important point—put a frivolous bonnet on the top of a grave and flowing garment that Albert Dürer might have designed for a mantle.[32]

Aesthetic dresses were satirized in countless articles and even in novels, but the most celebrated satire appeared in Gilbert and Sullivan's *Patience,* a comic opera in which Oscar Wilde was lampooned under the name of Bunthorne. Regularly, these audacious garments were pitilessly ridiculed by George du Maurier in the popular magazine *Punch;* ironically, these cartoons are now the main iconographic source for Aesthetic dress. However, not only the conservative partisans of fashionable clothing but also several artists criticized this attire. The best-known attack came from James Whistler, who, from an extreme "art for art's sake" perspective, denied in his famous lecture "Ten O'Clock" the very possibility of dress being considered artistic. In his opinion, art could never permeate life, as the Aesthetes claimed, and should never leave its ivory tower. To pretend it could do so was "blasphemous," denying the purity of art, and the pretty attempts of dress design could never "claim cousinship with the artist." Whistler concluded with the assertion "Costume is not dress. And the wearers of wardrobes may not be doctors of taste,"[33] an obvious reference to Oscar Wilde.

The Aesthetic dresses were worn mainly by the cultural elite. They were sold in exclusive places such as the famous shop Liberty's, founded in 1875 by Arthur Lasenby Liberty on Regent Street, which soon became the mecca of Aesthetic attire. E. W. Godwin, who was hired in 1884 to direct the dress department, made Aesthetic dresses readily available.[34]

The last attempt to produce artistic dress in England before the First World War was made by the Bloomsbury group and the Omega Workshops.[35] Opened in July 1913 at 33 Fitzroy Square in London under the direction of the artist and critic Roger Fry, the Omega Workshops sold, among many other objects, artistic dresses that were designed mainly by the painter Vanessa Bell. These dresses, cut in Omega fabrics with abstract patterns, were very different from the fashionable outfits of the time. Their geometrical shapes and their Cubist-influenced colors horrified many potential clients; they appealed mostly to fellow artists, such as the painter Nina Hamnett, who wore a Vanessa Bell dress in a portrait painted by Roger Fry. The bankruptcy of the Omega Workshops in 1919 put an end to the production of this experimental clothing.

HENRY VAN DE VELDE AND GERMANY

After having completed the embroidery *La Veillée des anges,* first exhibited in 1893 at the ninth *Salon des XX* in Brussels,[1] Henry van de Velde suddenly decided to abandon painting in favor of the decorative arts. As he acknowledged, this spectacular decision was influenced by his discovery of John Ruskin's and William Morris's writings. He was following Arts and Crafts' principles, and the main reasons for van de Velde's conversion were not just aesthetic but also moral and social: "The evolution of ideas and of the conditions of social life cannot make do solely with painting and statues. It is madness to consider only these for our material existence and it is blindness to believe they can satisfy all the art needs of our time."[2]

Limiting oneself to painting or sculpture meant being confined in the ivory tour of art for art's sake, a confinement that was obviously antisocial. The artist's mission was moral before being aesthetic, and its fulfillment required leaving the ivory tower for the real world. As a good disciple of Ruskin and Morris, van de Velde chose the decorative arts as the privileged field in which aesthetics and ethics can and should unite. Paintings and marble sculptures are unique pieces that decorate the sumptuous houses of the happy few. It is only in the decorative arts, which are more largely distributed, that the artist could break out of his confinement and practice his social responsibility. Fascinated by the aesthetic eugenics of Arts and Crafts, van de Velde was convinced that one could improve the human race through art. Living in an artistically created environment would necessarily make humans better. The ultimate goal of the battle against ugliness, "one of the scourges against which humanity has to defend itself," was moral redemption.

In 1895, van de Velde got an unexpected opportunity to realize his ideals. The project of his villa Bloemenverf in Uccle, near Brussels, was more ambitious than just building a residence for his family. Old public buildings—the temple, the church, the parliament, the city hall, or the court of justice—no longer had any meaning for him. Disappointed by society, he did not believe anymore in the possibility of collective redemption. Redemption could only be individual. Instead of expecting regeneration from building a new cathedral, "it is in the homes of each one of us that we can find the generating ideas behind all the monuments to which, rather naively, we have entrusted the idea of symbolizing the articles of our faith either in God, justice, or the community."[3]

Following the model of the celebrated Red House, built in 1859 by Philip Webb for William Morris in Bexleyheath, Kent, the Bloemenverf villa was designed as an example. It was to be a pedagogical instrument to be used in bringing up his own children, in whom "we want to inculcate true, healthy and moral ideas from their earliest childhood," and a model for the art of living for humanity as a whole. In building his home, the artist fulfilled his vocation as apostle: at last, he could prove to all the virtues of education through art. Conceived as a center for the dissemination of beauty, the Bloemenverf villa had to be protected from the virus of the surrounding ugliness: "we committed ourselves to ensuring that no ugly or corruptly inspired object . . . would dirty our children's eyes."[4]

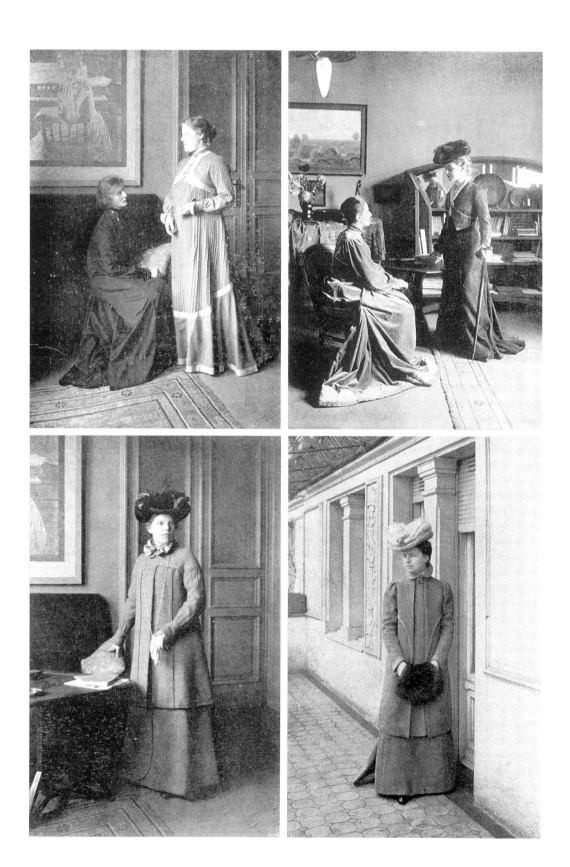

Mrs. E. B. wearing a dress created by Henry van de Velde, 1901–1902.

Henry van de Velde—Afternoon and street dresses, 1901–1902.

Maria van de Velde in a dress by Henry van de Velde, 1901–1902.

Henry van de Velde—Street dress, 1901–1902.

As he considered the obvious decline in quality of the products that contemporary industry could produce, van de Velde reached the same conclusion as his mentor William Morris—the only way to achieve the quality he desired was to produce the objects himself: "nothing . . . will enter our home except what I have conceived and designed myself."[5] According to his vision, his house had to symbolize the long-awaited synthesis of the arts. Obsessed by the idea of *Gesamtkunstwerk,* the total work of art, van de Velde wanted everything in Bloemenwerf to be coordinated: every object was to be created as a part of the whole design, whose harmony should be expressed in the slightest detail. Every element—from furniture to cutlery or kitchen utensils, from toilets to wallpaper or the shape of the handrail—had to express the unity of the whole.

The clothes of Maria Sèthe, whom van de Velde married in 1894,[6] were, of course, part of this global approach. In order that the visual coherence of the whole might be respected, the artist's wife had to pay the price: "my wife will wear toilettes made after my designs." The contrary would have been unthinkable: "In decor like that of the Bloemenwerf, the presence of a woman dressed by some haute couture firm would have been an insult. I do not remember any occasion in which my wife and I had to suffer a stain on the healthy and honest atmosphere of morality which was ours."[7]

It followed that Mrs. van de Velde's clothes were treated like any other object in the house, and it was said that van de Velde went so far in the refinement of this ideal as to match the color of her dresses with that of the vegetable puree served at their table. The simplicity of his designs was in total opposition to the ruffles and frills of fashionable dress at the time, and the contrast shocked their contemporaries. On a visit to the van de Velde's home, Toulouse-Lautrec had been outraged to be received by Mrs. van de Velde in what he believed to be her dressing gown, considering it a sign of gross disrespect toward him.[8]

The same principles were applied to another project of van de Velde's, the interior decoration designed in 1907 for the villa Hohenhof. The villa was the residence of Karl Ernst Osthaus, the art collector who had founded the Folkgang Museum in Hagen: "woe to the lady who enters such a room in a dress that is not artistically suitable."[9] To preserve the unity of the design, Osthaus's wife Gertrud was supposed to wear van de Velde's dresses.[10] The exaggeration in the *Gesamtkunstwerk* approach infuriated Adolf Loos, who, in a celebrated parody, ridiculed van de Velde's intransigence: an owner was scolded by the architect who built his home because he dared to wear slippers that had been coordinated with the bedroom . . . in the living room![11]

Van de Velde's example was followed by other famous modern architects, such as Frank Lloyd Wright, who designed most of the dresses of his wife, Catherine Tobin Wright.[12] He provided the same service for at least two clients' wives, designing a dress for Mrs. Coonley and a gown for Isabella Martin, the wife of one of his major patrons, Darwin D. Martin.[13] Both dresses were coordinated with the decoration of their respective dining rooms: as Wright's son recalled, "The Avery Coonley estate was one of Papa's most complete creations. He designed everything in and about the house including table service and linens—even some of Mrs. Coonley's dresses to harmonize with the interiors."[14]

The one exception to this formal totalitarianism was van de Velde's own clothes, which he did not design himself but which were instead cut for him by a good *faiseur.* That exception was justified by his belief that men's clothing was far more rational than women's clothing. This is so because "we men have less patience, and this trait of character has prevented tailors from exaggerating their inventions."[15] Therefore, since it was less often conceived as an instrument of seduction, men's dress was judged to be less subject to fashion and more a result of the search for greater convenience and practicality.[16] Indeed, whereas men's dress was "less dependent on merchants' opportunism," women were truly the victims of fashion. A woman who wants to appear attractive "is able to bear physical discomfort in order to please." Too passive, she is easily manipulated by the couturiers, being nothing but "docile and malleable" material in their hands.[17] The only way out lay in van de Velde's hope "to see women regain their self-confidence and finally recognize the contemptuous and unscrupulous way in which the sovereign masters of *haute couture* exploit their weak nature, fully realizing that as soon as she is confronted with finery, she loses her head and submits herself to the most foolish accoutrements."[18]

"Fashion is flighty, unfaithful, coquettish, and naturally delusive."[19] It is morally to blame, as it is primarily motivated by profit. However, it is also to blame from an aesthetic point of view. Its renewal is only apparent, affecting mere trifles, aspects of minor importance, through changes of silly details such as the width of skirts, the number of flounces, or the pleating. Since fashion is essentially immoral, being greedy, and ridiculous, because of its superficiality, it cannot be radically changed. Therefore, the only solution was an attempt to destroy the system of fashion itself, which, in van de Velde's eyes, was the most important obstacle to authentic creation:

The couturiere's best argument—that "this is fashion"—does not arouse the slightest protest or complaint. Fashion is the eye of Argus that surveys its own world of show. It is the great enemy that has caused the decline of all the decorative arts and has even contributed to the degeneration of "grand" art.[20]

However, van de Velde's theories had little practical impact in his own country, and in neighboring Holland the interest seemed to be limited to a few fellow artists.[21] Undoubtedly, Belgium was a territory too scanty for van de Velde's ambitions. It was his career in Germany that gave him a real opportunity to wage his war against fashion. There, his antifashion theories were more than favorably received for many reasons.

First, the recently unified German nation was experiencing the happy and promising years of the *Gründerzeit*—the time of the founders, the epoch of the economic boom following the 1870 victory at Sedan. One element of this economic and cultural dynamism was a great interest in *Kunstgewerbe* (applied art) and its relation to industry.

Second, Germany was the favorite place for the dress reform that had been initiated by feminists and hygienists. While Bloomerism had been considered a passing eccentricity in the United States and the impact of similar Pre-Raphaelite or Arts and Crafts' efforts had been limited to sophisticated persons belonging to the upper classes or the artistic world in the United Kingdom, it is undoubtedly in Germany that the *Reformkleid-ung* (Dress Reform) movement was the strongest. During the Internationaler Kongress für Frauenwerke und Frauenbestrebungen (International Congress for Women's Welfare and Endeavors), held in September 1896 in Berlin, the matter was thoroughly discussed. As a consequence of this debate, some of the delegates founded the Verein für die Ver-besserung der Frauenkleidung (Association for the Improvement of Women's Dress), an association that would be far more active and influential than its British counterpart, the Rational Dress Society founded in 1881. The public interest was strong enough to per-suade Wertheim's Department Store in Berlin to open a dress reform department in 1903.

For supporters of the *Reformkleidung,* fashion was a pernicious phenomenon that had to be abolished.[22] To begin with its economics, the yearly change in dress served only the interest of unscrupulous merchants who metamorphose women into spheres one year and spindles the next, generating useless spending that exhausted the savings of the German hausfrau. Next, fashion caused tension and resentment among different social classes. From an aesthetic point of view, fashion compelled women with different figures to submit to an identical mold, instead of selecting garments that were adapted to their individual anatomy. Moreover, fashion was unhealthy, because it imposed the use of the corset, the bête noire of dress reformers, who lashed out at its harmful effects on the fe-male body in countless books and articles.[23] Last but not least, the struggle against fash-ion closely matched the nationalist and chauvinistic trends of German society at the end of the nineteenth century. Because the anti-French feeling was still quite strong, to fight fashion was also, in a way, to fight the influence of Paris, the uncontested world capital of haute couture.

For Friedrich Deneken, fighting fashion was just another way of asserting *Deutschtum,* or Germanness, a struggle akin to the eradication of gallicisms in the Ger-man language. He wanted to abolish ornaments, spangles, and braids not only because they lacked taste but also because this French *pacotille* was contrary to the German spirit. He ridiculed German women who succumbed to the charms of French toilettes and who believed that trying to look Parisian made them in some way superior; contrasting the se-riousness of the typical *deutsche Frau* with the frivolity of French women could only rein-force German national identity.[24]

Deneken—a former assistant of Justus Brinckmann, the founder of the very influential Museum für Kunst und Gewerbe (Museum of Applied Arts) in Hamburg—was appointed in 1897 to be the first director of the brand-new Kaiser Wilhelm-Museum in Kre-feld. As an expression of his deep interest in the applied arts and in the relationship between art and industry, he organized a series of revolutionary exhibitions around these topics.

In 1900, the chosen subject was women's dress. This theme was of particular im-portance for Krefeld, a city where the textile industry was predominant. Furthermore, this exhibition was part of a more general endeavor to explore in a global way all fields in which art could be integrated into life. For Deneken, it was the continuation of a process in which dress was logically added to furniture, wallpaper, decorative objects, and books, which had already been approached by Arts and Crafts artists. The exhibition was a way

Marie Beyers de Graaff—"Reform"
dress, 1900s.

"Reform" dresses, about 1900.

DAS REFORMKLEID. Die Idee des heutigen Reformkleides entsprang einer natürlichen und künstlerischen Notwendigkeit. — Das Reformkleid ist künstlerisch durch die richtige Konstruktion und die erfinderische edle Handarbeit. Obige Kleider sind aus Tuch, das Jäckchen links Handweberei aus Schafwolle und Perlen von Frau Guttmann. Die Oberteile der unten stehenden Seidenkleider sind Handweberei von Fräulein Jutta Sicka aus Gold und Lilaseide; Ausführung sämtlicher Kleider durch den Salon Schwestern Flöge. Wien.

to pursue and complete their work. Many of the most important figures in German Art Nouveau, such as Margarete von Brauchitsch, Kurt Hermann, Franz August Otto Kruger, Bernhard Pankok, Richard Riemerschmid, and Hugo van der Woude, figured among the participants, but the star of the show was irrefutably the Belgian, Henry van de Velde: "The well-known art professional, Henry van de Velde, obsessed by 'a feeling of revolt against fashion and its collaborators,' was the first to announce the new renaissance of the art of dress."[25]

Exhibiting these dresses in the Kaiser Wilhelm-Museum represented a turning point in the perception of clothes. The museum's imprimatur brought about the awareness that dress could actually be a work of art: "From now on, shows of women's clothing will take their place among art exhibitions. Undoubtedly, we will begin to see clothing exhibited sometimes next to paintings and sculptures, as has recently been the case with other works of applied art."[26]

Alfred Mohrbutter—House dress, 1902–1903.

Alfred Mohrbutter—Silk dress, 1902–1903.

Wassily Kandinsky—Project for a dress, 1904.

Wassily Kandinsky—Project for a dress, 1904.

The exhibition was a great success and it was followed by similar shows—for instance, in Leipzig, Dresden, and Wiesbaden—and by a series of lectures that influenced other artists, like the architect Peter Behrens, to develop an interest in dress. Even Kandinsky, who tended to favor the idea that the applied arts were a minor field of creation, could not resist the temptation to design dresses for his lady friend at the time, the painter Gabrielle Münter.

Henry van de Velde exhibited six dresses designed for his wife, which were "one of the highpoints of the whole exhibition,"[27] and several dress projects. These designs were supposed to embody the ideal of *Künstlerkleid* (artistic dress), which for van de Velde was the only solution to the problem of dress. In his eyes, the *Reformkleidung* movement failed to eradicate fashion because of its lack of interest in beauty. The hygienic approach to clothing by the medical profession and the feminists made them miss the most important point, which was its aesthetic qualities. What is essential in a dress is the beauty of its structure. Fashion habitually concealed this, "having gone so far that it was no longer possible to see how a dress was made."[28] Just like the painters of the end of the

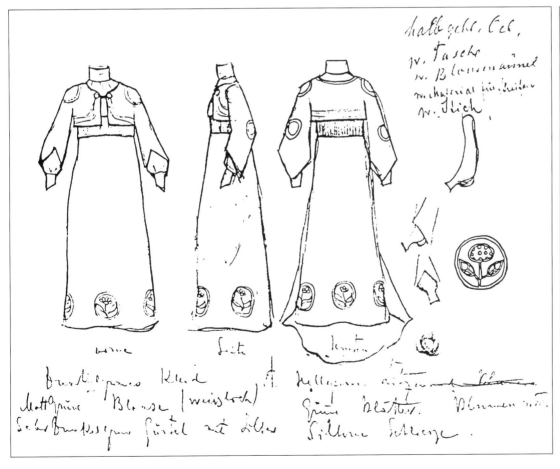

century who no longer concealed the compositional structure of their paintings, van de Velde asserted that the structure of dress should be made visible by apparent seams. As an architect, van de Velde felt that dress should be designed as rationally as a building.[29] In his lecture given in connection with the exhibition, he even proposed to the audience a thoroughly "rational" rereading of the history of dress in which the historical evolution of forms was explained according to Darwin's theory of the evolution of species.[30] It is ironic that several years before, Mary Haweis had used Darwin's theory of evolution as an argument in favor of the ornamentation of dress (a practice van de Velde was reluctant to accept): "The need of conspicuousness which Darwin tells us results in the survival of the fittest, it is at the root of this love of ornament, a healthy instinct not to be sneered at."[31]

Although he wrote that one should abandon all that is purely ornamental, van de Velde did not, in fact, rule out all ornament. In opposition to Adolf Loos, who believed that the only function of the decorative elements of woman's dress was to reinforce her sensuality and that when woman attained equal status with men through economic independence, "velvet and silk, flowers and ribbons will no longer have any effect and will disappear,"[32] van de Velde was convinced that ornament was indispensable. Nevertheless, ornamentation should not be applied in a decorative way; it had to be organic and underline the structure of dress. In practice, the sumptuous embroidery that van de Velde favored was placed at "strategic" places such as the hem, the neck, or the sleeves, in order to make the structure of the dress stand out. Van de Velde, who said that line was his demon, refused naturalistic ornamentation and favored abstract ornamentation, the only kind that could be adapted rationally to the form of the dress.

Convinced that it is possible to reconcile respect for individual character with a certain uniformity imposed by the need for harmony, van de Velde rejected the *Eigenkleid*,[33] the individual or personalized dress, in favor of the *Künstlerkleid:* "Actually, I almost think that all women could wear a really well-designed dress. If its beauty is based on the principles of its design and its ornamentation, then it will not lose anything if it is worn by Mrs. A rather than Mrs. B."[34] The uniformity created by fashion, he stated, should be rejected because not all women can adapt to the same cut or the same color. However, van de Velde praised the reasonable woman "who spontaneously agrees to sacrifice all individual dissonances and disparities to the unity and harmony of the whole." While the *Eigenkleid* could be tolerated at home, it could not be worn outside. On the streets of a modern city, our individuality disappears "because of the similarity of common conditions."[35]

The stylistic dictator of Bloemenwerf could not suppress his aesthetic pleasure watching a procession of people dressed in the same way, and the architect van de Velde dreamed about a possible extension of his *Gesamtkunstwerk* approach to the scale of a whole city. In a more modest way, Alfred Mohrbutter asserted that the uniform clothing of women in a choir would certainly improve the quality of their musical interpretation.[36] Thus, for both van de Velde and Mohrbutter, the sole solution would be to adopt artistic dress that could provide the individual and general harmony that only an artist could achieve. Nevertheless, one should not forget that the essential point in this search for

Peter Behrens—Visiting dress, 1902.

Peter Behrens—Visiting dress, 1902. Back view.

Henry van de Velde—Evening dress.

Anna Muthesius—Green silk dress.

perfect dress, liberated from the "despotism" of fashion, was "to rediscover the moral value,"[37] an essential requirement for the final reconciliation of art and life.

Later developments in artistic dress in Germany did not manage to attain the same degree of intensity as the Krefeld exhibition. The theoretical writings of Alfred Mohrbutter and Anna Muthesius were largely influenced by van de Velde, the Dress Reform philosophy, or both and did not offer any really new ideas.[38] Dress reform polemics had also become outmoded due to the new controversy between Hermann Muthesius's "type" (Typisierung) and van de Velde's "individuality," which was the central dispute of the newly founded Deutsche Werkbund.[39] If one leaves aside some minor contributions, like that of Bruno Rauecker,[40] dress was no longer a central issue for the Werkbund, and its debates increasingly focused on architecture and industrial design.

One exception was the dress, display and furniture designer Lilly Reich, one of the main Werkbund female personalities, who eventually become a member of its board of directors. Very concerned with dress, Reich attempted a synthesis between the development of clothing types, according to Muthesius's Typisierung theory, and the Eigenkleid. In a 1922 article,[41] Reich tried to find a compromise between clothes that were designed for large-scale industrial production and individual dress. Her idea was to personalize dresses cut from a similar pattern by using embroideries specific to each garment.[42] This type of advocacy was clearly influenced by contemporary architectural attempts to overcome the uniformity caused by standardization in building.

The last significant attempt to establish artistic dress in the 1910s Germany was the Modehaus Alfred-Marie, a fashion house opened in 1914 by the painter and dress designer Otto Ludwig Haas-Heye.[43] Although very successful, Haas-Heye's style was rejected by avant-garde personalities like Herwarth Walden, who believed it was too commercially oriented.

But the days of the German Künstlerkleid were numbered. The social conditions that followed Germany's defeat were less than favorable for the luxury firms such as Modehaus Alfred-Marie. The aesthetic of the new avant-garde trend of the twenties firmly rejected the Jugendstil's exuberance. Writing in 1924 for the Constructivist magazine G, the former Dadaist Raoul Hausmann adopted a primarily Functionalist approach.[44] He defined a suit as "a clothing object" and a hat as "a head covering." Accordingly, fashion was defined as "the function of the body made visible." However, even if the title of his article was "Fashion," these definitions were in fact antifashion. A suit designed in an absolutely rationalist way could never become obsolete and, therefore, would necessarily escape the system of fashion.

KLIMT AND THE WIENER WERKSTÄTTE

"Whatever is art is good" was a slogan that could be read in the *Ver Sacrum,* the famous publication of the Viennese Secession. This statement expressed the will of the *Jungen,* the young artists, to no longer accept the restrictive hierarchy that maintained a distinction between the major and minor arts. It arose not primarily from an abstract theory of art but mainly because the Modernist artists who lived during the Habsburg apogee, a period known as "the joyful apocalypse," considered the aesthetization of life to be their essential aspiration. To achieve this goal, the artist had to have a global vision of creation and should therefore be concerned with every aspect of life. Obsessed with the idea of *Gesamtkunstwerk,*[1] the Viennese avant-garde felt concern with the unity of the visual world, which they considered as a whole. If everything was to be directed by the artist, then obviously dress was part of the artistic realm.

Beyond any doubt, the most celebrated proponent of this view is Gustav Klimt, the leading artist of the Secession. He had, at least in part, opted out of the dominant trends of fashion by designing work and leisure dresses that soon became famous. These loose-fitting blue or brown robes looked more oriental than monastic. Curiously described as a mixture of "the oriental caftan and the Japanese No costume,"[2] Klimt's robes had in fact no connection with either. Adorned at the shoulders with applied arabesques very similar to those in his paintings, these garments expressed both Klimt's rejection of contemporary fashion and his search for an *Urkleid,* an imaginary primordial dress. Since they were designed as an archetypal model for all types of clothing, Klimt's robes were by far more essentially antifashion than a simple *Eigenkleid.* Undoubtedly influenced by Klimt, at least one of his friends, the poet and art critic Hermann Bahr, used to wear similar attire.[3]

Though one may not wholly agree with Elisabeth Rücker's assertion that "all [Klimt's] big portraits of ladies are at the same time documents of fashion,"[4] Klimt did more than paint extravagant dresses for his models. Like van de Velde, Behrens, Kandinsky, and many others,[5] Klimt was interested in the *Künstlerkleid* challenge and he designed some dresses for his companion Emilie Flöge.[6] Professionally concerned with dress and interested in life and dress reform, Flöge, together with her sisters Pauline and Helene, became the owner of one of the classiest haute couture salons in Vienna: the Schwestern Flöge, which opened on 1 July 1904 in the Casa Piccola on the posh Mariahilfenstrasse, with an interior designed by Josef Hoffmann and Koloman Moser.[7]

Although Emilie Flöge used a lot of embroidery inspired by traditional folklore for her commercial production, her own dresses, some of them designed by Klimt, were quite different. Very loose fitting, they contrasted sharply with the tight dresses in fashion at the time. They were cut from cloth printed with luxuriant lianas similar to those in Klimt's paintings or with black-and-white geometrical motifs: stripes, circles, or squares. Devoid of any "fashionable" applied decoration, they generated a remarkable kinetic effect on the body in movement, because of the interplay of their geometric designs.

However, the main contribution of the Viennese avant-garde to the renewal of dress was that of the Wiener Werkstätte artists. Founded in 1903 by Josef Hoffmann and

Koloman Moser on the model of the Century Guild of Arthur Mackmurdo and the Guild of Handicraft of Charles Robert Ashbee, the Wiener Werkstätte, "a society for the production of art craft," endeavored to be a place where any distinction between art and craft was abolished.[8] The struggle for the equal dignity for the *Kleinkunst,* the minor arts, was associated with a global approach to the world of objects. Though the model for the *Gesamtkunstwerk*-obsessed architect in Loos's parody was probably van de Velde, the story could very well also apply to Hoffmann, who was Loos's rival. For Hoffmann, the artist had to consider every detail of his surroundings from the point of view of the whole; in his eyes, this was the only way to achieve harmony.

A long-lived legend claims that the founding of the Wiener Werkstätte's *Modeabteilung* was a consequence of a visit to the Palais Stoclet in Brussels by one of Hoffmann's students, Eduard Wimmer-Wisgrill, who was called "the architect of fashion."[9] During this visit to the mecca of the synthesis of the arts preached by his master, Wimmer-Wisgrill is said to have been disturbed by the presence of the one element that had not

Gustav Klimt in one of his dresses, 1914.

Gustav Klimt—Dress.

Gustav Klimt and Emilie Flöge, 1905–1910.

Emilie Flöge in a dress that was probably designed by Klimt, 1905–1910.

Josef Hoffmann—Summer dress, 1911.

been designed by Hoffmann: Mme Stoclet's toilettes, which, with their Parisian lines, broke the harmony of the whole.

In reality, the interest of Hoffmann and Moser in the problem of artistic dress clearly predated 1911, the official date of the opening of the *Mode-abteilung* of the Wiener Werkstätte. Hoffmann had designed at least one dress himself,[10] and it is a fact that he was theoretically involved in the debate concerning dress reform. As early as 1898, he had published an article titled "The Individual Dress," in which he took a stand in favor of the *Reformkleidung.*[11] Regretting the leveling down brought by contemporary dress, Hoffmann reiterated the usual protest against the tyranny of fashion and agreed with the reform thesis, which stated that dress should be adapted to the personality of the individual who wears it and should express the person's character.

Yet this did not mean that he unconditionally accepted the *Eigenkleid,* the personalized dress that every woman was supposed to make for herself. Whereas four years before, Walter Crane had asserted that women may have an "innate" or instinctive sense that could eventually lead them to artistic dress,[12] Hoffmann was not willing to abandon responsibility for dress either to couturiers or to housewives. In his article, published two years before the Krefeld exhibition, Hoffmann had defined dress as one of the essential elements in our environment; as such, it naturally and rightfully concerned the artist, who

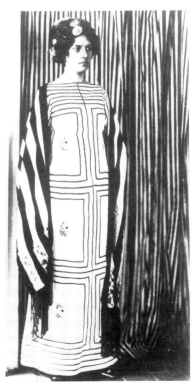

alone was qualified to design the world of forms. Already in the *Arbeitsprogram* of 1905, the Wiener Werkstätte manifesto, dress was listed as one of the objects that artists should deal with in order to express the harmony of the times:

As long as our cities, our homes, our rooms, our cupboards, our tools, our dress and finery, as long as our language and our feelings will not symbolize in a simple and beautiful way the spirit of our times, we will be relegated to an infinite distance from our ancestors, and no lie will ever be able to conceal these weaknesses.[13]

Nostalgically, Hoffmann also expressed his admiration for the Baroque, the Rococo, and, more surprisingly, the Biedermeier, when art "approached all fields of life" and was concerned with finding the right form "for the small things . . . dress, jewelry, and decorative elements that could be invented by the human mind."[14]

As a proponent of an all-embracing aesthetic imperialism, Hoffman could envision no other solution than the *Künstlerkleid,* the artistic dress, without apparently realizing how utopian this choice was; because of its exclusive nature, artistic dress could have only a very limited social impact. Created by an artist, such clothing is not primarily a practical object but rather a genuine work of art, whose foremost quality is beauty. His position was radically opposed to that of his main rival, Adolf Loos, who believed that talking about the beauty of clothing was a sort of heresy:

a painting by Botticelli, a melody by Burns, these are beautiful things. But a pair of trousers? . . . A jacket must have two or three buttons? The cut of the collar should be high or low? I am seized by anxiety when I hear people discussing the beauty of such things. I become nervous when one asks me about a garment, "Is this not beautiful?"[15]

According to Hoffmann's aesthetics, dress should never be designed separately; a garment is always just a part of a whole, and the artist should coordinate it with all the other elements. The integration of dress into the *Gesamtkunstwerk* was to a lesser degree the result of a peculiar cut, in general strongly influenced by the rather amorphous line of the *Reformkleid* that, for Bertha Zuckerkandl, the fashion critic of the influential *Wiener allgemeine Zeitung,* transformed dresses into "flour bags." The key element was decoration. The same square used by Hoffmann or by Moser to decorate furniture or perforated metal objects could be found as an ornament on a dress, and it was not uncommon for dress ornaments to be the same as those used in wallpaper patterns. Moser used this type of decoration for the striped black-and-white dress he designed for his wife Ditha in 1905–1906.[16]

Eduard Wimmer-Wisgrill, the leader of the *Mode-abteilung* from 1911 to 1922, followed the line of the *Künstlerkleid.*[17] Less geometrical in his approach than Hoffmann or his master Moser, Wimmer-Wisgrill favored a style that was halfway between the *Reformkleid* and the orientalizing costume. The frequent use, even for street dress, of "harem trousers," which were very similar to the bloomers that Amelia Bloomer had tried

Koloman Moser—Project for a dress, 1902.

Eduard Wimmer-Wisgrill—Project for a dress with "harem pants," 1914.

unsuccessfully to impose around 1850, is characteristic of his first period of creation. The sensuality of Wimmer-Wisgrill's designs deeply impressed Paul Poiret during his visit to Vienna and had a great success in Germany, where they were presented at the Hohenzollern Kunstgewerbehaus in 1912 and at the Werkbund exhibition in 1914.

Despite the quality of their design, the Wiener Werkstätte dresses frequently remained at the stage of projects, and the commercial results of the *Mode-abteilung* were mediocre. One reason is that they were conceived mainly as pictures and not as real fashion designs. Often, they were just superb sketches, which were almost impossible to realize in three dimensions. This is also true of the projects developed by Max Snishek and Dagobert Peche, who, like Wimmer-Wisgrill, had no practical training in dressmaking.

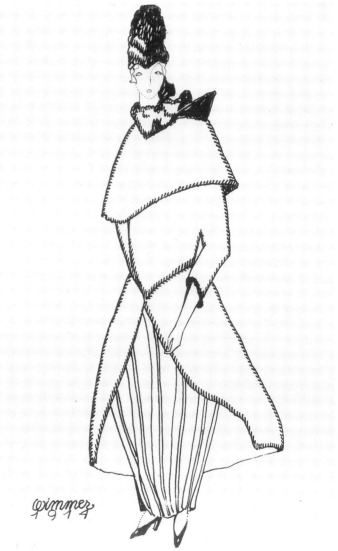

They did not usually take into account such problems as the choice and compatibility of materials or the difficulties of cutting—to the despair of their dressmaker, Marianne Zell, who was expected to actually make the clothes. The other reason is their search for an absolute quality of craftsmanship, as expressed by the famous Wiener Werkstätte slogan: "Better to work ten days on one product than to manufacture ten products in one day!" It is obvious that such an approach was suited to the needs of an elitist circle of well-to-do artistically minded customers, but totally inadequate to the imperative search for profitability.

The advent of the First World War modified the style of the Wiener Werkstätte dresses. Under the slogan *Los von Paris* (Away from Paris),[18] they were compelled to change their style, which was perceived as too frivolous for a time of war, and they had to adopt a more "Austrian" look—the sober *Alt-Wien* cut, which lasted until the beginning of the twenties.

FUTURISM AND DRESS

Today's woman loves luxury more than love. A visit to a great dressmaker's establishment, escorted by a paunchy, gouty banker friend who pays the bills, is a perfect substitute for the most amorous rendezvous with an adored young man. The woman finds all the mystery of love in the selection of an amazing ensemble, *the latest model, which her friends still do not have.*[1] (italics mine)

For Marinetti, fashion was undoubtedly evil: it corrupted women, who were too weak to resist the temptation of the latest garment, and he held it responsible for "the disdain for *amore.*" However, Futurism did not limit itself to a moral condemnation of fashion. In "Futurist Painting: Technical Manifesto of 1910," Umberto Boccioni, Carlo Carrà, Luigi Russolo, Giacomo Balla, and Gino Severini declared: "The harmony of the lines and folds of modern dress works upon our sensitiveness with the same emotional and symbolical power as did the nude upon the sensitiveness of the old masters."[2] The all-embracing ambition of the Futurists, who advocated the "Futurist reconstruction of the universe," could not ignore dress, which naturally belonged to the artistic domain. "A woman's dress brilliantly designed and well worn has the same value as a fresco by Michelangelo or a Madonna by Titian."[3] Their interest in dress was not motivated mainly by a wish to promote the "minor" arts; what they wanted was to extend the artistic realm to every aspect of life. In an interview given in 1920, Giacomo Balla emphasized the deep connection that, from a Futurist point of view, unites all activities related to the world of forms: "What was the Futurist painting from its beginnings till now other than a research of *an abstract chromatic decorativism*? That is why our art is essentially decorative and we direct it now toward the applied art and the industry."[4]

The Futurist artist wanted to act on all the elements of daily life, from architecture to furniture and carpets, from toys to food and music, and dress was no exception. Like all other objects, dress had to become essentially modern. This is not the relative and, in the end, deceptive modernity of fashion but the absolute "ever-changing" Futurist modernity, which was not submitted to the annual "fashionable" changes generated by marketing strategy. That is why, in my opinion, Enrico Crispolti, one of the leading experts in the field, was wrong to see just "a radical renewal of fashion" in the Futurist approach.[5] For even if the Futurists continued to use the word "fashion" for lack of a better word, their real aim was not simply to replace one fashion with another but to abolish the very system of fashion by designing clothes as works of art; as such, they were supposed never to become old-fashioned like the passéist fashionable clothes. Even if Balla wanted the new Futurist dress to be "short-lasting, in order to be able to renew incessantly the pleasure and animation of our body and to favor the textile industry,"[6] the renewal he imagined had more to do with the will to apply Futurist dynamism to all aspects of life than with the mercantile logic of fashion. The ephemeral aspect of Balla's dresses closely matched the ephemeral element of Futurist aesthetics as a whole.

In 1910, Arnaldo Ginna and Bruno Corra had already protested against the incompetence and traditionalism of women's dress manufacturers who should have studied the harmony of lines and colors in order to avoid the terrible dissonances of contemporary fashion. They dreamed of a visual symphony of the street of the future, which would be achieved by using dresses of different colors.[7] In 1920, Volt (Vincenzo Fani) demanded in a more radical way that fashion should be annexed to art. In his "Futurist Manifesto of Women's Fashion," he proposed that "A great poet or a great painter must assume the general directorship of all great firms of women's fashion."[8]

The first Futurist artist who actually designed clothes was, undoubtedly, Giacomo Balla. He began to do so in 1912, as shown by a letter that Balla, then decorating the living room of the Löwenstein family villa in Düsseldorf, sent to his wife in Rome.[9] These clothes, made up by Mrs. Eliza Balla according to her husband's directions, were an unprecedented rupture not only with contemporary fashion of the day but with fashion as such.

In his letter, Balla mentioned "a clear small-checked suit" whose whereabouts, unfortunately, are unknown. In another letter, from November 1913, Balla mentioned another suit that is also probably lost but is documented by a drawing, almost certainly a self-portrait. This is the costume that Grethel Löwenstein liked so much that she asked Eliza Balla to made another one for her.[10] It was a black outfit with a white border that was coordinated with the black furniture of the Löwensteins' living room. This suit totally transgressed conventional notions of a jacket. The collar and symmetrical lapels were eliminated and the jacket was held together by a big triangle. To dynamize the suit, the triangle was underlined by the large white border that cut through its silhouette. The same white border zigzagged down the trousers. In opposition to van de Velde, who used linear ornament to emphasize the structure of the dress, Balla de-structured the dress by optically destroying the anatomy of the wearer. The goal of his systematic use of an asymmetrical cut and interpenetrating colors was to achieve a general dynamic effect, similar to that in his paintings.

It is highly significant that Balla's first sartorial creation aimed at abolishing fashion was an item of male dress. In her article on Futurist fashion, Emily Braun has argued that Balla's choice displayed a "gender bias . . . typical of the Futurist movement on the whole, especially in the prewar years."[11] However, this explanation is, in my opinion, too restrictive and, ultimately, biased. Historically, male dress had not been a primary interest of dress reform supporters, who considered it an example of the rationality missing in women's dress. While a woman's clothes were a good indication of her husband's economic status, the male suit was also highly symbolic. As Gilles Lipovetsky has noted, "the neutral, austere, sober masculine costume reflected the consecration of egalitarian ideology as the conquering bourgeois ethic of thrift, merit, and work."[12] But most of all, the audacity of women's fashion was absent from male dress. At the beginning of the twenties, it was still possible for Le Corbusier to write that "a judgment passed on a really elegant man is more definitive than on an elegant woman, because male dress is standardized."[13] More than its symbolic dimension—the acceptance of an established order and of bourgeois values—male dress was such an attractive territory for an artistic intervention pre-

30

Giacomo Balla—Project for a scarf, 1925–1930.

Giacomo Balla—Project for a dress, 1920s.

cisely because of its normalized aspect. The focus on the male dress was an obviously strategic decision in accordance with Futurist logic, gaining coverage through scandal. Balla knew very well that the same effronteries perpetrated on women's dress, which was subject to much vaguer rules, would have shocked far less.

On 20 May 1914, Balla published the Futurist manifesto on clothing, "Male Futurist Dress." The first version of this text, in French (translated in this volume), may have been written at the end of 1913.[14] Earlier dress was accused of representing "the negation of the muscular life, which suffocated in an antihygienic passéisme of weighty fabrics and boring, effeminate, or decadent halftones.[15] To escape from the depressing established approach to clothing, Balla wanted to completely abolish mourning dress; dark or faded colors; striped, checked, or spotted fabrics; symmetry in cut; uniformity of lapels; useless buttons; and the detachable collar and starched cuffs. In contrast to the clothes of the

past, the new Futurist dress would be dynamic, asymmetrical, nimble, simple and comfortable, hygienic, joyful, illuminating, willful, flying, and, most of all, variable. The main reason for these qualities was "the need to vary the environment very frequently, together with sport."[16] Balla's Futurist clothes were made variable, or transformable, by the use of *modifiers,* "appliqué pieces of cloth (of different size, thickness, or color) that can be attached at will to any part of the dress with pneumatic buttons."[17] The impact of modifiers was not limited to their color or texture, as some of them were perfumed.

When Balla imagined variable shapes and colors for his clothes, he did much more than "invent the kinetic work of art in the Futurist sense: a work, which could be manually transformed through the manual intervention of its user."[18] The modifiers fundamentally changed the relationship between the dress and the person who wore it. Dress was no longer a given object to which its owner had to submit. "Thus, anyone can not only modify but also invent a new dress for a new mood at any instant."[19] In this way, clothing escaped fashion, which thereby lost its raison d'être. The responsibility for controlling changes in dress was given instead to its wearer, who had to enter the aesthetic realm and collaborate with the designer. Within the limits fixed by the artist, the wearers of clothing could express their own creativity, and in this way attire became an "open" work of art. The first modifiers were in cloth, but the next were in colored paper. The "Male Futurist Dress" manifesto also mentions the "perfumed" modifiers, indicating Balla's intention to integrate the other senses. In a later manifesto, "Tactilism," released on 11 January 1921, Marinetti pursued the idea of integrating the other senses, proposing the design of "tactile" shirts and dresses.[20]

The concept of perpetually changing dress was taken up in another manifesto, "The Futurist Reconstruction of the Universe," jointly signed by Giacomo Balla and Fortunato Depero; in it, they defended "the transformable clothes" made using "mechanical trimmings, surprises, tricks, disappearance of individuals."[21] The idea of a dress freed from the whims of fashion and that, when modified by its owner, could metamorphose according to his or her mood, the time of the day, or the season also fascinated Marinetti. In a less-known manifesto from 1935, "Latin Pleasures for the Mind," he advocated "tactile resonant metaphorical dress tuned according to the hour, the day, the season, and the mood to convey sensations of dawn, noon, evening, spring, summer, winter, autumn, ambition, love, etc."[22]

Concerning the "light-giving" quality of his clothes, Balla went beyond the manifesto's requirement that phosphorescent cloth be used. In his memoirs, Bragaglia wrote that Balla had made a Futurist tie consisting of a transparent celluloid box in which he put a battery and an electric bulb that lit up to emphasize electrifying passages of his speeches.[23] One immediately thinks of Marinetti's "Futurist Proclamation to the Spaniards" (1910), in which he praised "sublime Electricity, the one and only divine mother of future mankind, Electricity with its fidgeting quicksilver torso, Electricity with a thousand violet and lightning arms!"[24]

On 11 September 1914, Balla published an Italian version of the manifesto, different from the one in French, with a new title, "The Antineutral Dress." According to

Giacomo Balla—Male suit with modifiers, 1913–1914.

Giacomo Balla—Modifiers, 1914.

LE VÊTEMENT MASCULIN FUTURISTE

Manifeste

L'humanité a toujours porté le deuil, ou l'armure pesante, ou la chape hiératique, ou le manteau traînant. Le corps de l'homme a toujours été attristé par le noir, ou emprisonné de ceintures ou écrasé par des draperies.

Durant le Moyen-Âge et la Renaissance l'habillement a presque toujours eu des couleurs et des formes statiques, pesantes, drapées ou bouffantes, solennelles, graves, sacerdotales, incommodes et encombrantes. C'étaient des expressions de mélancolie, d'esclavage ou de terreur. C'était la négation de la vie musculaire, qui étouffait dans un passéisme anti-hygiénique d'étoffes trop lourdes et de demi-teintes ennuyeuses efféminées ou décadentes.

C'est pourquoi aujourd'hui comme autrefois les rues pleines de foule, les théâtres, et les salons ont une tonalité et un rythme désolants, funéraires et déprimants.

Nous voulons donc abolir:

1. — Les vêtements de deuil que les croque-morts eux-mêmes devraient refuser.

2. — Toutes les couleurs fanées, jolies, neutres, fantaisie, foncées.

3. — Toutes les étoffes à raies, quadrillées et à petits pois.

4. — Les soi-disants bon goût et harmonie de teintes et de formes qui ramollissent les nerfs et ralentissent le pas.

5. — La symétrie dans la coupe, la ligne statique qui fatigue, déprime, contriste, enchaîne les muscles, l'uniformité des revers et toutes les bizarreries ornementales.

Costume gris
Dessins noirs
Modifiants rouge bleu
Gilet vert *Jours.*

Modifiants.

Giacomo Balla—Projects for Futurist ties, 1925–1930.

Giacomo Balla—Projects for scarves, 1919.

Giacomo Balla—Projects for Futurist jackets, 1914.

Balla's daughter Elica, he was not very satisfied with Marinetti's modifications but finally he reluctantly accepted them.[25] This text—whose motto was Marinetti's famous phrase from the "Futurist Manifesto," "We will glorify war, the world's only hygiene"—was soaked in the interventionist rhetoric of Futurist circles, which favored Italy's entry into the First World War. The protest targeted "the distressing peace" and "Teutonic hues." The joint use of black and yellow, the German colors, was proscribed. The differences between the first and the second manifestos are significant: in order to adapt the text to the coming war, the new Futurist clothes had to be bellicose and their main qualities became aggressiveness, "to increase the courage of the strong and to disrupt the sensitivity of cowards"; nimbleness "to increase the flexibility of the body and to favor its surge to fight"; and dynamism, "to inspire the love of danger, of speed and assault, [and] the hatred of peace and immobility."[26] While the first manifesto promoted simple, comfortable clothes, in the second comfort was associated with military practicalities such as rifle

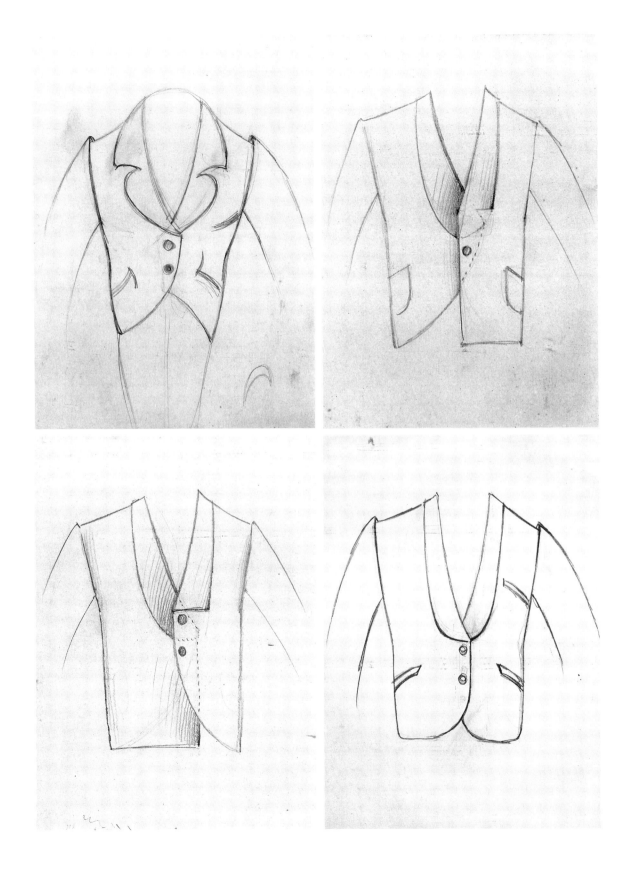

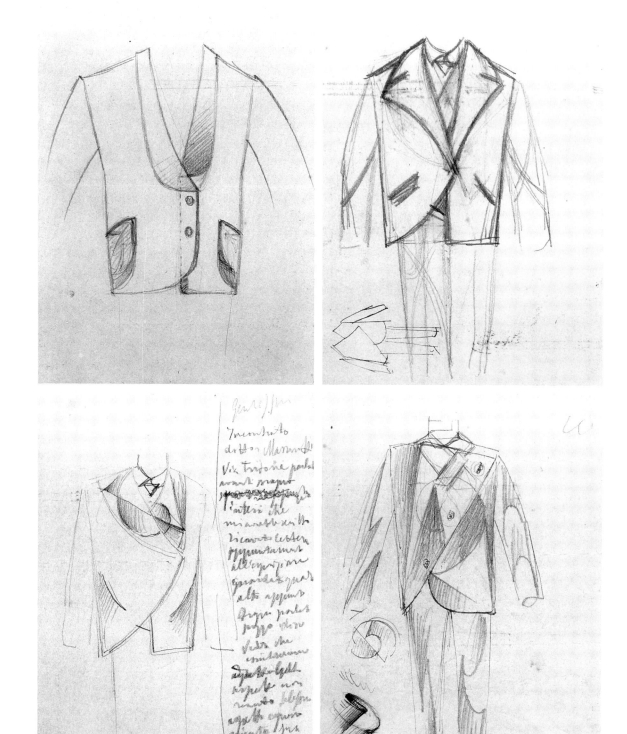

Giacomo Balla—Projects for Futurist suits, 1913–1914.

shooting. Even the rejection of mourning dress, present in the first version, had been modified to fit the new situation: the heroic dead should not be wept over but celebrated by wearing red clothes. The modifiers that were illustrated are identical to those of the French version, but the explanations were changed to make them "warlike."

It is interesting to compare Balla's proposals with the evolution of the standard military uniform. At a time when the British army had changed its uniforms to khaki after the Boer War, the German army had changed to field gray, and even the French, inspired by Cubist painting, had finally abandoned their celebrated red trousers for camouflage battle dress,[27] Balla's gaudy "artistic" uniforms would have been disastrous for the Italian soldiers.

Earlier than the Russian Constructivists, Balla was convinced that dress was able to influence the psyche of its wearer. While in "Male Futurist Dress" he wanted to use clothes to render people more joyful, in "Antineutral Dress" he imagined that clothes could be used to prepare them for war.

Another important change was the replacement of the earlier generic dress designs by clothes specifically designed for some of his Futurist companions; the white-red-green (the colors of the Italian flag) morning suit for the *parolibero* Marinetti, the white-red-blue suit for the *parolibero* Francesco Cangiullo, a white-red-green evening suit for Umberto Boccioni, a red all-piece suit for Cardo Carrà, and a green pullover with a coordinated white-and-red jacket for the *rumorista* Luigi Russolo, who was to join the Lombard Volunteer Cyclist Battalion. In the definitive version, published in 1915, the colors of Cangiullo's suit were "Italianized"—that is, changed from red-white-blue to red-white-green. In this way, to quote Marinetti, Cangiullo was transformed into "a living flag."[28] Giacomo Foà, a tailor who was Balla's friend, made the suits.[29] It is on record that Cangiullo actually wore the garment during the demonstration of university students in Rome against their neutral and pro-German professors. One element of his attire was a hat topped by a silver star—a clear reference to the "Italian star," one of the symbols of the Risorgimento.[30]

After the war, Balla designed several Futurist suits, which he frequently wore. In *Lettres sur la Jeune Italie,* Lucien Corpechot described him wearing a Futurist tie, which was shaped like an airplane propeller, and Futurist white-and-yellow shoes.[31] Public reaction to this attire was rather negative, and it is said that Balla, who in 1925 had wanted to visit the Exposition Internationale des arts décoratifs et industriels modernes in Paris, had to try thirty-one hotels to find a room. Every concierge who saw him in his Futurist suit, with his cap peak painted with colored "force lines," told him with some distrust: "Je regrette, Monsieur, c'est complet!"[32]

These aggressive clothes had to be worn in an aggressive, Futurist way. Crispolti rightly emphasized that

This intrinsic provocation in Futurist dress is not only based on imagination, it also involves behavior . . . a behavioral input aimed at the achievement of greater ability and nonchalance in everyday actions and social relations. This type of behavioral induction is an integral part of Futurist ideological proselytism, for which the garment is a visible

Giacomo Balla—Projects for Futurist
shoes, 1928–1929.

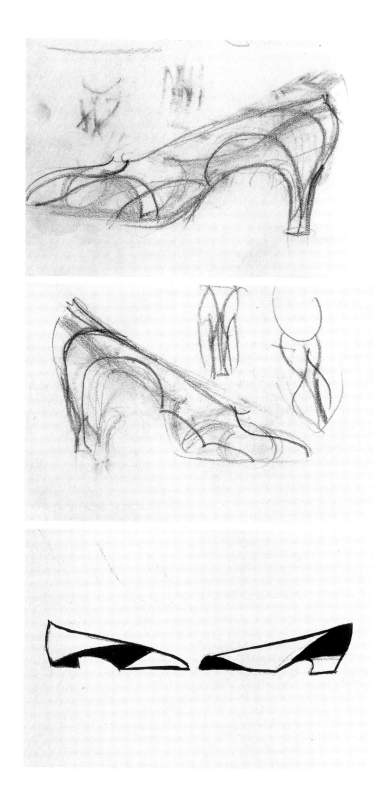

Giacomo Balla—Futurist shoes, 1916–1918.

Giacomo Balla—Futurist shoes, 1929.

Giacomo Balla—Dress, 1930.

sign. It is not possible to be Futurists without acting in the real world in a Futurist manner, and the correct dress is the visible sign of this intention.[33]

While one is aware of the influence of the "force lines" in his male suits of 1914–1915 or in certain jackets, some of Balla's later designs, such as his home dress or his *panciotti* (waistcoats), are based on a different chromatic system that is significant in terms of the evolution of his painting. This connection with painting would increase in the dresses that Balla designed in the twenties for his daughters, Luce and Elica. The direct relationship between Futurist painting and Futurist dress had been clearly expressed in the

Tullio Crali—Synthetic jacket, 1932.

Tullio Crali—Jacket, worn by the artist, 1931.

"Futurist Manifesto of Women's Fashion," written by Volt in 1920: "We will use the most aggressive lines and the gaudiest colors of our Futurist paintings upon the feminine profile."[34] But in comparison with Balla's male dress, his clothes for women appear quite restrained. Surprisingly, the cut of his women's clothes, like the dress for Luce or the blouses of 1920 to 1930, is almost banal, and the dynamic effect is generated only by Balla's use of color, which visually destroys form.

Fortunato Depero, who co-signed the "Futurist Reconstruction of the Universe" manifesto, also designed Futurist dresses, which are mostly influenced by Balla. His designs, however, are softer and more decorative. In his famous collage portrait *Marinetti temporale patriotico* (1924), the founder of Futurism is represented in a smart gray-black asymmetrical suit and an elegant red-white-green bow tie, but there is no information whatsoever on whether this suit ever really existed. On the other hand, it is known that Depero designed a waistcoat, now in a private collection in Milan, which was worn by Marinetti. In any case, artistic dress was a relatively small, albeit important, part of Depero's production, which encompassed stage, graphic, and furniture design together with painting.

Despite Balla's claims that Futurist art was directed toward industry, in practice his and Depero's artistic dress were always unique pieces created mainly for personal use, or the use of family or friends. From 1919 on, their favorite fabric was a kind of felt, called *panno lenci,* which was sold by the Austrian Helena Koenig and her husband Ettore Scavini in *Ars lenci,* their shop in Turin.[35] Both the design and the fabric, a Tirolian specialty, were wholly inappropriate for industrial production.

Many other more or less well-known artists, following Balla's example, became interested in dress design; in my opinion, two of the "second generation" of Futurists, each with a radically different approach, best exemplify the different ways of designing clothes within the Futurist movement in the thirties.

In the summer of 1932, Tullio Crali, the first of these artists, designed a "synthetic dress"—a very short Futurist jacket, with a single left lapel behind which a pocket for pencils had been astutely hidden.[36] Normal outer pockets had been abolished. These Futurist jackets were in very vivid shades and the lapel was usually in a contrasting color. Faithful to his principle of "eliminat[ing] what is superfluous,"[37] in 1932 Crali designed for his own use *una giacca a modo* mio—a plain, collarless jacket, without lapels, in gray flannel with a single chrome-plated button. As there were no angles to the design, the jacket seemed astonishing fluid. These jackets had to be worn with a special, personally designed shirt, which Crali was still using when I met him in 1992. The plain shirt had no buttons or cuffs and was closed at the neck with a cuff link. This type of collar prevented the use of ties. Despite Balla's experiments, Mino delle Site's research on ties, and the metallic antitie of Renato di Bosso and Ignazio Scurto, (who published a manifesto on the Futurist tie), Crali considered ties to be anti-Futurist; for him, they were passéist objects that have to be discarded.

After the Second World War, Crali created for his personal use a fire-red jacket and a *giacca di raccolta,* designed for his Egyptian trip in 1961. This lapelless jacket had

big front pockets in which he collected stones for his *sassisintesi,* strange photographs of minerals that express nature's creative powers.

Though ties were banished from his new Futurist man's wardrobe, Crali added other new accessories to it. In 1951, he invented the *borsello,* a bag for men, and attempted to enter the Louvre carrying one. As he expected, they stopped him at the entrance on the grounds that bags were allowed only for women, thereby giving him the opportunity to make a scandal in the purest Futurist style.

Crali was also interested in women's dress, and in 1931 he sent his designs to Benedetta Marinetti and to Balla's daughters. Because he created these dress designs without thinking precisely about how to produce them,[38] he had total artistic freedom. Superbly rendered graphically, these designs are extraordinary dynamic: in one of them, multicolored spirals roll up around the body; in a second, the dress is an "assemblage" of different sized triangles; and in yet another, complex-shaped pieces are held together in an apparently miraculous way. The general effect of these dresses is almost kinetic. Every element is of a different color; and sometimes complimentary contrasts, such as violet and yellow, are used, as in the "Sun/shadow" garment. In several designs, certain details, such as a breast or a shoulder, are emphasized, almost always in an asymmetrical way, giving the dresses an arousing sensuality in spite of their "geometricality."

Diametrically opposed to this extremely refined aestheticism, Ernesto Thayaht (Michahelles) in 1919–1920 created the *tuta,* a kind of synthetic one-piece dress. According to Crali, Thayaht developed an older idea of Carlo Carrà, who had designed a *tuta* several years before.[39] The *tuta*'s main characteristic was its universality. It could be worn by anyone, at any time, thereby abolishing class distinctions in clothing. Although Thayaht developed several variants, the *tuta* was a unique type of dress, wearable on any occasion and all year round, thus making all other clothes useless and the very idea of fashion obsolete.

The principles of the *tuta* were comfort, simplicity, and hygiene. It was so simple that it could be made for oneself, without any specialized help; and it seems that more than a thousand patterns were sold in a few days.[40] The infatuation with the *tuta* was sufficiently widespread to give birth to a new social group known as *i tutisti.* Because it was aiming for practicality and simplicity, the *tuta* had to be plain-colored and all decorative elements were left out. However, it was not supposed to be unisex, as Thayaht designed a model for women, a female *tuta,* in which the trousers had been replaced by a skirt. This garment was supposed to become the single style of dress, under the utopian expectation that it would replace the untidy variety in the wardrobes of the weaker sex.

Crispolti described the *tuta* as a proposal motivated by the economic precariousness of the immediate postwar period, its "economy" being a reaction to scarcity and a protest against the cost of traditional clothes.[41] But if one compares Thayaht's *tuta* with quite similar designs by Aleksandr Rodchenko or László Moholy-Nagy,[42] it is obvious that the three were just variations on American overalls.

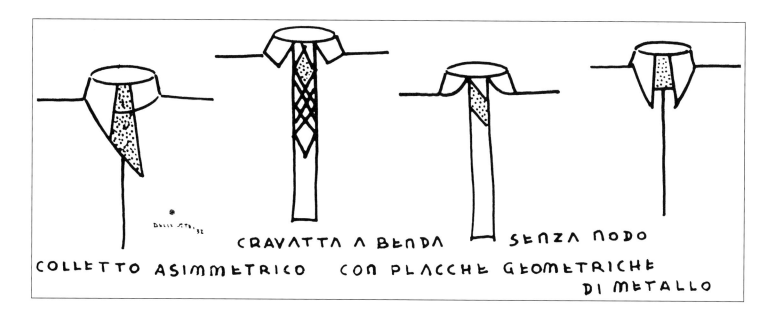

COLLETTO ASIMMETRICO   CRAVATTA A BENDA   SENZA NODO
CON PLACCHE GEOMETRICHE
DI METALLO

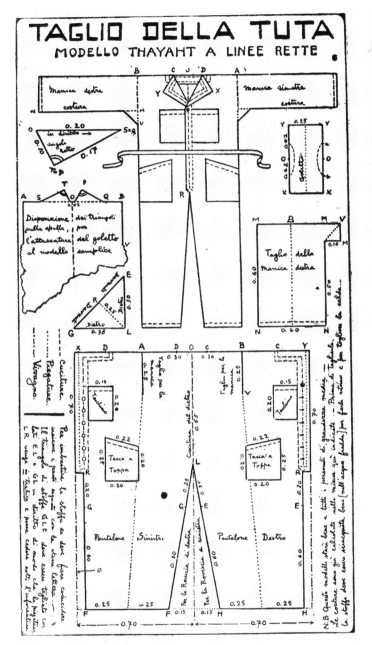

One year later, Thayaht imagined the *bituta,* a two-piece garment that was a development of *tuta.* Later still, in 1932, another Futurist, Mino delle Sitte, developed Thayaht's ideas even further and designed the *tuta termica* for women. The simple and practical outfit, which anticipated women's suits of the 1980s, was provided with a *giberna portatutto,* a bag attached to the belt, which again anticipated the waist bag of recent years.

In 1932, with his brother Ruggero Michahelles (the Futurist painter Ram), Thayaht signed the "Manifesto for the Transformation of Male Dress." From a hygienist's perspective, Thayaht asserted that male dress should be designed according to norms based on comfort and practicality. Everything that was purely decorative or physically constraining, everything that restricted the free circulation of the blood or freedom of movement, was to be avoided absolutely. "Puritan and Anglo-Saxon, Northern, and anti-Mediterranean" clothes had to disappear and be replaced by a new type of dress.[43] The innovations were also linguistic, as the new garments also had new names: *toraco,* a sleeveless undershirt; *corsante,* a half-sleeve chest cover; the *femorali* (the "thighbones"), a kind of thigh cover that was supposed to replace the passéist underpants, *asole* (the "asun"), a summer hat with a special adjustable light protection device; and the *radio-telfo,* an ultralight travel helmet with a built-in miniature radio, which anticipates modern-day headsets. Notwithstanding his radicalism, Thayaht was tempted by activities that were more profitable. Despite these radical antifashion sartorial statements, from as early as 1921, he designed more commercial designs for Madeleine Vionnet.[44]

THE RUSSIAN AVANT-GARDE AND DRESS

There is no other country in which fashion was so attacked as in revolutionary Russia. The reproaches of the dress reformers who had accused fashion of being unhealthy and immoral were replaced by an ideological stance: fashion was essentially a bourgeois phenomenon and, as such, it was expected to die together with the social class that produced it.

The debate concerning dress that took place in the first years after the October 1917 revolution cannot be dissociated from the polemic about the role of art in the new communist society that was under construction. For the Productivists, the most radical group of the Russian avant-garde, utility was the only valid criterion that could give legitimacy to artistic activity in the communist future. "Pure" art, which had no social utility was considered socially unacceptable in the new revolutionary society and, therefore, it could not survive. For the Productivists and certain Constructivists, the disappearance of traditional art was inevitable; as Aleksei Gan wrote, "Marxists must work in order to elucidate its death scientifically and to formulate new phenomena of artistic labor within the new historic environment of our time."[1]

In a conference given at INKhUK (the Institute for Artistic Culture) in 1921, Nikolai Tarabukin provocatively announced: "The last painting has been painted!" The reason for this inevitable end was that "as a typical form of visual art, 'painting' has lost its meaning as a social phenomenon."[2] For Tarabukin, painting was an elitist and strongly individualistic form of art that had been too closely connected with museums and the decoration of bourgeois residences. It thus could not have any significant impact on the masses—a failure that, in itself, signed painting's death warrant, because the art of the new communist society had to be a "mass art." This, as Tarabukin asserted, led to the real question: "Painting is dead. Rodchenko is the murderer and the suicide. But if painting is dead, is art dead as well?"[3]

"Easel painting"—wrote Osip Brik, the critic of the magazine *LEF*—"is not only useless for our contemporary artistic culture, but it is also a powerful hindrance to its development."[4] If easel painting was no longer socially justified, artists had only one chance to avoid being sucked up into the whirl of art that was in the process of dying: they had to give up "pure" art and get involved with real life, with "production." In 1921, Rodchenko emphatically declared:

Constructive life is the art of the future.

Art that fails to become a part of life will be catalogued in the museum of archeological antiquities.

It is time for *art* to organize itself and become a part of life.[5]

What was at stake was the very survival of the artist. In a famous debate concerning Constructivism in 1921, Varvara Stepanova asked her fellow artists not to forget that "our task is to find ourselves a place in real life."[6] To survive socially, artists had to play an active role in the construction of the new society. Art was no longer considered a

separate domain and the artist was no longer a specific individual. Under the new conditions, art became just one of the multiple levers to be used to establish communism, and the artist became no more than an art worker who was expected not to "create" but to produce. Consequently, the work of art had to get rid of its aura: it had to become a thing and enter the realm of daily life.[7] Paraphrasing the famous formula developed by Marx, the Constructivist critic Aleksei Filippov asserted that "artists in varying ways have merely depicted the world but their task is to change it."[8]

In order to accomplish this ambitious project of changing the world and replacing the creation of art with the "construction of life," artists had to abandon their "petty" personal aesthetic goals and dedicate themselves to the collective aim of building a new communist lifestyle. In practical terms, this radical transformation of life had to begin with the reshaping of the world of objects. The Productivists were convinced that objects employed every day had a great influence on human behavior and could, therefore, be used to modify the way of thinking of the masses. An object had no value in itself; its value could be judged only by its ability to influence the psyche and to act on people's consciousness, and ultimately by its capacity to speed up the construction of a communist society. As artists were expected not to help preserve the old world but to contribute instead to its destruction, they had to create new types of objects to match the new revolutionary values.

Since the social impact of dress could not be minimized, clothing was an essential member of the large family of everyday objects. The social importance of dress was a common theme in the libertarian tradition. Pyotr Kropotkin had already called for the abolition of fashion and "the communalization of clothing." As this could not be realized simply by the redistribution of the existent clothes,

the communal outfitters would soon make good these shortcomings. We know how rapidly our great tailoring and dressmaking establishments work nowadays, provided as they are with machinery specially adapted for production on a larger scale.

"But every one will want a sable-lined coat or a velvet gown!" exclaim our adversaries. Frankly, we do not believe it. Every woman does not dote on velvet, nor does every man dream of sable linings. Even now, if we were to ask each woman to choose her gown, we should find some to prefer a simple, practical garment to all fantastic trimmings the fashionable world affects.[9]

More than any other everyday object, dress symbolically preserved class distinction. Since class differences were not supposed to exist in the new revolutionary world, they had to be abolished in the new dress. Previously, clothes had maintained these differences, and they were therefore socially harmful. Following this line of thought, the Productivists called for the elimination of the clothes of the past, a totally utopian suggestion at a time of terrible shortages of fabric and clothing. In 1919, Kerzhentsev had already exhorted artists to design the new, different clothes that the revolution so badly needed in order to express its fervor. Old dark suits, feathered hats, and bowlers were obviously in opposition to the new Bolshevik style; however, the forms of the revolutionary dress to come were still vague, with concrete proposals simply mentioning the ordinary blouse or a revival of the Phrygian cap.[10]

According to the historian Richard Stites,

The "revolt in dress," which could have been predicted by the sartorial culture of pre-revolutionary Russia, by the studied codes of the nihilist sloppiness, and by symbolic use of certain garments in revolutionary posters to indicate corrupt plutocracy, never reached a high level of self-consciousness. The major responses were to dress down, to dress up, to dress equally, and not to dress at all.[11]

Yet the creation of new types of clothing adapted to the new revolutionary life was considered a priority. The primary function of these clothes-to-be was to express revolutionary change symbolically. From this perspective, it is not surprising that the competition to create the new uniforms for the Red Army stipulated that the designs should be "democratic."[12] Epaulettes, one of the distinctive signs of the old hierarchy of Czarist officers and therefore heavily invested with ideological connotations,[13] were reintroduced only at the beginning of the Second World War. The new revolutionary clothes had to express the new egalitarian values; and, as they were believed to directly affect the behavior of those who wore them, they were expected to reinforce the social cohesion of a communist society.

Some voices were even raised to demand compulsory, identical dress for all: this, in their eyes, was the only possible type of clothing appropriate for the classless society they imagined they were building. The idea of suppressing sartorial differences, of standardizing the social body by using a unique model of dress, has been a constant element in egalitarian utopias since the inhabitants of the first utopia—Thomas More's—had to wear similar clothes.[14] In one of the first Marxism-inspired Russian science fiction novels, Aleksandr Bogdanov's *Red Star* (1908), the communist Martians wore identical unisex garments. During the years of the communism of the war, the threat of this being realized on earth was not improbable: in Yevgeny Zamiatin's prophetic satire *We* (1924), the citizens of the Single State, who had been reduced to the status of numbers, had to wear blue "unifs" coordinated with the bluish color of the identical cells that had replaced individual homes, since "being original destroys equality." In another famous dystopia, described in George Orwell's *1984* (1949), all citizens forcibly enrolled as members of the sole party had to dress in the same blue overalls to homogenize the social body. Moreover, reality was to go beyond fiction as Mao's puritan-style dress that disregarded gender differences became the compulsory unisex uniform of the Chinese Cultural Revolution.

Under such a conception of clothing, the persistence of the institution of fashion could not be tolerated. In the first years after the October revolution, "the very word 'fashion' was an insult; it became synonymous with bourgeois prejudice; it was considered fundamentally hostile to the spirit of the new society."[15] This aggressive opposition is characteristic of the Constructivist and Productivist approach to fashion. In 1923, Sergei Tretiakov, the editor of *LEF,* ruled out fashion on ideological grounds: "And the question of a rational suit—is it possible to encroach upon the fashion magazine which dictates the masses the will of the capitalist manufacturers!"[16]

The answer was obviously no. The "constructed" clothes of Vladimir Tatlin, the founder of Constructivism, exemplify an "antifashion" perspective as the starting point of the creative process. In his "Answer to a Letter to the Futurists" (1918), Tatlin regretted that "the Futurists were more interested in cafés and different embroideries for the Czar or a few ladies"[17] and, were artists willing to go into "production," he pointed out the way to follow. After announcing that he would "not create any more useless counterreliefs but would produce useful pans instead,"[18] Tatlin dedicated his efforts for a while to the production of utilitarian objects: pans, a special economical oven, and, last but not least, clothes. For the Constructivist Tatlin, dress was not an object to draw but a *constructed* thing. Dress had to be put together as a machine, and the same criteria of efficiency and effectiveness should apply to it. The clothing created by the Section of Material Culture of the Petrograd *GINKhUK* (State Institute for Artistic Culture) led by Tatlin was typically antifashion. It was designed solely with regard to practical criteria. For instance, color was cho-

Vladimir Tatlin—Man's suit and
overcoat, 1924.

sen never for its expressive power but for its ability to conceal dirt. Consequently, the results were almost "scientifically" ugly.

In accordance with the Productivist theory, Tatlin was not interested in the
"style" of his dress designs. Instead, he wanted his clothes to be comfortable, long lasting, and easy to clean. Their cut had been carefully calculated to accommodate all body
positions and to permit complete freedom of movement. The placing of pockets was not
the result of formal research into the structure of a garment; the only parameter taken into
account was the length of the arms. The straight-cut jacket, buttoned up almost to the
throat, had a strange trapezoidal form that was broader at the shoulders and narrower
at the waist. The trousers were also narrower at the ankles. These unusual forms, which
were not really elegant, had many practical advantages in Tatlin's eyes. They stopped the
wind from entering from below, the loose-fitting cut prevented the cloth from sticking to
the body, and the trapezoidal shape trapped a considerable amount of air that acted as
a thermal regulator. It is significant that Tatlin did not call his suit "beautiful," describing
it instead as a "warm and hygienic garment."[19] But the most interesting item of those

Vladimir Tatlin—Project for a dress, 1924.

Vladimir Tatlin—Project for an overcoat, 1924.

Vladimir Tatlin—Overcoat (detail of ill. on p. 49), 1924.

produced by the Section of the Material Culture was an overcoat. For its design, Tatlin pushed utilitarian criteria to their utmost limits. The shape of the overcoat was a strange ovoid, and it was made in waterproof cloth. In order to ensure that it could be worn for two seasons, Tatlin gave it two removable linings, one in flannel for the autumn and one in fur for the cold Russian winter. The collar was specially designed so that it could be buttoned up without using a mirror.

The truly revolutionary innovation, however, was a new way of designing clothes according to a modular concept. Aware that different parts of an overcoat wear out in different ways, Tatlin conceived the design in three modules, which could be replaced one after another as needed. This modular overcoat could therefore last much longer than traditional clothes. Undoubtedly fascinated by Tatlin's idea, the art critic Boris Arvatov specifically mentioned "the outfits with detachable parts" among the items that the Productivists had to design for the New Man and the New Woman.[20] From a practical point of view, Tatlin's innovation was greatly appreciated at a time when cloth was so scarce that even the tiniest piece was considered a small treasure. This led the Leningrad Odezhda textile company to adopt the overcoat as a prototype for production on a large scale—a decision that, unfortunately, was never been put into practice.[21]

At the end of 1924, these clothes and their patterns were reproduced in the journal *Krasnaia Panorama.* The caption "Normal Dress" shows clearly the link between

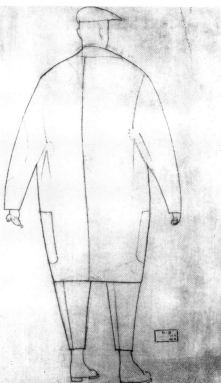

Varvara Stepanova wearing a
Constructivist dress, 1924.

Caricatures of Liubov Popova and
Varvara Stepanova, 1924.

Caricatures of Varvara Stepanova and
Aleksandr Rodchenko, 1924.

Tatlin's clothes, which were ideally designed as prototypes for the textile industry, and the
ideas of "normalization" and "standardization," key concepts of Taylorism. As the design
criteria were only practical, economic, or hygienic, any arbitrary elements were suppos-
edly excluded from the creative process, which had to become totally objective. This perfectly matched Tatlin's slogan: "Not toward the new, not toward the old, but toward what
is necessary."[22]

These bizarre garments evoked many sarcastic remarks: Konstantin Miklashevski, for instance, caustically compared the refinement of English tailors with the
coarseness of Tatlin's clothes.[23] In a famous photomontage, Tatlin replied by showing himself dressed in his "Normal Dress" against a contrasting backdrop showing two elegantly
dressed gentlemen who had been knocked to the ground. The bourgeois suit was described as hindering movement, as not being hygienic, and as worn only because it was
considered beautiful. Tatlin's suit, on the other hand, was, according to its caption, "designed to be warm, to facilitate freedom of movement, to be hygienic, and to last."[24]

The determination to design antifashion clothing was also central to the creations of Varvara Stepanova and Liubov Popova. They were directly involved in "production," as they worked for the First Cotton-Printing State Factory in Moscow.[25] In an
important article published in *LEF* in 1923, "Present-Day Dress—Production Clothing,
Stepanova asserted that the notion of fashion should be replaced by a conception of
dress based on use.[26] Consequently, clothes should be designed that were adapted to
production. Stepanova defined three types of dress: *prozodezhda, spetsodezhda,* and
sportodezhda. The first, a "production dress," was a garment that was perfectly adapted
to the requirements of its wearer's profession. Designed from a Taylorist perspective,

the *prozodezhda* had to provide maximum comfort for its wearer as he or she worked. According to Stepanova, her clothing designs were intended for mass production. However, she had never really accomplished this goal.

Her fellow artist Liubov Popova applied these principles to designing actors' *prozodezhda* for Vsevolod Meyerhold's theater. The garments were used as costumes for Meyerhold's staging of *The Magnanimous Cuckold* in 1922. That same year, the "constructor" Stepanova created her version of actors' *prozodezhda* for Aleksandr Sukhovo-Kobylin's play *The Death of Tarelkin,* staged by Meyerhold with the aid of Sergei Eisenstein and Meyerhold's assistant, Inzhinov.[27] Interviewed by the theater magazine *Zrelishcha* in 1922, Stepanova declared:

Prozodezhda cam be created for various spheres of labor, physical exercises, in the theatre for biomechanics—where there is a precise productional task and an operative system. That is why I set myself the following tasks in working on the actor's clothing. . . .

The *prozodezhda* I created were of two types—the *spetsodezhda* of the workmen (the costume for Pakhom the janitor) and the *spetsodezhda* for the assistant producer, where protection was provided for the parts of the clothes subject to heavy wear and the scheme of the cut of the outfit was revealed (in the case of the assistant producer, the pockets and the fastenings were highlighted).[28]

Stepanova's husband, the "artist-constructor" Aleksandr Rodchenko, was also interested in *prozodezhda* and designed one for himself. According to Aleksandr Lavrentiev, Rodchenko's grandson, Stepanova made up that garment in wool and leather, on a

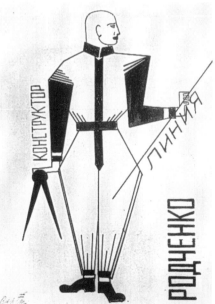

Singer sewing machine. The artist's working suit "had multiple pockets to hold precious instruments: a ruler; one compass; red, blue, and black pencils; scissors; one watch; etc."[29] Nevertheless, Rodchenko's working suit was obviously influenced by American overalls, thus indicating the impact of Americanism on the Russian avant-garde in the twenties.[30]

In 1931, the art critic Aleksei Fedorov-Davydov took up these ideas again and asserted that universal garments—the jacket, for example—should be abandoned precisely because of their universality; without a specific use, the jacket is not really adapted either for work, leisure, or gymnastics. The wardrobe of the communist future should be determined by utility, and Fedorov-Davydov dreamed of a worker owning different *prozodezhda*s to be used on various specific occasions: for production, for leisure, for sports activities, and why not "a special dress for eating in the factory cafeteria?"[31]

According to Fedorov-Davydov, universal dress should be abandoned for an important ideological reason: it perpetuates individualism. Even in capitalist societies, standard specialized dress was used for collective activities, such as in the army, the railways, the factories, or big shops. Such attire was even more important in a socialist society, where common specialized dress not only functioned as a protective garment but also had an organizational character that could reinforce the feeling of belonging to the community. It followed that the revolutionary task of the designer of communist clothes was "the organization of the socialist environment, the organization of the behavior of collectivist man, and, through the organization of behavior, the transformation of man's character, psyche, and emotions."[32]

As with the common houses or the workers' clubs, which were meant to be "social condensers," the first quality of dress should be its power to act as an instrument of socialization. In Fedorov-Davydov's eyes, the most important clothes were those used for demonstrations or for children who, dressed identically, were being educated for the collective life.

But *prozodezhda* should not be confused with *spetsodezhda,* a specialized garment with a specific productive function. For Stepanova, *spetsodezhda* designated the special protective clothes needed by surgeons, pilots, firefighters, workers in acid factories, or arctic explorers. Although the idea of a specialized dress had already been developed by Henry van de Velde, who spoke of the need for different specific types of clothes when riding bicycles, driving cars, or working in factories,[33] *prozodezhda* is distinguished by its primary anti-aestheticism. The decisive element in its design was not the aesthetic dimension but its social impact. In a text of 1921–1922, Stepanova approvingly quoted Arvatov, who had written that "the aesthetic form exists only because of its separation from life."[34] Not surprisingly, from this perspective evening dress was considered a socially unworthy subject for a revolutionary dress designer, who should abandon such preoccupations in favor of designing *spetsodezhda* for workers in hazardous environments.

As we have seen with *prozodezhda* and *spetsodezhda, sportodezhda* was a category that had priority because of its social impact. From Lenin to Orwell's Big Brother—including of course Mussolini, Stalin, and Hitler—all totalitarian leaders have been fond of sport. The totalitarian state claimed not only the soul of its citizens but also their bodies.

Considered an affair of state in the Soviet era, sport was a favorite subject for agitprop; physical exercise was almost a revolutionary duty. Quite often, stadiums were used not only as sports fields but also as a place for celebrating the mass of uniform thinking, whether in Moscow or in Nuremberg. In a rather obscure passage from his infamous *Mein Kampf*, Adolf Hitler wrote:

The clothes of the young people also have to be adapted to this purpose. It is truly miserable to be compelled to see how our youth is also subject to a lunacy of fashion which helped in converting the meaning of the old proverb *Kleider machen Leute:* (Clothes make people) into a detrimental one. Particularly with youth, clothes have to be put into the service of education. The young man who in summer walks about in long pipe-like trousers, covered up to the neck, loses, merely through his clothing a stimulant for his physical fitness.

For ambition, too, and we may as well say it, vanity also, have to be applied. Not the vanity in beautiful clothes which not everyone is able to buy, but the vanity in a beautiful, well-shaped body which everyone can help in building up.[35]

For both the Soviet and the Nazis, sport garments were thus thought to be essential to spurring patriotic activity: the "New Man" had to have a physically fit, "new" body, which was naturally devoted to the service of the state. Consequently, if sport was judged according to its social utility, it followed that team sports were the most highly appreciated, because they were supposed not only to strengthen the athlete's body but to reinforce the cohesion of the social body as well.

When she decided to create jerseys for football and basketball teams, Stepanova was not simply designing clothes—she was fulfilling an ideological mission. Some outfits for *The Death of Tarelkin* had been designed not only as theatrical costumes but also as "prototypes . . . of a sporting character" for a possible wider use.[36] Sport clothes had to be easy to wear, cut simply and without buttons, which limit freedom of movement. This type of clothing raised the interesting question of how to vary a specific type of dress; clothed in the same way, the members of the two teams had to be identifiable from a distance, and the distinctive element for achieving this goal was color. The rigor of Stepanova's geometric patterns and her combinations of colors recall the precision of her Constructivist painting. However, this graphic approach lost much of its appeal when it was translated into the three dimensions of an actual garment. Nevertheless, the students at the Social Education Academy in Moscow used her sport outfits in 1923.[37]

For Fedorov-Davydov, this was not enough. The design of such clothing had to emphasize particularly that it was a proletarian sportsman's dress: "The designer of clothing for sportsmen should make a clear distinction between socialist and capitalist sport and should emphasize the relationship between Soviet sport and the general tasks of the socialist construction, its link with the defense of the country.[38]

In 1928, Stepanova published an article in which she complained that the integration of the artist in the process of making clothing was an almost complete failure.[39]

The artist remained an "appendix" to production and "became the decorative tool of such factors as 'demand' and 'market requirements,' which take shape without his involvement."[40] In her eyes, one of the major causes of this situation was the division of work between the creator of the fabric and the designer of dress. This "lack of continuity between the fabric and the finished garment is becoming a serious hindrance for the improvement of the quality of production of our clothing."[41] Like Sonia Delaunay, Varvara Stepanova firmly believed that the only solution was to make it possible for the artists to be responsible for both tasks, thus ensuring unity of design.

In the same article, Stepanova apparently reconsidered her previous views on fashion writing:

It would be a mistake to think that fashion could be eliminated or that is an unnecessary profit-making adjunct. Fashion presents, in a readily understandable way, the complex set of lines and forms predominant in a particular time period—the external attributes of the epoch. It never repeats already-used forms, and persistently and steadily advances towards rationalization, just as our daily life in gradually becoming more and more rational.[42]

But while Stepanova saw the novelty of fashion as a positive factor, her understanding of fashion was not generally accepted. She continued to reject its mercantile dimension, which tied the artist's hands and kept him "bogged down in mediocre bourgeois taste."[43] Fashion's novelty was the newness of the artistic creation, and its evolution would necessarily lead to increasingly rationality, according to the Productivist ideals. The utopian ideal that she had in mind was a fashion that obeyed not the logic of the market but that of the artist.

In addition to developing the actor's *prozodezhda,* Liubov Popova, who shared Stepanova's Productivist ideas, created a whole series of designs for dresses that had a certain elegance, in spite of their deliberately popular style and the intentional simplicity of the ordinary printed cotton cloth that was used. This cloth was designed as part of Popova's work at the cotton-printing factory;[44] but her use of geometrical forms originating in her previous abstract painting did not appeal to the masses, who obstinately continued to prefer cloth printed with floral motifs.

Contrary to the theses of Bolshevik propaganda—which claimed that the "New Man," ineluctably produced by the communist revolution, would be immune to all temptations—old desires did not vanish. Not only the remnants of the decomposing bourgeoisie but also, as Vladimir Fon-Meck noted with regret,[45] the urban proletariat and peasantry aspired to copy Parisian fashion. In addition, the problem was not limited to the NEP (New Economic Policy) period.[46] In his classic account *The Revolution Betrayed,* Leon Trotsky lamented that

The young Soviet clerks, and often the workers too, try both in dress and manner to imitate American engineers and technicians with whom they happen to come in contact in

the factories. The industrial and clerical working girls devour with their eyes the foreign lady tourist in order to capture her modes and manners. The lucky girl who succeeds in this becomes an object of wholesale imitation. Instead of the old bangs, the better-paid working girl acquires a "permanent wave." The youth are eagerly joining "Western dancing circles." In a certain sense all this means progress, but what chiefly expresses itself here is not the superiority of socialism over capitalism, but the prevailing of petty bourgeois culture over the patriarchal life, the city over the village, the center over the backwoods, the West over the East.[47]

In a 1932 article about her recent trip to the Soviet Union, Margaret Bourke-White corroborated this observation, noting that although some women preferred dressing like men to wearing the latest Western fashions, this preference mainly reflected their desire to avoid being considered traitors to Communist ideals. Despite her revolutionary dedication, "the factory girl in Moscow is just as eager to adorn herself and to enhance her attractiveness as is the lady of Park Avenue."[48]

The designs of Popova and Stepanova were in complete discrepancy with the social and economic conditions of the times and, therefore, hardly ever got beyond the stage of prototypes. Of about 120 printed cloth designs by Stepanova, only about 20 were ever mass-produced.[49] In his 1932 review of the condition of decorative arts, the critic David Arkin was obliged to confirm the failure of the avant-garde attempts to revolutionize clothing.[50]

Less radical than the Productivist Popova or Stepanova, Nadezhda Lamanova and Aleksandra Exter were also opposed to "the tyranny of fashion and recklessness in the field of dress."[51] Lamanova, who had a successful career as a designer of haute couture before the revolution and who was one of Paul Poiret's friends, evolved toward a hybrid position. She tried to escape the tyranny of fashion by mixing Dress Reform methods with elements of Russian folk costume that "developed out of the collective creativity of the people" and "could serve as ideological and plastic material to be integrated in our urban clothing."[52] Her formal solutions are often a compromise: she agreed to design utilitarian everyday "clothes for street wear" but was unwilling to abandon the formal or evening dress that the Productivists wanted to outlaw.

It is revealing to compare Lamanova's sport clothes with Stepanova's designs; her rather long, modest, pleated skirt and something akin to knickerbockers replaced the daring shorts of the Constructivist designer. Following the traditions of haute couture, Lamanova paid special attention to the relationship between the type and properties of cloth used and the form of the dress. Nevertheless, she did take an antifashion stand, albeit one far less radical than Popova and Stepanova's position. According to her, the modern, correct conception of dress was no longer dependent on fashion. Using Dress Reform arguments, she criticized fashion because it "levels people without taking into account the characteristics and shortcomings of their bodies."[53] This was unacceptable, as everyone had the right to a harmonious figure—and it is precisely the aim of the dress designer to improve the appearance of the wearer by developing the most harmonious figure

Nadezhda Lamanova—Pioneer's attire, 1925.

Nadezhda Lamanova—Projects for sport clothes, 1925.

possible. Such a claim would have seemed ridiculous to Stepanova, whose intentionally sloppy clothes were not designed to enhance the appearance of an individual body, and who therefore paid no attention to draping.

For Lamanova, the future of dress was not *prozodezhda* but an outfit adapted to the individual figure, an idea that was very similar to the old Dress Reform concept of the *Eigenkleid,* or "personalized dress." In order to have a clearer representation of a silhouette, one should mentally divide the body into geometrical forms and thereby facilitate the construction of the dress. The application of these "artistic-constructive" ideas could, in her opinion, "wipe out the prejudice of fashion, this false idea that has, until now, forced working women to submit to bourgeois fashion instead of elaborating their own creative principles in the field of dress."[54] The utopian character of such proposals was evident, however, as this approach could not be reconciled with the demands of industrial clothing production.

At the beginning of the thirties, this attempt to modify the wearer's silhouette
was continued by one of Kandinsky's students, Sofia Beliaeva-Ekzempliiarskaia, who tried
to apply the laws of perception formulated by Gestalt psychology to optically correct a
body's shortcomings.[55]

The relationships between the cloth of a dress and its form were also a main interest of Aleksandra Exter. Clearly influenced by Tatlin's theory of the culture of materials,
Exter asserted that "every object is submitted to the laws imposed by its material."[56] The
design of a dress was therefore a direct consequence of the cloth that was to be used. Like
Lamanova, Exter declared that clothes should be not cut but "constructed." Indeed, ac-

Sofia Beliaeva-Ekzempliiarskaia—
Studies of visual perception laws
applied to dress design, 1934.

cording to the art critic Iakov Tugenkhold, the main characteristic of Exter's clothes was that "they are not drawn but constructed as an assemblage of different surfaces, which act as reminiscences of her Cubist paintings."[57]

Although she had experimented with the *prozodezhda,* designing a garment adapted to the needs of women working in offices, Exter never really abandoned a certain formal elegance. Her statements in favor of simplicity and practicality in dress sometimes contradict the "artistic" refinement of her designs. Although in her articles she mentioned the necessity of designing outfits for workers, one feels that her preference was for "individual dress," whose practical realization was to be based on the collaboration between the artist and a technician that she viewed as fundamental to solving the problem of clothing.

Openly opposed to Productivist theories announcing the death of "pure" art and its replacement with "production," Kazimir Malevich, the founder of Suprematism, was nevertheless interested in dress. Like other art objects, dress should be absolutely modern: "Do we need wardrobes with the braids of ancient costumes while modern tailors make the metallic clothing of the contemporary era?"[58]

Though Suprematism began as "a purely philosophical and instructive movement that expressed itself through color," in a second stage it became "the form that could be applied, thereby constituting the new style of the Suprematist ornament."[59] As the movement was inaugurated by his celebrated *Black Square,* which claimed to be a total approach to existential as well as formal problems, Malevich asserted that artistic

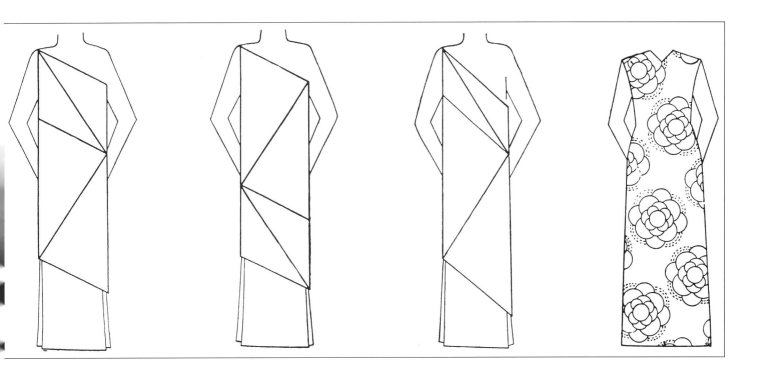

Aleksandra Exter—Project for a dress, 1923.

Aleksandra Exter—Project for an overcoat, 1923.

creation had to be concerned with the whole of human existence. As it evolved out of the narrow painterly frame of his initial phase, Suprematism reached the scale of architecture and attempted to present itself as a global principle for organizing life in its entirety. Malevich's interest in clothing is not transferred from the artistic realm into production, as was the case for the Constructivists. He annexed dress, including it in his empire, because every element of life should become Suprematist. The journal *Supremus,* a periodical meant to support Suprematism but never actually published, had planned "a section exclusively devoted to Suprematist clothing and embroidery designs."[60]

Not surprisingly, Malevich's students did not wait long to use Suprematist forms in clothing. Olga Rozanova had already decorated her dress and handbags with Supre-

Ilia Chashnik—Project for a young
girl's dress, 1924.

Ilia Chashnik—Project for a
Suprematist dress, 1924.

matist motifs in 1916. These were exhibited the following year at the *Second Modern Decorative Arts Exhibition* in Moscow.[61]

After the revolution, Malevich tried to establish a link between his Suprematist project of remaking the universe and the political program of the Bolsheviks. In a UNOVIS manifesto titled "We Want," a text intended not just for artists but also for "textile workers, apparel makers, milliners," Malevich stated: "We will create new clothes and we will give the world a meaning it has never had, as we now possess rights and liberties that have never existed before."[62] Yet despite Malevich's attempts, the expected collaboration with the new regime did not occur, and his dream to see the streets of Moscow full of people dressed in Suprematist clothes walking amid Suprematism-inspired architecture never came true.

In 1923, however, Malevich created two watercolor sketches of Suprematist outfits that were coordinated with the Suprematist forms of the new world to come. The text, written in Malevich's hand at the right of one of the designs, reads:

Harmonizing of architectural forms in whichever style of industrial architecture whether Suprematist-dynamic, static or Cubist will require a change in existing furniture, ceramics, clothes, murals, and painting. Foreseeing that the movement of architecture will carry a predominantly Suprematist harmony of functional forms, I have made a dress design in accordance with the mural painting based on color contrast.[63]

These sketches were not really dress designs, because they were not detailed enough to be put into practice. In a sense, they were the ultimate example of dress as work of art: totally utopian and functioning only in Malevich's own creative realm. The same can be said about a number of Malevich's paintings—such as *Sportsmen* (1928–1932), *Self-Portrait* (1933), the portrait of his wife Natalia (1933), and *Male Portrait* (probably a portrait of the art critic Nikolai Punin; 1933)—in which the models are dressed in what one could call the new Suprematist clothes.

Some other artists influenced by Malevich also tried to use Suprematist models for their clothing designs. However, as the case of Ilia Chashnik illustrates, they did not truly respect "the fifth dimension of art," the Suprematist principle of economy. According to this principle, the Suprematist dress had to voluntarily abandon all decoration. Chashnik's projects of 1924 violated this rule, and he used Suprematist forms in a decorative manner, applied superficially to traditionally designed dress.

SONIA DELAUNAY

Like all other fields of the visual environment, fashion was affected by the formalist experiments of the avant-garde at the beginnings of the twentieth century. Working toward the recognition of fashion as an art and wishing to be considered as artists themselves,[1] the great couturiers were deeply interested in painting. They expressed this interest not just as collectors—the painting collections of Jacques Doucet or Paul Poiret, for instance, were famous—but also as dress professionals, constantly looking for new sources of inspiration. A detailed history of the influence of the visual arts on clothing at the beginning of the twentieth century has yet to be written;[2] however, this influence was widespread. Traces of the impact of the avant-garde on dress can be found even in the popular press in advertisements, and in cartoons associating new tendencies in dress with Cubism or Futurism.

But in France, the frequent contacts between painters and couturiers did not often result in a real professional collaboration. Unlike in Germany and in Austria, the Dress Reform movement never really succeeded in Paris, the international bastion of fashion, where the great representatives of haute couture jealously guarded their monopolies. In most cases, the contributions of artists were limited to illustrations for fashion magazines—for example, the drawings of Paul Iribe and Georges Lepape for Poiret.[3]

Before the First World War, there was just one major exception to this rule—the Russian Sonia Delaunay, who became interested in dress design as a consequence of the simultaneous painting with which she and her husband Robert had experimented in the early 1910s. For Robert Delaunay, Simultaneism,[4] a style of painting based on contrasts of color, had to transcend painting and penetrate the world of objects, asserting itself in every area of life. Later on, Blaise Cendrars claimed that *"simultané* is an art of depth that technically expresses in the raw material—painting, music, dresses, posters, books, furniture, color—the universal matter: the world."[5]

In 1911, Sonia Delaunay made a cradle blanket for her son Charles—a type of covering traditionally used by the Russian peasants. While the influence of Russian folk art can be seen in the patchwork technique, the contrasts of color were chosen according to the new principles, and this item "became the precursory model of all her simultaneous objects."[6] She would apply simultaneous principles to a variety of objects, such as painted furniture, cushions, lamp shades, curtains, book bindings, and, naturally, clothes. The first *robe simultanée* was designed in 1913. Sonia Delaunay wore it for an evening event at the Bal Bullier, a legendary meeting place located at 31 Avenue de l'Observatoire, where avant-garde artists and writers mixed with the Parisian demimonde and shared the dance frenzy of the prewar years.[7] The dynamic and colorful atmosphere of "the last stronghold of the vanishing bohemia of Paris"[8] inspired one of Sonia Delaunay's most important paintings—the *Bal Bullier* (1913). She was accompanied to the Bal by her husband Robert, dressed in "a violet jacket, a beige waistcoat, and black trousers" or in "a red overcoat with a blue collar, red socks, yellow and black shoes, black trousers, green jacket, and a minuscule red tie."

Sonia was dressed in "a violet suit, a long green-and-violet sash and, under her jacket, a bodice divided into areas of vivid, tender and faded colors, in which there were mixed old pink, yellowish-orange, Nattier blue and scarlet." The outfits were sensational enough to earn these descriptions from Apollinaire in an article in which he called the Delaunays "the reformers of dress."[9] Blaise Cendrars was so impressed with Sonia's dresses that he immediately wrote the famous poem "Sur la robe elle a un corps" ("On Her Dress, She Has a Body"), later collected in *Dix-neuf poèmes élastiques (Nineteen Elastic Poems)* and dedicated to her.[10]

Under Delaunay's influence, some other artists adopted extravagant clothing. Blaise Cendrars wore unusual painted ties, and the Russian painter Vladimir Baranoff-Rossiné wore "trousers with black and white horizontal stripes 10 cm high."[11] One evening, dressed in a scarlet tuxedo, Robert Delaunay wanted to enliven Arthur Cravan's clothes and "painted scarlet tattoos on his friend's starched shirt front[;] . . . to give his posterior a dash of 'simultaneity' Arthur sat down on Robert's palette."[12]

According to Blaise Cendrars, Gino Severini, who was a good dancer and another habitué of the Bal Bullier, was so impressed by the Delaunays' attire that he immediately sent a telegram to his Futurist friends in Milan:

The great beanpole telegraphed about our dress in general, but more particularly about the details of Mrs. Sonia Delaunay's dress, *la robe simultanée*.

He was a true intelligence agency. Milan spread his piece of news around the world as a Futurist event.[13]

While one could reasonably question the literal truth of Cendrars's assertion,[14] the polemics concerning the Futurist inspiration of Sonia Delaunay's simultaneous clothes (and painting!) have not yet ended. At that time, the competition between the Delaunays and the Italian Futurists was at its peak, and the new simultaneous clothes played an important role in the contest between Milan and Paris. Although Balla's primary importance in creating Futurist clothes is unquestionable, the influence of Delaunay's clothes on the further development of Futurist dress was suggested by one contemporary critical comment:

It does not appear to us to be the moment for launching new fashions. Intelligent buffoonery in time of peace and calm can have its own reason for existing. Today the moment is too serious to be able to accept it. This buffoonery here, moreover, does not have the excuse of being new. It's a copy of Cubist clothes that the French painter Delaunay and friends wore some evenings at Bullier.[15]

With rare perspicacity, Apollinaire realized the specific character of Sonia Delaunay's approach: she "did not try at all to innovate on the level of the form of the cut, following the fashion of the day."[16] Many years later, Sonia Delaunay's confirmed the poet's intuition: "We were not interested in contemporary fashion; I tried to innovate not in terms of the form of the cut but to brighten and liven up the art of dress by using new fabrics with a wide range of colors."[17]

As an extension of painting, simultaneous clothes were clearly antifashion, using painterly techniques to attack traditional fashion. The combinations of colors destroyed any well-defined shape of the cut, and the association of different fabrics with varied textures contributed to this breaking up of form. The ties to Delaunay's Orphist experiments in painting and to the Cubist principle of assemblage are obvious. In a later interview, Sonia Delaunay asserted that "In 1913, the more or less stylized floral patterns were in fashion. I wanted to escape fashion, to do something absolutely new and modern. My starting point was the laws of color. A dress, an overcoat, and a star are all fragments of space."[18]

A simultaneous outfit was in fact a work of art that was produced on a support that was different from the usual canvas and, as such, it totally escaped the logic of fashion. Robert Delaunay was fully aware of the *robe simultanée*'s antifashion essence when he defined it as "a living painting, so to speak, a sculpture of living forms."[19] As dynamism

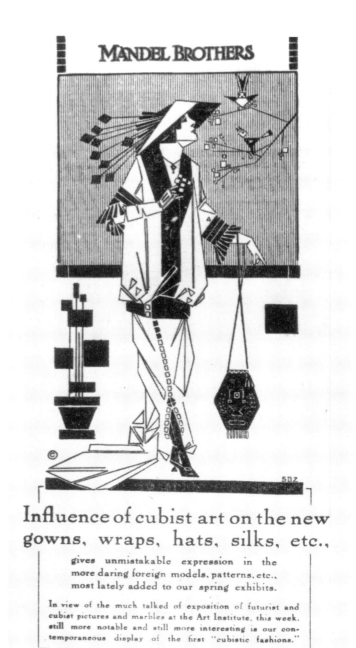

was one of the major goals of Simultaneism, the new living medium was ideal because body kinetics increased the dynamic effect of the painterly composition of the dress.

Some have attempted to explain Sonia Delaunay's temporary abandonment of painting by pointing to her sudden financial difficulties caused by the Russian Revolution, which forced her to find a way of earning a living.[20] While such economic factors are undeniably important, one must remember that the first simultaneous clothes were designed at a time when the Delaunays had no money problems. In her memoirs, Sonia Delaunay emphasized that this concentration on simultaneous dress was not frustrating to her as an artist.[21] She did not share Kandinsky's aversion to the applied arts or his fear that abstract art applied to common objects would be perceived as purely decorative. For her, there was no division between her painting and her interest in applied arts, which she saw as a natural extension of the same fundamental research into color. Her family's financial ruin had only made her look for markets for designs that had previously been reserved for herself or her immediate family and circle of friends.

During her stay in Spain, Sonia Delaunay was commissioned, on Diaghilev's recommendation, to design tunics, raffia hats, and parasols for the marquis d'Urquijo's four daughters. The success of these creations and of those for the family of the director of *La Epoca,* the influential marquis de Valdeiglesias, brought her a rich clientele; such patronage enabled her to open a fancy shop in Madrid, the Casa Sonia, on the Calle Columela. Business went well and branches were opened in Barcelona and Bilbao.

Despite these financial successes, homesickness and a wish to participate in the artistic life of Paris made the Delaunays return to France. Once there, Sonia continued to design simultaneous dresses and scarves, like the one worn by Tristan Tzara in his portrait by Robert. She began to create a new category of clothes, the *robes-poèmes.* These were a hybrid work that transgressed generic boundaries by combining poetry and dress; shortly after the first poem-dresses appeared, the Surrealist painter Victor Brauner attempted a synthesis between painting and poetry, which he called *pictopoetry.*[22]

Besides their poetic dimension, Sonia Delaunay used letters for their decorative and ornamental value, and apparently she preferred some characters to others. Her very free "typography" reminds one of Apollinaire's *Calligrammes* combined with a pinch of Marinetti's *Parole in libertà.* It seems that the Spanish avant-garde poet Ramón Gómez de la Serna, who had written a poem on a fan, suggested the idea to her. He liked the concept of the poem-dress and imagined a longer poem that would cover two or three dresses, or even a whole series to be brought out in weekly installments. The same concept was used for a *rideau-poème* with a text by Philippe Soupault, for blouses and scarves, and even for some *cabans-poèmes* (poem-three-quarter coats). Sonia Delaunay, who had already received Blaise Cendrars's tribute, was adored by poets, and she could use texts by great avant-garde literary figures such as Tristan Tzara and Philippe Soupault, who dedicated a poem to her titled "Manteau du soir de Madame Sonia Delaunay." René Crevel, who visited her apartment for the rehearsal of Tristan Tzara's *Cœur à gaz,* was amazed by the novelty of her clothes:

you enter her home and she shows you dresses, furniture, furniture drawings, sketches for dresses.

Neither the dresses nor the furniture resemble anything you can find at the couturiers' or in the furniture shows.[23]

In 1924, Jacques Delteil dedicated to her the poem "La mode qui vient," staged as a part of a poetry evening accompanied by a show of Delaunay's dress and costume designs at the Claridge Hotel. The success of this event and also that of the Baraque à mode (a clothing stall that Sonia Delaunay presented on 23 February 1923 at the Grand Bal Travesti-Transmental organized by the Russian Artists' Union at Bullier) attracted the attention of the furrier and couturier Jacques Heim, who became her associate. The result of this partnership, the Ateliers simultanés, was very encouraging and led to the triumph at the *Exposition internationale des arts décoratifs* of 1925. Her shop, the Boutique simultanée, became famous, and well-known personalities, including Gloria Swanson and Nancy Cunard, were among her clients.

The techniques employed by Sonia Delaunay were always based on her theories of the simultaneous and on combinations of fur and fabric, or even metal, which added a tactile element to the visual pleasure. "For her," wrote Robert Delaunay, "a dress or an overcoat was a fragment of space that was designed and structured according to its material and dimensions, forming an organized whole obeying laws that become a standardization of her art."[24]

In 1927, Sonia Delaunay's notoriety was so great that she was invited to lecture at Sorbonne.[25] In her talk, "The Influence of Painting on Fashion," Sonia Delaunay drew a parallel between the evolution of modern painting and the liberation of dress from the academicism of couturiers, claiming that the construction and cut of a dress should be conceived at the same time as its decoration. Consequently, the traditional separation between the design of the printed cloth and that of the dress had to be abolished. This abolition had been already achieved in the first *robes simultanées,* in which contrasts of color were used to fuse the wearer's body with the dress.

The idea of integrating the separate fields of fabric and dress design was commercially exploited by the patenting of *tissu-patron,* the "fabric-pattern."[26] This invention was a dress kit that combined dress-cutting marks with an appropriate decorative pattern, both printed on the piece of fabric cut to the required dimensions. There is an obvious analogy between the idea of a prefabricated dress and modern architecture's concept of the prefabricated house. The *tissu-patron* was conceived in order to maintain the unity between fabric decoration and dress design. However, the buyers of these *tissu-patron* dress kits did not respect the cut that was intended for a specific pattern, often replacing it with their own designs; this lack of control finally made Sonia Delaunay abandon the idea.

The economic crisis of 1929 led to the bankruptcy of Ateliers simultanés, thereby putting an end to Sonia Delaunay's experiments in the field of clothing.

FASHION AND MODERNITY

1. See, for example, Jennifer Craik, *The Face of Fashion: Cultural Studies in Fashion* (London, 1994), or Dorothy Ko, "Bondage in Time: Footbinding and Fashion Theory," *Fashion Theory: The Journal of Dress, Body and Culture* 1, no. 1 (1997): 3–27.

2. For a discussion of the relationship between fashion and change, see Fred Davis, *Fashion, Culture, and Identity* (Chicago, 1992), pp. 14–15. The change from traditional Muslim dress to Mongol costume in the thirteenth century in the conquered areas of the Middle East or the Westernization of clothing in the Muslim territories from the nineteenth century on cannot be considered "fashion changes" in the modern sense of the term; see Bernard Lewis, *The Middle East: A Brief History of the Last 2,000 Years* (New York, 1995), pp. 3–7.

3. "Fashion as we know it in the west is not, and never was universal, it is a product of Europe and is of comparatively recent date" (Quentin Bell, *On Human Finery* [London, 1947], p. 60).

4. Gilles Lipovetsky, *The Empire of Fashion: Dressing Modern Democracy* trans. Catherine Porter (Princeton, 1994), p. 55 (originally published as *L'empire de l'éphémère: La mode et son destin dans les sociétés modernes* [Paris, 1987]).

5. See Thorstein Veblen, "Dress as an Expression of the Pecuniary Culture," chap. 7 of *The Theory of the Leisure Class* (1899; reprint, New York, 2001). Pierre Bourdieu, *Distinction: A Social Critique of the Judgement of Taste,* trans. Richard Nice (Cambridge, Mass., 1987), (originally published as *La distinction: Critique sociale du jugement* [Paris, 1979]).

6. Lipovetsky, *The Empire of Fashion,* pp. 3–4, 5.

7. Ibid., p. 5.

8. Robert Radford, "Art and Fashion, a Love Affair or a Shoot Out? An Application of Lipovetsky's Cultural Theory of the Ephemeral," *Issues in Architecture, Art, and Design* 3, no. 2 (1994): 83. See also Radford, "Dangerous Liaisons: Art, Fashion, and Individualism," *Fashion Theory: The Journal of Dress, Body, and Culture* 2, no. 2 (1998): 151–164.

9. Charles Baudelaire, *Œuvres complètes* (Paris, 1968), p. 547.

ROMANTICISM: FROM ECCENTRICITY TO ARTISTIC DRESS

1. Louis Magron, *Le Romantisme et la mode: D'après des documents inédits* (Paris, 1911), p. 57.

2. Ibid., pp. 56–57.

3. Theophilus Gautier, *Fashion* (Paris, 1858), p. 1. This work originally appeared as Théophile Gautier, *De la mode* (Paris, 1858); the earliest English translation was in *Artist* (1858), and the first separate edition was published by the *Newspaper of Ladies and Messenger from Ladies and from Young Ladies,* March 1858.

RATIONAL, ARTISTIC, AND AESTHETIC DRESS IN ENGLAND

1. On Amelia Bloomer, see Dexter C. Bloomer, *Life and Writings of Amelia Bloomer* (Baltimore, 1972); Anne S. Coon, *Hear Me Patiently: The Reform Speeches of Amelia Jenks Bloomer* (Westport, Conn., 1994), and Gayle V. Fischer, *Pantaloons and Power: A Nineteenth-Century Dress Reform in the United States* (Kent, Ohio, 2001).

2. William Morris, "The Lesser Arts, Delivered before the Trades' Guild of Learning, December 4, 1877," in *Hopes and Fears for Art; and, Signs of Change* (Bristol, 1994, p. 24; John Ruskin, quoted in Anne Buck, "John Ruskin and Dress, 1882," *Costume* 32 (1998): 80. In his letter, Ruskin also called for "unusually comfortable" clothes.

3. Though it has not been proven that Morris designed his wife's clothes, it is likely that he did so and persuaded her to wear such dresses.

4. William Morris, "The Beauty of Life: Delivered before the Birmingham Society of Arts and School of Design, February 19, 1880," in *Hopes and Fears for Art,* p. 76.

5. William Morris, "On Art and Industry," in *Collected Works,* vol. 22, (London, 1914), p. 265.

6. William Morris, *Art under Socialism: A Lecture Delivered before the Secular Society of Leicester* (London, 1884), p. 12.

7. Morris, "On Art and Industry," p. 263.

8. Ibid., p. 262.

9. Edward William Godwin, "A Lecture on Dress" (1868), *The Mask,* 6 April 1914; reprinted in this volume, p. 92.

10. Ibid., pp. 92.

11. Ibid., p. 93.

12. Edward William Godwin, *Dress and Its Relation to Health and Climate* (London, 1914).

13. John Ruskin, *The Ethics of Dust* (1865; reprint, London, 1925), p. 121; quoted in Buck, "John Ruskin and Dress, 1882, p. 80.

14. Godwin, "A Lecture on Dress," p. 94.

15. Godwin, quoted in Stella Mary Newton, *Health, Art, and Reason: Dress Reformers of the nineteenth Century* (London, 1974), p. 74.

16. Lionel Lambourne, "Edward William Godwin; Aesthetic Polymath," in Susan Weber Soros, ed., *E. W. Godwin: Aesthetic Movement Architect and Designer* (New Haven, 1999), p. 34.

17. Diana de Marly, *The History of Haute Couture, 1850–1950* (London, 1980), p. 63.

18. On this aspect of Rossetti's art, see Leonée Ormond, "Dress in the Painting of Dante Gabriel Rossetti," *Costume* 8 (1974.).

19. de Marly, *The History of Haute Couture,* p. 66.

20. The best overview of the subject of *Reformkleid* is still Stella Mary Newton's *Health, Art, and Reason.*

21. Alison Smith, "The 'British Matron' and the Body Beautiful: The Nude Debate of 1885," in Elizabeth Prettejohn, ed., *After the Pre-Raphaelites: Art and Aestheticism in Victorian England* (New Brunswick, N.J., 1999), p. 224.

22. Patricia Cunningham mentions the use of the Venus de Milo as an aesthetic standard for the female body as early as 1865. Later on, the comparison will become a commonplace, and it was still used in the twentieth century—for example, by Paul Schultze-Naumburg in his *Die Kultur des weiblichen Körpers als Grundlage der Frauenkleidung* (Leipzig, 1903).

23. Mary Eliza Haweis, *The Art of Beauty* (London, 1878), pp. 45–46.

24. Oscar Wilde, "Woman's Dress," *Pall Mall Gazette* 40, no. 6114 (October 14, 1884); reprinted in this volume, p. 114. Wilde's appreciation of the costume was not absolute, however. He once wrote that "Greek dress was in its essence inartistic. Nothing should reveal the body but the body" (Wilde, "Phrases and Philosophies for the Use of the Young," in *Art and Decoration: Being Extracts from Reviews and Miscellanies* [London, 1920], p. 3).

25. Wilde, "Woman's Dress," p. 114.

26. Frank Harris, *Oscar Wilde* (London, 1938), p. 89.

27. Wilde, "Phrases and Philosophies for the Use of the Young," p. 3.

28. Oscar Wilde, "More Radical Ideas on Dress Reform," *Pall Mall Gazette* 40, no. 6224 (November 11, 1884); reprinted in this volume, p. 118.

29. Oscar Wilde, "Slaves of Fashion," in *Art and Decoration;* reprinted in this volume, p. 111.

30. Oscar Wilde, *The Writings of Oscar Wilde* (London, 1907), p. 254.

31. See Mary Warner Blanchard, *Oscar Wilde's America: Counterculture in the Gilded Age* (New

Haven, 1988). For details of Wilde's wardrobe during the tour, see Alicia Finkel, "A Tale of Lilies, Sunflowers, and Knee-breeches: Oscar Wilde's Wardrobe for His American Tour," *Dress* 15 (1989).

32. Max Beerbohm, "1880," in *The Yellow Book* (London, 1994), p. 72.

33. James Whistler, "Ten O'Clock" (1885), in Ian Small, ed., *The Aesthetes: A Sourcebook* (London, 1979), pp. 28–29.

34. On Liberty's, see Alison Adburgham, *Liberty's: The Biography of a Shop* (London, 1975), and Mervin Levy, *Liberty Style: The Classic Years* (New York, 1986).

35. On the Omega Workshops, see Isabelle Anscombe, *Omega and After: Bloomsbury and the Decorative Arts* (London, 1981), and Richard Shone, ed., *The Art of Bloomsbury* (London, 1999).

HENRY VAN DE VELDE AND GERMANY

1. The work is now in the Bellerive Museum in Zurich.

2. Henry van de Velde, "Première prédication de l'Art," *L'Art Moderne,* 13, no. 53 (December 1893): 420.

3. Henry van de Velde, *Aperçus en vue d'une Synthèse d'Art* (Brussels 1895), p. 30.

4. Van de Velde, quoted in Françoise Aubry, "Henry van de Velde ou la négation de la mode," *Revue de l'Institut de Sociologie* (Brussels) 1 (1977): 295.

5. Van de Velde, quoted in Claude Lemaire, "Abandon, grâce, souplesse," in *Art Nouveau Belgique* (Brussels, 1980), p. 179.

6. See Birgit Schulte, "Ich bin diese Frau, die um jeden Preis Ihr Glück will . . . Maria Sèthe und H. van de Velde—eine biographischen Studie," in Klaus-Jürgen Sembach and Birgit Schulte, eds., *Henry van de Velde: Ein europäischer Künstler seiner Zeit* (Cologne, 1992).

7. Van de Velde, quoted in Lemaire, "Abandon, grâce, souplesse," p.179.

8. *Toulouse-Lautrec en Belgique* (Paris, 1955), p. 18.

9. Siegfried Giedion, "Mode oder Zeiteinstellung," *Information* (Zurich), 1 June 1932, p. 9; quoted in Mark Wigley, *White Walls, Designer Dresses: The Fashioning of Modern Architecture,* (Cambridge, Mass., 1995), p. 70.

10. I am indebted to Dr. Birgit Schulte, the curator of Henry van de Velde foundation in Hagen, Germany, who brought to my attention a photograph of Gertrud Osthaus dressed in one of van de Velde's creations.

11. Adolf Loos, "The Poor Little Rich Man," in his *Spoken into the Void: Collected Essays, 1897–1900,* trans. James O. Newman and John H. Smith (Cambridge, Mass., 1982), pp. 124–127.

12. David A. Hanks, *The Decorative Designs of Frank Lloyd Wright* (London, 1979), pp. 24–25.

13. A photograph dated 1910 is in the Archives of the State University of New York at Buffalo.

14. John Lloyd Wright, *My Father Who Is on Earth* (New York, 1946), pp. 41–42; quoted in Hanks, *The Decorative Designs of Frank Lloyd Wright,* p. 103.

15. Henry van de Velde, *Die künstlerische Hebung der Fraunetracht,* (Krefeld, 1900); trans. in this volume as "The Artistic Improvement of Women's Clothing," p. 127.

16. For a recent discussion of the perception of the male dress at the end of the nineteenth century, see Anne Hollander, *Sex and Suits: The Evolution of Modern Dress,* (New York, 1995): "What was entirely forgotten was that male dress was equally the product of fantasy, a deeply erotic fashionable just like the female version. But men's clothes had long been striking the eye in a different way, appearing somehow naturally sensible in themselves, just as they had been carefully designed to do so" (p. 125). See also Christopher Breward, "Manliness, Modernity, and the Shaping of Male Clothing," in Joanne Entwistle and Elizabeth Wilson, eds., *Body Dressing* (Oxford, 2001).

17. Van de Velde, "The Artistic Improvement in Women's Clothing," p. 127.

18. Van de Velde, quoted in "Henry van de Velde," p. 296.

19. Henry van de Velde, *Les mémoires inachevés d'un artiste européen,* ed. Léon Ploegaerts (Brussels, 1999), 2: 778.

20. Van de Velde, "The Artistic Improvement of Women's Clothing," p. 127.

21. See Marianne Carlano, "Wild and Waxy: Dutch Art Nouveau Artistic Dress," *Art Journal* 54, no. 1 (spring 1995): 30–33.

22. On dress reform, see Wolfgang Krabbe, *Gesellschafts-Veränderung durch Lebensreform: Merkmale einer Sozialreformatorischen Bewegung in Deutschland der Industrialisierung-Période,* (Göttingen, 1974); Stella Mary Newton, *Health, Art, and Reason: Dress Reformers of the Nineteenth Century* (London, 1974); and Angela

Völker, "Kleiderreform, Künstlerkleid und Mode," in *Drüber und Drunter: Wiender Damenmode von 1900–1914* (Vienna, 1987).

23. The literature on the corset is plentiful. Among the most important recent titles, see Birgit Stamm, "Auf dem Werk zum Reformkleid—Die Kritik des Korsetts und der diktierend Mode," in Ekkard Siepmann, ed., *Kunst und Alltag* (Giessen, 1978); David Kunzle, *Fashion and Fetishism: A Social History of the Corset, Tight-lacing, and Other Forms of Body-Sculpture in the West* (Totowa, N.J., 1982); Mel Davies, "Corsets and Conception: Fashion and Demographic Trends in the Nineteenth Century," *Comparative Studies in Society and History* 24, no. 4 (October 1982): 611–641; Sabine Welsch, *Ein Austieg dem Korsett: Reformkleidung um 1900* (Darmstadt, 1996); Valerie Steele, *The Corset: A Social History* (New Haven, 2001); and Leigh Summers, *Bound to Please* (New York, 2001).

24. Friedrich Deneken, "Künstlerkleid und Eigenkleid," in *Zweiter Bericht des Städtischen Kaiser-Wilhelm Museum,* (Krefeld, 1904); trans. in this volume as a "Artistic Dress and Personalized Dress," p. 146.

25. Max von Boehn, *Bekleidungskunst und Mode,* (Munich, 1918), p. 109. See Gerda Brauer, "Der Künstler ist seiner innersten Essenz nach glühende Individualist: Henry van de Veldes Beiträge zur Reformierung des Krefelden Industrie Grenzen einer Geverbeförderung durch Kunst," in Sembach and Schulte, eds., *Henry van de Velde..*

26. Van de Velde, "The Artistic Improvement of Women's Clothing," p. 126.

27. Deneken, "Artistic Dress and Personalized Dress," p. 144.

28. Van de Velde, "The Artistic Improvement of Women's Clothing," p. 128.

29. For the relationship between modern architecture and modern dress, see the seminal work of Mark Wigley, *White Walls, Designer Dresses:* "Modern architecture cannot be separate from dress design. . . . The modern architect is first and foremost a creator of dress" (p. 86).

30. Van de Velde, "The Artistic Improvement of Women's Clothing," pp. 129–130.

31. Mary Eliza Haweis, *The Art of Beauty* (London, 1878), p. 98.

32. Adolf Loos, "La mode feminine," in *Paroles dans le vide* (Paris, 1981), p. 116.

33. For *Eigenkleid,* see von Boehn, *Bekleidungskunst und Mode,* p. 119.

34. Van de Velde, "The Artistic Improvement of Women's Clothing," p. 133.

35. Van de Velde, *Les mémoires inachevés d'un artiste européen*, 2, pp. 780–781.

36. Von Boehn, *Bekleidungskunst und Mode*, p. 109.

37. Van de Velde, "The Artistic Improvement of Women's Clothing," p. 135.

38. Alfred Mohrbutter, *Das Kleid der Frau* (Darmstadt, 1903), and *Das künstlerische Kleid der Frau* (Leipzig, 1904); Anna Muthesius, *Das Eigenkleid der Frau* (Krefeld, 1903).

39. For a good summary of these debates, see John Heskett, *German Design, 1870–1918* (New York, 1986), esp. pp. 119–136, and the recent monograph by Frederic Schwartz, *The Werkbund: Design Theory and Mass Culture before the First World War* (New Haven, 1996).

40. In his article "Expressionism in the Discourse of Fashion" (*Fashion Theory: The Journal of Dress, Body, and Culture* 4, no. 1 [2000]: 56), Sherwin Simmons quotes an attempt by Bruno Rauecker to discuss dress in connection with the "type" theory.

41. Lilly Reich, "Modefragen," *Die Forms* (1922), trans. in this volume as "Questions of Fashion."

42. Sonja Günther, *Lilly Reich, 1885–1947: Innenarchitektin, Designerin, Ausstellungsgestalterin* (Stuttgart, 1988), p. 86. On Lilly Reich, see also Magdalena Droste, "Lilly Reich: Her Career as an Artist," in Mathilda McQuaid, ed., *Lilly Reich, Designer and Architect* (New York, 1996).

43. On Haas-Heye's activity, see Simmons, "Expressionism in the Discourse of Fashion," pp. 56–60.

44. See Brigid Doherty, "Fashionable Ladies, Dada Dandies," *Art Journal* 54, no. 1 (spring 1995): 46–50.

KLIMT AND THE WIENER WERKSTÄTTE

1. For an analysis of how the concept of *Gesamtkunstwerk* was understood in Vienna, see the excellent study by Werner Hofmann, "Gesamtkunstwerk Wien," in *Der Hang zum Gesamtkunstwerk* (Zurich, 1983).

2. Christian Brandstätter, *Klimt et la mode* (Paris, 1998), p. 9.

3. See Susannna Partsch, *Gustav Klimt: Painter of Women* (Munich, 1994), p. 48. Partsch reproduces a photograph of Hermann Bahr dressed in a Klimt-like robe (p. 50).

4. Elisabeth Rücker, *Wiener Charme: Mode 1914/1915: Graphiken und Accessoires,* (Nuremberg, 1984), p. 34.

5. Among those interested in *Kunstlerkleid* was Alfred Roller, the celebrated set and costume designer and one of Klimt's dear friends, who designed indoor attire for his wife, the artist Mileva Stoisavljevic. For information on Roller, see Manfred Wagner, *Alfred Roller in seiner Zeit* (Salzburg, 1996).

6. Ten dress designs were reproduced in *Deutsche Kunst und Dekoration* of 1906. Sometimes attributed to Klimt alone, these designs may be a joint creation of both Klimt and Flöge. See Partsch, *Gustav Klimt,* p. 45.

7. The most comprehensive study of Klimt and Flöge is Wolfgang Georg Fischer, *Gustav Klimt and Emilie Flöge: An Artist and His Muse,* trans. Michael Robinson (New York, 1992) (originally published as *Gustav Klimt und Emilie Flöge: Genie und Talent, Freundschaft und Bessessenheit,* [Vienna, 1987]). On Flöge's interests, see Partsch, *Gustav Klimt,* p. 36, who mentions the possible influence of the psychoanalyst Otto Gross, and Ulrike Steiner, "Die Frau im modernen Kleid: Emilie Flöge und die Lebensreform-Bewegung," in *Gegenwelten: Gustav Klimt—Künstlerleben im Fin de Siècle* (Munich, 1996).

8. The literature on the Wiener Werkstätte is huge; the best monograph remains Werner J. Schweiger's *Wiener Werkstätte: Kunst und Handwerk 1903–1932* (Vienna, 1982).

9. Mark Wigley, "White Out: Fashioning the Modern," in Deborah Fausch, Paulette Singley, Rodolphe El Khoury, and Zvi Efrat, eds., *Architecture: In Fashion* (New York, 1994), p. 193. Wimmer-Wisgrill's visit actually took place in 1912—that is, after the opening of the *Mode-abteilung.*

10. This summer dress was published in *Mode* (Vienna) in 1911; it is reproduced in Traude Hansen, *Wiener Werkstätte: Mode, Stoffe, Schmuck, accessoires* (Vienna, 1984), p. 46.

11. Josef Hoffmann, "Das individuelle Kleid," *Die Waage,* 1, no. 15 (9 April 1898); trans in this volume as "The Individual Dress."

12. Walter Crane, "Of the Progress of Taste in Dress in Relation to Art Education," *Aglaia* 3 (1894); reprinted in this volume.

13. The manifesto is quoted in Schweiger, *Wiener Werkstätte,* p. 285.

14. Hoffmann, quoted in *Vienne 1880–1938: L'Apocalypse joyeuse* (Paris, 1986), p. 272.

15. Adolf Loos, "La mode masculine," in his *Paroles dans le vide* (Paris, 1981), p. 18.

16. Werner Fenz, *Koloman Moser: Art graphique, art appliqué, peinture* (Paris, 1989), p. 196.

17. See *Wimmer-Wisgrill-Modeentwürfe 1912–1927* (Vienna, 1983).

18. For the repercussions of the "Away from Paris!" slogan in Germany, see Sherwin Simmons, "Expressionism in the Discourse of Fashion," *Fashion Theory: The Journal of Dress, Body, and Culture* 4, no. 1 (2000): 55–56.

FUTURISM AND DRESS

1. Filippo T. Marinetti, "Destruction of Syntax—Imagination without Strings—Words-in-Freedom" (1913), in Umbro Apollonio, ed., *Futurist Manifestos* (London, 1973), p. 97.

2. Umberto Boccioni, Carlo Carrà, Luigi Russolo, Giacomo Balla, and Gino Severini, "Futurist Painting: Technical Manifesto of 1910," in Apollonio, ed., *Futurist Manifestos,* p. 29.

3. Volt (Vincenzo Fani), "Manifesto della moda femminile futurista," *Roma Futurista* 3, no. 72 (20 February 1920); trans. in this volume as "Futurist Manifesto of Women's Fashion," p. 160.

4. Enrico Santamaria, "Conversando con Balla," *Griffa* 1, no. 10 (15 August 1920); quoted in Giovanni Lista, *Giacomo Balla futuriste* (Lausanne, 1984), p. 143.

5. Enrico Crispolti, *Il Futurismo e la moda: Balla e gli altri* (Venice, 1986), p. 7.

6. Giacomo Balla, "Futurist Manifesto of Men's Clothing, 1913," in Apollonio, ed., *Futurist Manifestos,* p. 132.

7. Arnaldo Ginna and Bruno Corra, *Arte dell'avvenire* (Ravenna, 1910).

8. Volt, "Futurist Manifesto of Women's Fashion," p. 160.

9. The letter has been published by Maurizio Fagiolo dell'Arco in his *Futur-Balla* (Roma, 1970).

10. Elica Balla, *Con Balla* (Milan, 1984), p. 280.

11. Emily Braun, "Futurist Fashion: Three Manifestoes," *Art Journal* 54, no. 1 (spring 1995): 37.

12. Gilles Lipovetsky, *The Empire of Fashion: Dressing Modern Democracy,* trans. Catherine Porter (Princeton, 1999), p. 74 (originally published as *L'empire de l'éphémère: La mode et son destin dans les sociétés moderne* [Paris, 1987]).

13. Le Corbusier, *Vers une architecture* (Paris, 1986), p. 115.

14. Another version has been published in Apollonio, ed., *Futurist Manifestos,* under the title "Futurist Manifesto of Men's Clothing."

15. Giacomo Balla, (Milan, 20 May 1914), trans. in this volume as "Male Futurist Dress: A Manifesto," p. 155.

16. Giacomo Balla and Fortunato Depero, "Futurist Reconstruction of the Universe," in Apollonio, ed., *Futurist Manifestos,* p. 199.

17. Giacomo Balla, "Male Futurist Dress," p. 156.

18. Lista, *Giacomo Balla futuriste,* p. 70.

19. Giacomo Balla, "Male Futurist Dress," p. 156.

20. F. T. Marinetti, "Il Tattilismo," in Maria Drudi Gambilla and Teresa Fiori, eds., *Archivi del Futurismo* (Rome, 1958–1962), 1:60.

21. Giacomo Balla and Depero, "The Futurist Reconstruction of the Universe," 199.

22. Marinetti, quoted in Luigi Scrivo, *Sintesi del futurismo* (Rome, 1968), p. 203.

23. Crispolti, *Il Futurismo e la moda,* p. 100.

24. F. T. Marinetti, "Proclamation futuriste aux Espagnols," in his *Le Futurisme* (Lausanne, 1980), p. 74.

25. Elica Balla, *Con Balla,* p. 350. Recently, Giovanni Lista has contested Balla's authorship of "The Antineutral Dress," which he attributed to Marinetti: "the Marinettian style is perfectly recognizable in the Italian variant of the text and it is obvious that Balla could not have conceived the new manifesto" (Lista, *Le Futurisme: Création et avant-garde* [Paris, 2001], p. 153). In support of his arguments, Lista mentioned the case of the Futurist Pratella, who admitted that the manifestos he signed were in fact written by Marinetti (Giovanni Lista, "La mode futuriste," in *Europe 1910–1939: Quand l'art habillait le vêtement* [Paris, 1997], pp. 30–31). However, while Marinetti's influence cannot be denied, many of the ideas expressed in the manifesto belonged to Balla, who was the only one who signed the 1914 text.

26. Giacomo Balla, "Il vestito antineutrale: manifesto futurista." (Milan: Direzione del Movimento Futurista, 11 September 1914); trans. in this volume as "The Antineutral Dress: A Futurist Manifesto," p. 157. In a manifesto of the same period, "L'Orgoglio italiano," Marinetti called the Italians "the most mobile of all people" (in Drudi Gambilla and Fiori, eds., *Archivi del futurismo,* 1:33).

27. For the influence of the Cubist painting on the introduction of camouflage in the French army, see Stephen Kern, *The Culture of Time and Space, 1880–1918* (Cambridge, Mass., 1983), pp. 302–304.

28. Marinetti, quoted in Giovanni Lista, *Balla* (Modena, 1982), p. 57.

29. Elica Balla, *Con Balla,* p. 358.

30. Lista, "La mode futuriste," p. 31.

31. Lucien Corpechot, *Lettres sur la Jeune Italie* (Nancy, 1919), pp. 42–43.

32. Pier Luigi Fortunati, "I futuristi italiani all'Esposizione d'Arte Decorativa di Parigi-intervista con Giacomo Balla e Guglielmo Janneli," *L'Impero*, 20 June 1925; quoted in Lista, *Giacomo Balla futuriste*, p. 145.

33. Enrico Crispolti, "Balla beyond Painting: The 'Futurist Reconstruction' of Fashion," in Fabio Benzi, ed., *Balla. Futurismo tra arte e moda: Opere della Fondazione Biagiotti Cigna* (Milan, 1998), p. 64.

34. Volt, "Futurist Manifesto of Women's Fashion," pp. 160–161.

35. Rosalia Bonito-Fanelli, "Le dessin textile et l'avant-garde en Europe, 1910–1939," in *Europe 1910–1939*, p. 134.

36. See Alessandra Quattordio, "Moda e aerogioielli," in *Crali aeropittore futurista* (Milan, 1987), pp. 75–79, and "Crali moda futurista," in *Crali futurista* (n.p., n.p.), fascicle 22.

37. "Crali moda futurista," fascicle 22.

38. Tullio Crali interview with the author, 1992.

39. "Crali moda futurista," fascicle 22.

40. Viviana Benhamou, "Ernesto Thayaht (1893–1959): nouvelles perspectives," in *Europe 1910–1939*, p. 44.

41. Crispolti, "Balla beyond Painting," p. 131.

42. On László Moholy-Nagy's overall, see Gabriele Mahn, "Autour de Sophie Tauber et Johannes Itten," in *Europe 1910–1939*, p. 117. Mann quotes the Hungarian art historian and Moholy-Nagy expert Kristina Passuth, who asserted to her that this garment was originally a fisherman's working attire.

43. Ernesto Thayaht and Ruggero Michahelles, (Tonfano, Fonte dei marmi, 20 September 1932); trans. in this volume as "Manifesto for the Transformation of Male Clothing," p. 167.

44. On the collaboration between Thayaht and Vionnet, see Betty Kirke, "Vionnet: Fashion's Twentieth Century Technician," *Thresholds* 22 (2001).

THE RUSSIAN AVANT-GARDE AND DRESS

1. Aleksei Gan, "Constructivism," in Stephen Bann, ed., *The Tradition of Constructivism*, (1974; reprint New York, 1990), p. 32.

2. Nikolai Taraboukine [Tarabukin], *Le dernier tableau: Écrits sur l'art et l'histoire de l'art à l'époque du constructivisme russe* (Paris, 1972), p. 42.

3. Nikolai Tarabukin, "Communication to the INKhUK Praesidium," in Selim O. Khan-Magomedov, *Rodchenko: The Complete Work*, ed. Vieri Quilici (Cambridge, Mass., 1986), p. 292.

4. Osip Brik, "Ot kartini k sittsu," *LEF*, 2, no. 2 (1924): 30.

5. Aleksandr Rodchenko, "Slogans," in Richard Andrews and Milena Kalinovska, eds., *Art into Life: Russian Constructivism, 1914–1932* (New York, 1990), p. 71.

6. "Transcript of the Discussion of Comrade Stepanova's Paper 'On Constructivism,' December 22, 1921," in Andrews and Kalinovska, eds., *Art into Life*, p. 78.

7. For the debate over the concept of a work of art as a "thing," see Hubertus Gassner, "The Constructivists: Modernism on the Way to Modernization," in *The Great Utopia: The Russian and Soviet Avant-Garde, 1915–1932* (New York, 1992), pp. 305–308.

8. Aleksei Fillipov, "Production Art," in Bann, ed., *The Tradition of Constructivism*, p. 23.

9. P. Kropotkin, *The Conquest of Bread* (New York, 1906), p. 110.

10. Platon Kerzhentsev, "Upriok khudozhnikam," *Sovetskaia strana* 3 (10 February 1919): 3. Kropotkin himself was not more explicit, writing only that "fashion in vogue at the time of the Revolution will certainly make for simplicity" (*The Conquest of Bread*, p. 110).

11. Richard Stites, *Revolutionary Dreams: Utopian Vision and Experimental Life in the Russian Revolution* (New York, 1989), p. 137.

12. Tatiana Strijenova, *La mode en Union Soviétique 1917–1945* (Paris, 1991).

13. Stites mentions that "captured White officers sometimes had the epaulettes nailed into their shoulders as symbolic retribution before being executed" (*Revolutionary Dreams*, p. 132).

14. On the relationship between utopias and dress, see Richard Martin, "Dress and Dream: The Utopian Idealism of Clothing," *Arts Magazine* 62, no. 2 (October 1987): 58–60; Richard Martin, "The Deceit of Dress: Utopian Visions and the Arguments against Clothing," *Utopian Studies* 4 (1991): 79–84; and Aileen Ribeiro "Utopian Dress," in Elizabeth Wilson and Juliet Ash, eds., *Chic Thrills* (Berkeley, 1992).

15. Strijenova, *La mode en Union Soviétique*, p. 112.

16. Sergei Tretiakov, "From Where to Where? (Futurism's Perspectives)," in Anna Lawton, ed., *Russian Futurism through Its Manifestoes, 1912–1928* (Ithaca, N.Y., 1988), p. 215.

17. Vladimir Tatlin, "Otvechaiu na 'Pismo k Futur-istami,'" *Anarkhiia,* 27 September 1918, p. 29.

18. Taraboukine, *Le dernier tableau,* p. 59. For an analysis of Tatlin's reliefs as a preparatory phase of his utilitarian designs, see Radu Stern, "'Ni vers le nouveau, ni vers l'ancien, mais vers ce qui est nécessaire.' Tatlin et le problème du vêtement," in *Europe 1910–1939: Quand l'art habillait le vête-ment* (Paris, 1997), p. 66.

19. Tatlin, quoted in "Novyi byt," *Krasnaïa Panorama,* 4 December 1924, p. 17.

20. Boris Arvatov, "Organizatsiia byta," in *Al'manakh Proletkul'ta* (Moscow, 1925), p. 81.

21. In her article "Les objets quotidiens du con-structivisme russe" (*Les Cahiers du Musée Na-tional d'Art Moderne,* no. 64 [summer 1998]: p. 51), Christina Kiaer asserts that "these models had been effectively produced in one of the facto-ries of Leningrad textile trust (Leningradodezhda) owned by the State." Unfortunately, her claim is not substantiated by any evidence.

22. On Tatlin's conception of design, see Elena Sidorina, "Konstruirovanne byta i sootvestvie bytu. Proektnaya kontseptsiia V. Tatlina," in her *Skvoz' ves' dvadtsat'ii vek: Hudojestvenno-proektn'ie konctseptsii russkogo avantgarda* (Moscow, 1994), pp. 287–298. His slogan appears on a banner in his studio.

23. Konstantin Miklashevski, *Gipertrofia iskusstve* (Petrograd, 1924), p. 61.

24. The photomontage is now in the TSGALI archives in Moscow. In a rather perplexing read-ing, Kiaer interprets it as an encoded work. Ac-cording to her, the four patrons reproduced around Tatlin from with his figure a "subtle im-age" of a hammer. In her even more puzzling analysis, this hammer is part of the well-known Soviet symbol of hammer and sickle and hits "the elegance of the ancient world" ("Les objets coti-diens, p. 50).

25. For details concerning the activity of Steponova and Popova at the factory, see Christina Lodder, *Russian Constructivism* (New Haven, 1983), pp. 291–292, and Alexandre Lavrientiev, "Mini-malisme et création textile ou l'origine de la mode constructiviste," in *Europe 1910–1939,* pp. 72–79. In her article on Popova, Christina Kiaer ex-plained their engagement: "the Constructivist women were most likely invited to work there, while their male colleagues were not, because of the feminization of the textile industry" (Kiaer, "The Russian Constructivist Flapper Dress," *Criti-cal Inquiry* 28, no. 1 [autumn 2001]: 192). How-ever, in a text from 1931 cited by Lavrentiev, Stepanova mentioned that the director went to VKhUTEMAS without finding interested artists and then approached Pavel Kuznetsov and Aris-tark Lentulov. The first wanted his name printed on every meter of cloth and the second one asked a very high price. Moreover, Lavrentiev asserted that in 1924, Stepanova and Popova were "practi-cally the only two women who dared to work for the textile industry," then totally dominated by men ("Minimalisme et création textile," p. 75).

26. Varst [Varvara Stepanova], "Kostium segodni-ashnego dnia—prozodezhda," *LEF* 1, no. 2 (1923); trans. in this volume as "Present-Day Dress—Production Clothing," p. 172.

27. On Stepanova's theater costumes, see Alexan-der Lavrentiev, *Varvara Stepanova: A Construc-tivist Life,* ed. John E. Bowlt (London, 1988), pp. 61–78.

28. Stepanova, quoted in *Zrelishcha,* no. 16 (1922); quoted from "A Conversation with V. F. Stepanova," in Peter Noever, ed., *The Future Is Our Only Goal: Aleksandr M. Rodchenko, Var-vara F. Stepanova* (Munich, 1991), p. 205 (I have slightly modified the translation).

29. Lavrentiev, "Minimalisme et création textile," p. 71.

30. See Radu Stern, "American Models for Social-ist Goals: *Amerikanizm* and the Russian Avant-Garde in the 1920s," paper presented at the session "*Americanisme:* The Old World Discovers the New," chaired by Wanda Corn, Seventy-seventh Annual Meeting of the College Art Asso-ciation, San Francisco, 15–18 February 1989 (summarized on p. 130 of the conference pro-ceedings).

31. Aleksei Fedorov-Davydov, "Iskusstvo textilia" (1931), in his *Russkoe i Sovetskoe Iskusstvo,* (Moscow, 1975), p. 195.

32. Ibid., p. 65.

33. Henry van de Velde, *Die künstlerische Hebung der Fraunetracht* (Krefeld, 1900); trans. in this vol-ume as "The Artistic Improvement of Women's Clothing," p. 125.

34. Stepanova, quoted in Lavrentiev, *Varvara Stepanova,* p. 173.

35. Adolf Hitler, *Mein Kampf* (New York, 1939), p. 619.

36. "A Conversation with V. F. Stepanova," p. 205.

37. In another odd reading, Kiaer gives a feminist interpretation to the photograph of the students wearing the sport outfits: "The dark striped pattern of the pants, in particular, seems designed to override the conventional signs of gender difference. The illusion of a diamond-within-a-diamond design when the legs of the pants are pressed together makes the lower half of the students' bodies look like some completely third, hermaphroditic appendage—phallic in its form but distinctively vaginal in its patterning, with the lines emanating out from the 'central core' of the diamond shape" ("The Russian Constructivist Flapper Dress," p. 220).

38. Fedorov-Davydov, *Russkoe: Sovetskoe Iskusstvo,* p. 203.

39. Varvara Stepanova, "Ot kostiuma k risunku i tkani," *Vechernaia Moskva* 49 (28 February 1929): 3; translated as "From Clothing to Pattern and Fabric" in Lavrentiev, *Varvara Stepanova,* p. 180. A longer version of this text, translated from a manuscript, is published under the title "Tasks of the Artist in Textile Production" in Novoer, ed., *The Future Is Our Only Goal.*

40. Stepanova, "Tasks of the Artist in Textile Production," p. 190.

41. Ibid., p. 193.

42. Ibid., p. 191.

43. Ibid., p. 190.

44. Lavrentiev, "Minimalisme et création textile," pp. 74–75.

45. Vladimir Fon-Meck, "Kostium, i revolutsiia," *Atel'e,* no. 1 (1923): 31–32.

46. On the debates over dress in the NEP period, see Mark Allen Svede, "On What the Soviet Dandy Will Be Wearing This Next Five-Year Plan," in Susan Filin-Yeh, ed., *Dandies: Fashion and Finesse in Art and Culture* (New York, 2001).

47. Leon Trotsky, *The Revolution Betrayed: What Is the Soviet Union and Where Is It Going?,* trans. Max Eastman (1937; reprint, New York, 1965), p. 173.

48. Margaret Bourke-White, "Silk Stockings in the Five-Year Plan," *New York Times,* 14 February 1932, sec. 6, p. 4.

49. Lavrentiev, "Minimalisme et création textile," p. 75.

50. David Arkin, *Iskusstvo bytovoi veshchi* (Moscow, 1932), p. 151.

51. Nadezhda Lamanova, "O sovremenem kostiume," *Krasnaia Niva,* no. 27 (1923); trans. in this volume as "Concerning Contemporary Dress," p. 174.

52. Nadezhda Lamanova, "Ruskaia moda," *Krasnaia Niva,* no. 30 (1923); trans. in this volume as "Russian Fashion," p. 177.

53. Lamanova, "Concerning Contemporary Dress," p. 174.

54. Ibid., p. 176.

55. Sofia Beliaeva-Ekzempliiarskaia, *Modelirovanie odezhdy po zakonam zritel'nogo vospriiatiia* (Moscow, 1934).

56. Aleksandra Exter, *Atel'e,* no. 1 (1923); trans. in this volume as "The Constructivist Dress," p. 178.

57. Tugenkhold, quoted in Strijenova, *La mode en Union Soviétique,* p. 112.

58. Kazimir Malévitch [Malevich], "Du musée," in his *Ecrits,* trans. Andrée Robel-Chicarel (Paris, 1986), p. 252.

59. Kazimir Malévitch [Malevich], "Le Suprématisme," in his *Ecrits,* p. 226. On the role of color in Suprematism see Radu Stern, "Le suprématisme comme 'sémaphore de la couleur,'" in Philippe Junod and Michel Pastureau, eds., *La couleur: Regards croisés sur la couleur du Moyen-Age au XX siècle* (Paris, 1994).

60. Charlotte Douglas, "Suprematist Embroidered Ornament," *Art Journal,* 54, no. 1 (spring 1995): 43.

61. Ibid., p. 42.

62. Kazimir Malévitch [Malevich], "Nous voulons . . . ," in his *Ecrits,* p. 263. UNOVIS—Unia novogo iskusstva or Utverditeli novogo iskusstva, Union of the New Art or Affirmers of the New Art—was an artist's group formed in 1919 by Malevich's students. Its members included Ilia Chashnik, El Lissitzky, Evgenia Magaril, Nikolai Suetin, and Lev Yudin.

63. *Malevich: Artist and Theoretician,* [trans. Sharon McKee] (Paris, 1991), p. 241.

SONIA DELAUNAY

1. In an interview of 1913, Paul Poiret declared: "Ladies come to me for a gown as they go to a distinguished painter to get their portraits put on canvas. I am an artist, not a dressmaker" ("Poiret Here to Tell of His Art," *New York Times,* 21 September 1913, p. 11; quoted in Nancy J. Troy, "The Logic of Fashion," *Journal of the Decorative Arts Society,* no. 19, [1995]: 2).

2. Valerie Steele's book *Paris Fashion: A Cultural History* (Oxford, 1988) is an excellent beginning of the much-needed research spanning broad periods.

3. Diana de Marly, *The History of Haute Couture, 1850–1950* (London, 1980), pp. 83–86.

4. The term *simultanéisme* came from Michel-Eugène Chevreul's famous treatise on color, *De la loi du contraste simultané des couleurs* (Paris, 1839).

5. Blaise Cendrars, *Inédits secrets* (Paris, 1969), p. 356.

6. Sandor Kuthy and Kuniki Satonobu, *Sonia et Robert Delaunay* (Bern, 1991), p. 63.

7. On the Bal Bullier, see the excellent study by Jody Blake, *Le Tumulte Noir: Modernist Art and Popular Entertainment in Jazz-Age Paris, 1900–1930* (University Park, Pa., 1999), pp. 43–49.

8. Marjorie Howard, "The Vanishing Bohemia of Paris," *Vanity Fair,* July 1914; quoted in Blake, *Le Tumulte Noir,* p. 46.

9. Guillaume Apollinaire, "Revue de la quinzaine: Les Réformateurs du costume," *Mercure de France,* no. 397, 1 January 1914; trans. in this volume as "The Fortnight Review: The Reformers of Dress," p. 181.

10. For modern analyses of "Sur la robe elle a un corps," whose translation is reprinted in this volume, see Jean-Pierre Goldenstein, *19 Poèmes élastiques de Blaise Cendrars* (Paris, 1986), and Carrie Noland, "High Decoration: Sonia Delaunay, Blaise Cendrars and the Poem as Fashion Design," *Journal X* 2, no. 2, (spring 1998).

11. Giovanni Lista, *Balla* (Modena, 1982), p. 59.

12. Axel Madsen, *Sonia Delaunay: Artist of the Lost Generation* (New York, 1989), p. 121.

13. Blaise Cendrars, *Le Lotissement du ciel* (Paris, 1949), p

14. Giovanni Lista, "La mode futuriste," in *Europe 1910–1939: Quand l'art habillait le vêtements* (Paris, 1997), p. 30.

15. Giuseppe Prezzolini, *La Voce,* October 1914; quoted in Lista, *Balla,* p. 57.

16. Apollinaire, "The Reformers of Dress," p. 181.

17. Sonia Delaunay, *Nous irons jusqu'au soleil* (Paris, 1978), p. 96.

18. Hélène Demoriane, "Interview de Mme Sonia Delaunay à propos de l'Exposition 'Les Années 1925' au Musée des Arts Décoratifs en 1966," *Connaissance des Arts,* no. 171 (1966):

19. Robert Delaunay, quoted in Jacques Damase, *Sonia Delaunay: Rythmes et couleurs* (Paris, 1971), p. 44.

20. This explanation is repeated many times in the literature on Sonia Delaunay. See, among others, Arthur A. Cohen, *Sonia Delaunay,* (New York, 1975), p. 76; Sherry A. Buckberrough, *Sonia Delaunay: A Retrospective* (Buffalo, N.Y., 1980), p. 50; Elizabeth Morano, *Sonia Delaunay: Art into Fashion* (New York, 1986), p. 19; and Monique Schneider Manoury, "Sonia Delaunay: The Clothing of Modernity," in Celant, Sischy, and Tabatai Asbaghi, eds., *Art/Fashion,* p. 60.

21. Sonia Delaunay, *Novis irons jusqu'au soleil,* p. 96.

22. An example of pictopoetry is reproduced in *75 HP* (Bucharest), October 1924.

23. Crevel, quoted in Damase, *Sonia Delaunay,* p. 133.

24. Robert Delaunay, *Du Cubisme à l'art abstrait* (Paris, 1957), p. 205.

25. The text of Sonia Delaunay's lecture, "L'lufluence de la peinture sur la mode," was published in the obscure journal *Bulletin d'Etudes Philosophiques et Scientifiques pour l'examen des tendances nouvelles* (1927); trans. in this volume as "The Influence of Painting on Fashion."

26. To make her invention known in the Soviet Union, Sonia Delaunay published an article about the "fabric-pattern" in *Iskusstvo Odevatsia,* no. 2 (1928).

TEXTS

ELIZABETH CADY STANTON THE NEW DRESS *The Lily* 4 (April 1852)

Why do not the women put it on? All the reasons given can be summed up under two heads.

1st. It is not the Fashion!! To hear people talk on the fashions, one would think they were fixed as the laws of the Medes and the Persians—that they were all got up by some sovereign power, with peculiar reference to the comfort and beauty of the race; when the fact is, they are ever varying the device, generally, of an individual, to conceal some special deformity, or set off some peculiar charm. There is great tyranny in this idea of a universal dress. Only look at the difference in the face, form and manners of those around you, and is it not fair to infer that a different style of dress would become each? Why should I, a short woman, with a short plump arm, destroy the proportions of my figure by wearing a great flowing sleeve, and a bag of an undersleeve, because some tall thin woman, with an endless arm must resort to some such conceit, to break up the monotony of its length? Why should I cover my ears with my hair, because the Duchess of R. slit her's down by wearing heavy ear-rings, and must cover them to hide the deformity? Why must I wear a *tournour,* a thing so vulgar in fact, and in idea, because my Lady V. wears one to conceal a great wen, growing in the centre of her back?—Why should I trail my clothes upon the ground because royal fools, having no true dignity or nobility in themselves, impose upon an ignorant populance by the show of it, with their lofty plumes, jewelled crowns, and trails of rich brocade.—Suppose we should hear of some Chinese mother, who being convinced of the folly and cruelty of compressing her daughter's feet, had suffered them to grow, and left them to use their powers of locomotion naturally and free, in the Celestial Empire, in spite of ridicule and odium. If in reply to the question, "why do you make yourself ridiculous by such a course? Why not do as others do? If all the women would let their feet grow, why then, of course it would be a great blessing to them, but it is absurd for one to stand up alone to change a long established fashion. It seems to me you wear the crown of martyrdom for a very small matter. I do not see but the women get on very well with the small feet. A large foot is a masculine appendage, pray do not ape the men"—suppose the Chinese mother should say, "this fashion is cruel, wicked and unnatural, that so cramps the energies of woman, and trammels all her movements, has already existed long enough. Shall my country women always suffer this outrage, because no one has the heroism to stand up alone, and say this shall not be? Evils can never be remedied by a suspine endurance of them. Shall I who see the truth neither proclaim it, nor live it, because the mass are not ready to go with me? No; I am willing to encounter a life long of ridicule and rebuke, if the blessing of free powers of locomotion can be gained thereby, for those who come after me—for my children, who are dearer to me than my own case and comfort—yea, than life itself." Who would not admire the noble independence, the lofty self-sacrifice, the straight forward common sense of the Chinese mother? And why should we not ourselves be, what we so much admire in story and in song? Are there no evils from which American mothers would fain shield their daughters? Shall we through fear of ridicule, sail on with the multitude, doing no good work for those who come after us, whilst we are in the full enjoyment of blessings won for us by the heroes of the past?

2d. The long dress and bodice is most graceful. Let us see. Do you mean the woman moves with more grace with her vital organs all pinched into the smallest possible compass, with her legs and feet bound together in triple mail of cotton wool and silk? Does she walk, run, climb, get in and out of the carriage, go up and down stairs with more grace? Certainly not. Two elements essential to grace are wanting in all her movements, namely, ease and freedom. It is not the woman, but the drapery that strikes you as more graceful. A long, full, flowing skirt, certainly hangs more gracefully than a short one; but does woman crave no higher destiny than to be a mere frame work on which to hang rich fabrics to show them off to the best advantage?—Are not the free easy motions of the woman herself, more beautiful than the flowing of her drapery? Just veil the exquisitely harmonious motions of yonder danseuse, in drapery of the softest folds and richest shades, and tell me, in the mazes of that mystic dance is she as beautiful as when her limbs were free?

The most you can say of the long skirt is, it conceals ugly feet, crooked legs, and awkward attitudes. But we look upon these things as diseases, unnatural conditions. It is the violation of some law that makes people crooked and ugly. And some false state of mind that makes them awkward. She made it to a point to fall in and out of a carriage, seemed to walk with a painful consciousness of security, a dread uncertainty as to where her next step would lead her. Her legs seemingly refused to make any compromises with her petticoats, hence she was continually assuming the horizontal position when the perpendicular would have been much more becoming. Now her whole appearance is really graceful. She walks off with a dignified, majestic step, apparently as joyous and free as some poor captive who has just cast off his ball and chain.

AMELIA BLOOMER DRESS REFORM *The Lily* 5 (March 1853)

We are in the receipt of many letter[s] which show that there is a great deal of feeling on this subject, and that, though scattered, the wearers of the short dress are quite numerous.

It is a matter of joy that much of the prejudice that first existed against this dress is wearing away, or at least, its manifestations are not so apparent. Ridicule and frowns have failed to accomplish their object, and have done harm to none save those who re-sorted to them. The advantages of this style of dress over the old are so apparent, that no good argument can be brought against its adoption; and a silent acknowledgement of woman's right to fashion her dress according to her own taste and necessities is now yielded on every hand. A woman can travel from one end of our State to the other in this dress without annoyance; and though she may occasionally hear a passing remark, or see a curious eye directed towards her, there will be nothing to make her feel uncomfortable, and seldom any thing to remind her that she is differently dressed from others. Even in the City of New York, where it has been said a woman could not appeared so attired without being mobbed, we have freely walked the streets, and been as respectfully and courte-ously treated as though our dress had been a street-sweeper. So far as we have had the opportunity of judging there is about as much self-respect and civilization existing among the New Yorkers as with people in the country.

There is really nothing to hinder the universal adoption of this comfortable and convenient style of dress, except the fact that the fashion has not yet come to us from the corrupt Parisian Court. On every hand we hear the admission of its superiority, and the wish expressed that it might become fashionable. There is, however, hope for our faint-hearted, fashion-led women, for we see it stated that "the new Emperor has directed a change in court costume, and that the ladies are to wear short skirts, coats and vests, but no pantaloons." This fashion will doubtless take; as the pantaloons have been the great scare-crow with both men and women, in adopting our style of dress. This garment being dispensed with by the Parisian ladies there can be no objection raised against the fashion introduced by the Emperor. So we shall expect in a short time to see *all* our ladies adopt-ing this style. *We* prefer however to retain our dress as it is—"pantaloons" and all.

E. W. GODWIN A LECTURE ON DRESS (1868) *The Mask,* 6 April 1914

Ladies and Gentlemen,

We are met at the outset of the subject which I have selected for our consideration tonight by the question, What has Dress to do with the study of Architecture and Archeology? It is quite possible, too, that those who give up to us in everything else, who allow us the right to dogmatise about arches and pillars, . . . who accept our art views of buildings without question and our antiquarian conclusions as gospel will also meet us at the outset with the advice that we should mind our own business and leave dress where we at present find it, i.e., under the arbitrary power and sole despotic sway of the French milliners and the west-end tailors.

It will be my endeavour in the few following remarks to answer the "question" by showing dress in its relation to architecture and archeology and to prove to you that we ought to decline accepting the "advice" for the simple reason that the study of dress is or ought to be so much the business of the architect as the study of animal or vegetable life or indeed of any of the studies accessional to the main science of building.

Again, to people unaccustomed, as we are, to the free use of figure as an architectural decoration the subject may at first sight appear of too trifling a nature to be ventilated before a society like this. But it must be remembered that although the figure has been gradually estranged from architecture during the last four centuries and historical portraiture has been suffered to become altogether a thing of the past there is at the present time a very strong disposition on the part of some architects to employ sculpture in its old and only legitimate function, viz., as a handmaid to architecture.

Nor will the service of the figure stop here. Already there are very significant works completed and in contemplation other than those of the plastic art where the human figure forms the base of the decorations. We find it painted on our ceilings and on our walls, we find it inlaid in mosaic on our floors, walls and roofs, and in some few cases animating the whole skeleton of architecture. Nor need we hesitate to predict that it will not be long before this revived delight in God's noblest and final work of creation will make itself felt more generally, when mere millinery will give place to art in textile fabrics; when in our churches cloth and vestment and hanging the human form as saint or angel will be "wrought about with gold and divers colours."

Now in art, if we omit altogether the barbarism of academic blankets, there are only two systems of dress. The one historical, the other conventional. The one by clothing a person represented in a habit as he lived when he belongs to a past age involves the study of archeology; the other by clothing him in the fashion of the artist's own time (which last may also become historical when the person represented is contemporary with the artist) involves the study of the fashion of the day.

This last system was almost invariably adopted in past times under all conditions.

It is manifest that the more perfect course, (that indeed which we should take) is to adopt both systems, the first for the representations of the past, the second for the portrayal of the present. From the science of archeology diligently followed we may certainly learn one system. The question is, are fashions of today capable of raising to any, even the lowest level in the temple of Art?

I think there are. Let us consider how.

It has been said, and I see no reason why to question the assertion, that all art is the expression of man's delight in God's works. We may take it for granted that no one wishes to dress *unartistically.* Even if gentlemen be indifferent it would be heresy to suppose for one moment that the time and money which ladies spend upon dress were purposely devoted to the production of the unnatural unartistic and therefore ugly results which we so often see. The evil rests not with ladies and gentlemen except in so far that passiveness and indifference are evils, but is rather to be found in the restless brains of milliner and tailor. To fight against these is no slight work and rather than engage in it people submit their necks to the yoke. Much good however might be done if there was more home-made work. For we can scarcely imagine that anyone with a power of apprehending form and an eye for seeing colour could consciously watch and permit the execution of such things as those illustrated in the fashion books of this month.

Of course I have not such unbounded faith as to suppose that everyone possesses an eye for form and colour, besides which there are degrees in art as in everything else. There are some people who will be always talking, to whom the myriad glories of nature and the highest excellencies of art are all equally "charming," or "pretty" or "beautiful" or "nice." These are the people who wear things not because of any beauty in the articles but because they are "worn just now" and because they are the last things out. There are happily others to whom nature and art are something more than pretty or nice, people who can take in the Beautiful and the message which it bears them quietly and peacefully with just perhaps a little more electricity as the spirit yearns to thankfulness and praise. These are those who robe themselves in purity of colour, in simple graceful forms, subtle harmonies and delicate contrasts for their own sakes and not because "they are worn."

Between these two extremes the many may be classed, and it is with the many we have to do, for the lowest will follow the many although always in the rear and the highest may generally be left to themselves.

There is perhaps an imperfection from which even the highest are not exempt, and it may be that their very gentleness is one reason why the imperfection clings to them. If the English nation were not so rude, if our men and boys could allow people whose dress was slightly different from others to pass unmolested, if all our schools, national and others, gave the sense of vision the instruction it ought to receive, the obtruding ugliness of crinoline would long since have quite disappeared: but the low observations of street boys and the rude stares of many both in the lower and in the middle classes which the absence of popular ugliness evokes require to be met with more courage than is perhaps consistent with that tenderness which is such a special attribute to the gentle life. Nevertheless we all doubtless know those who have passed this ordeal but not without at first some self-denial and some little pain. Be this as it may there is no reason why popular and particular forms of ugliness should not be dispensed with in the house.

But the important features of dress to which I wish to call your attention tonight are:

1. The cut of the sleeves.

2. The neck piece.

3. The trimming.

Now I shall ask your attention to a few illustrations showing how they managed those things in days of old.

We may pass by Egypt, Greece and Rome inasmuch as our climate forbids us to profit much by the dresses of those nations however beautiful and appropriate they may have been. One thing however worth noticing is that both in classic and mediaeval fashions the shape of the arm was almost always maintained either by being left bare or, as in the middle ages, by tightly fitting sleeves at least from the wrist to the elbow.

An examination of the manuscripts, monuments, marbles and ivories in the British Museum alone will be sufficient to convince us of the great importance of this fashion and will enable us to account for its long continuance, for there can be no question that much of the life, action, vigour and grace of the figure work of the past depends on the limbs we are considering being unencumbered.

From the few rough diagrams before you taken from the examples of the most popular dresses of the best periods of mediaeval art you may observe that the complete visible outdoor dress of both men and women principally consisted of three garments: the undermost was the gown, robe or tunic; over that was the dalmatic, surcoat, cyclas or super-tunic, and then come the mantle. Hoods, caps and kerchiefs were worn upon the head either singly or in combination: whilst coloured or embroidered hose and leather shoes or boots showed beneath the tunic.

Of the smaller articles of dress then commonly in use such as girdles and other mercery, we have a long list in a 13th century song called "The Mercer." It includes:

Fine gloves for little dames

Furred gloves

Wimples dyed in saffron

Kerchiefs with ties of silk and of linen embroidered with flowers or birds for the young beaux to coif themselves in presence of their sweethearts

Hempen ones for the clowns

Muffles for the hands

Hose of Bruges

Stamped leather red and green, white and black

Pretty little girdles

Buckles for girdles

Leather purses with buttons

Silk and linen purses

Little chains of steel

Laces for surcoats with knots

Laces for lacing sleeves

Lace tags

Shoe buckles

Broaches of brass and of laten gilt or silvered

Fine tassels for fixing with great buttons of gold or silk

Silver and brass pins

Needles

Thimbles

Jewel cases, Tablets, Good soap of Paris and all the utensels necessary for a lady's toilet. (Razors, forceps, looking glasses, tooth brushes, tooth picks, bandeaux, crisping irons, combs, Rose Water with which they furbished themselves, cotton with which they rouge and whitening with which they whiten themselves.)

All borders or anything approaching what we now call trimming were either woven or stitched in the stuff itself or embroidered and sewn on. The materials of which the dresses of the 13th and 14th centuries were made were of every degree of quality from home-spun woollen fabric to cloth-of-gold from over the sea. The favourite colours in the beginning of the 13th were green and red as we see by reference to the MSS, effigies and wall-paintings of that period. The devices and embroidered work were chiefly in gold and silver appliqué work was sometimes used, the animal and other forms cut out in silk or dyed linen as in a fragment preserved in the British Museum.

In Henry III's reign it would appear that the dresses of the higher classes in England were bordered with fringes. The Pope was so pleased, says Matthew of Paris, with the effect of some gold fringe worn by some English in their choral copes and head dresses that he exclaimed "Of a truth England is our garden of delights; truly is an inexhaustible well in which many things abound;" from many things many may be "extorted" and thereupon ordered the Cistercian Abbots to send him some choice gold fringe without delay.

The furs of sables, foxes, ermines, martens and squirrels with vair, (minevair or minulo) were used as linings to the winter mantles and super-tunics. There were also two distinct kinds of mantle; one the mantle proper or state dress, the other the travelling dress, cloak, *supertotus* or over-all.

The only changes of importance which took place in the civil dress of the period I am speaking of were those made in the cut and form of the super-tunic and the substitution of buttons for laces.

Two great extravagances, however, mark the close of this period. I mean the length of the ladies' trains and particular form of head-dress, both of which have been repeated within our own time.

The attention of the mediaeval satirist was often directed to these follies of the costume. "I have heard of a proud woman" writes one "who wore a white dress with a long train which trailing behind her raised a dust even as far as the altar and the crucifix. But as she left the church and lifted up her train on account of the dirt a certain holy man saw a devil laughing and having adjured him to tell why he laughed the devil said 'a companion of mine was just now sitting on the train of that woman using it as it were his chariot but when she lifted her train up my companion was shaken off into the dirt and that is why I was laughing.'" Again these ladies are advised if their legs be not handsome, nor their feet small and delicate, to wear long robes trailing on the ground to hide them. Another writer compared the ladies to peacocks and magpies because they delight in strange habits and have long tails that trail in the dirt.

The false hair introduced into the head-dress fashionable during the reign of Edward I and the whole style of the head-dress at the time received, and justly so, bountiful condemnation. In the Imperial Library at Paris a satirical song, written in the beginning of the 14th century, after telling us that the Bishop of Paris is a theologian and a philosopher, makes this great authority observe that a woman is too foolish a hussey who puts a false hair on her head and paints herself to please the world. A woman is not free from sin, says the bishop, who has her hair dark or blonde according to nature when she places her intention and care in fixing the false hair along on her tresses. Another critic, attacking the frisettes of his day, says that between the towel or gorget and the temple and the horns there is a space through which a rat might pass or the largest weasel between this and Arras.

With the approach of the 14th century was resuscitated also the custom of tight lacing. At first it was little more than a close fitting neatly-laced body such indeed as we see in the best effigies and illuminations. But the almost Greek simplicity, purity and grace of the 13th century gradually disappeared in the 14th until it was ultimately lost in the full tide of the restless luxuriousness of the 15th century, and it was not until *then* that tight-lacing in the sense we unfortunately know it became a general fashion.

It is time, however, that I returned to the cut of the sleeves, the neck or collar, and the trimming.

Amongst the list of mercery which I quoted just now from a manuscript of the 13th century you may remember that besides Lace tags and Laces for surcoats with knots there was another kind described as *Laces for lacing sleeves.* If we accept the authority of this manuscript, (and there is no reason why we should not), there can be no doubt that the *Lace* fastening whether for body, foot or arm was that which was generally adopted by well-dressed people during the reign of the third Henry. That such laces are not apparent either in the drawings or sculpture of the 13th century is no argument against their use because it must be remembered that, like the fringes to which I have referred and the use of which Matthew of Paris places beyond question, they were by no means easy to represent unless the artist sacrificed some of that breadth and wise conventionality of treatment that it was his chief aim to attain and which constitute now his chief claim to our reverences and admiration.

In the early sleeves the upper part from the elbow to the shoulder was very loose and wide so that the lacing extended only as far as from wrist to elbow, in many cases probably not more than half that distance. As the century advanced the love of finery grew greater and greater and the reader of the chronicles of that time will not fall to observe how presents and necklaces and jewels become more frequent towards the approach of the 14th century.

So in dress the lace gave place to the enamelled and jewelled button, but, whether laced or buttoned, the sleeve was as a rule always tight fitting. As the button fashion became established these little excrescences extended further and further until they even reach the shoulder, and with this excess tight fitting was also carried to excess and applied to the entire sleeve of the tunic.

It may be worth while pausing here for a moment to note how easily a new fashion irreproachable in itself may drift into the preposterous.

The button fastening which took the place of the lace fastenings in the last quarter of the 13th century are possibly preferable to the latter on practical grounds as offering not only less hindrance in dressing but more opportunity for obtaining a greater variety of *useful* ornament. In all the early and good examples it will be found however that in no station of life were they employed in any other way than as *fastenings,* rarely reaching and never going beyond the waist. In our wise modern copyism we have in this as in other matters imitated only the extravagance and folly of the past.

The neck piece of the tunic both in men and women was at first cut closely round the base of the neck and an opening made in front just long enough to allow the dress to be easily slipped over the head and give room to admit the arms into the sleeves. After the 13th century the neck piece was cut lower and square but there was a transitional shape which is occasionally met with and of which I give an example taken from the superb manuscript the Arundel Psalter.

We come now to the consideration of the super-tunic, a garment which must perforce enlist the sympathies of us all from the similarity which its history bears to the history of modern dress.

The super-tunic, unlike the tunic or the mantle, was always changing. Fashion seems to have been as restless then as she is now only in those artistic days her restlessness was limited; and for nearly a century she was satisfied to confine her frolics within the border of the super-tunic.

1 Henry van de Velde—Ornament for a dress, 1896–1898.

2 Wiener Werkstätte—Women's shoes, 1914.

3 Koloman Moser—Visiting dress, 1905.

5 Eduard Wimmer-Wisgrill—Project
for the Norne dress, 1922.

6 Eduard Wimmer-Wisgrill—Project
for sport clothing in wool, 1921.

Eduard Wimmer-Wisgrill—Project
for a summer dress, 1911.

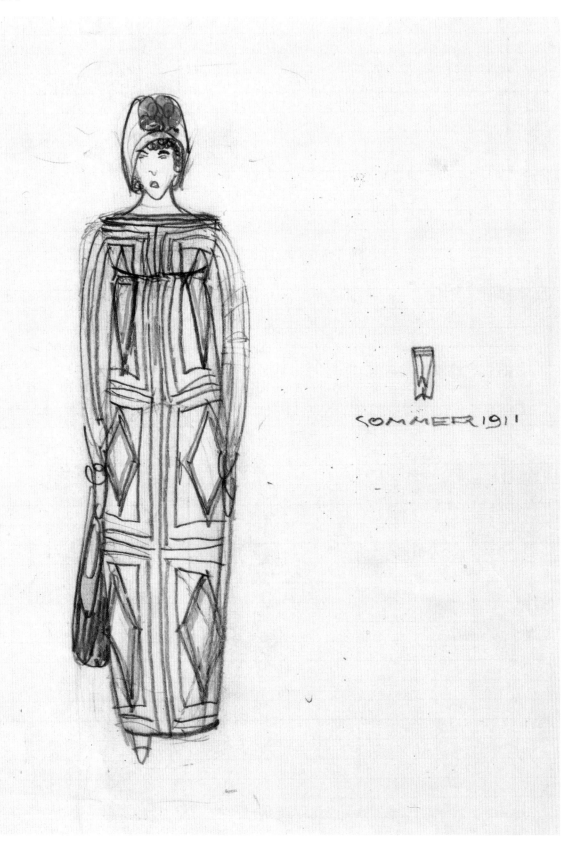

10 Max Snischek—Project for an evening dress, 1918.

12 Piet Zwart—Projects for clothing,
1916–1917.

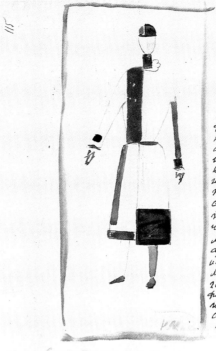

14 Varvara Stepanova—Projects for
sport clothing, 1924.

КАФТАН ИЗ 9Х2 = ВЛАДИ МИР =СКИХ ПОЛОТЕНЕЦ

Кафтан сделан из двух холщевых кустарных полотенец; юбка сделана или из такого же холста, или из какой-либо другой материи синего или черного цвета. Кафтан определяется шириной полотенец. Боковые полотнища сдернуты на резинку на высоте бедер или немного ниже (в зависимости от фигуры), но только отнюдь не над талией, чтобы не нарушалась форма прямоугольника. Естественная ширина полотенца спадает с плеча наподобие короткого рукава. Эту же форму можно делать и из другой ткани — бумажной или шерстяной; в этом случае вышивка заменяется полосатой материей. Рис. 1—развернутый план кафтана. Рис. 2—спина.

ДОМАШНЕЕ ПЛАТЬЕ ИЗ ГОЛОВНОГО ПЛАТКА

В этом платье за основу взят квадрат головного кашемирового платка, и поэтому весь план его построен на квадрате. Добавочная черная материя—такой же кашемир, как и платок. Требуется ее 3½ до 4 метров. Зеленые полосы сделаны из легкой шелковой материи; можно делать их и из шерстяной. Излишнюю ширину кафтана в бедрах надо заколоть в складку с левой стороны или опоясать узким черным кушаком (отнюдь не над талией).

На рисунке 1—пунктиром обозначена форма нижней рубахи, верхнюю часть которой можно делать из более легкой материи. Для более худой фигуры рукав можно делать приблизительно на ладонь уже и ставить ластовицу зеленого цвета. Один рукав показан нам в плане, другой — сшитый.

Это платье можно делать также из бумажной материи с применением бумажных головных платков.

17 Giacomo Balla—Projects for
blouses and sweaters, ca. 1930.

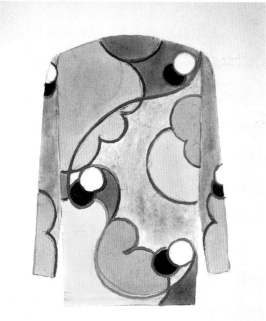

PER TENNIS   FUTURBALLA

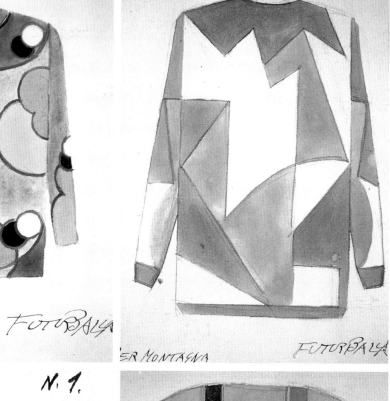

PER MONTAGNA   FUTURBALLA

N. 1.

FUTURBALLA

MODELLO FUTURFASCISTA

FUTURBALLA

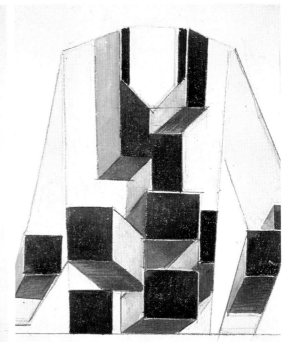

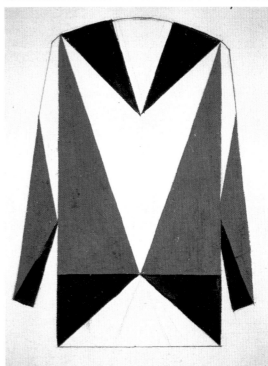

18 Giacomo Balla—Three projects for Futurist suits: morning, afternoon, and evening, 1914.

19 Giacomo Balla—Three projects for Futurist fabrics, 1913.

20 Giacomo Balla—Project for a scarf, 1922.

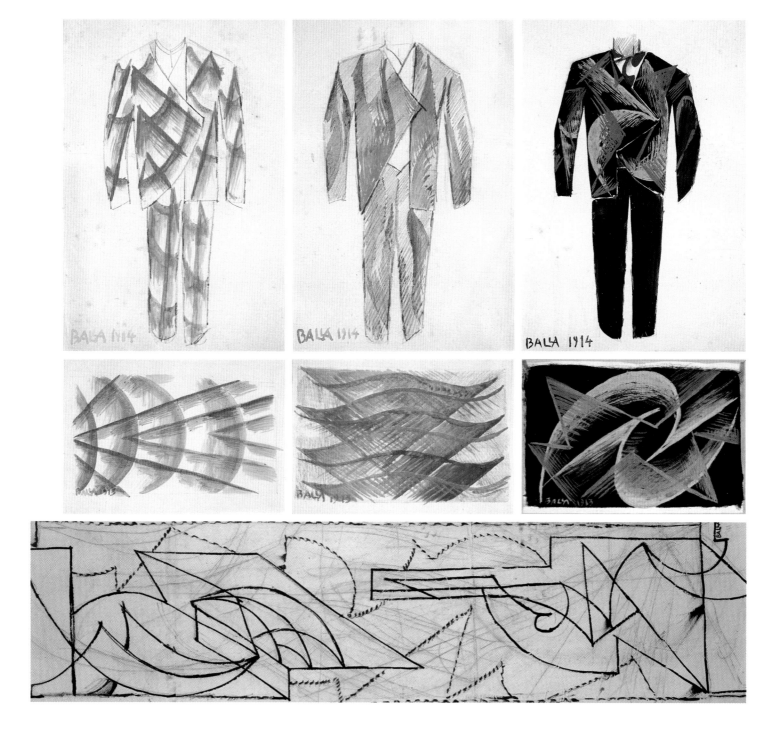

21 Giacomo Balla—Project for a sweater, 1920.

22 Giacomo Balla—Two projects for a sweater, 1929.

23 Giacomo Balla—Three Futurist ties, 1914.

24 Giacomo Balla—Project for a Futurist tie, 1916.

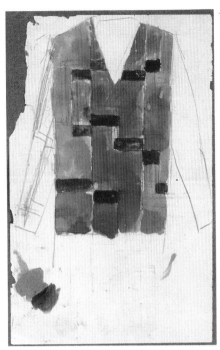

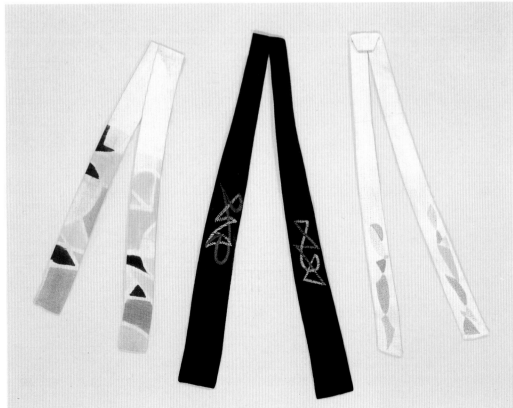

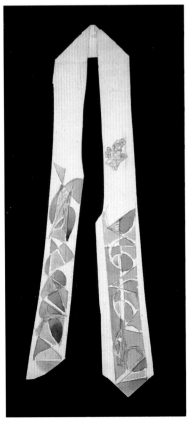

25 Giacomo Balla—House dress worn by the artist, 1925.

26 Giacomo Balla—Embroidered
waistcoat worn by the artist, 1924.

27 Giacomo Balla—Project for a bag, 1916.

28 Giacomo Balla—Eight modifiers, 1914.

29 Giacomo Balla—Project for a fan, 1918.

30 Giacomo Balla—Study for a modifier, 1914.

31 Giacomo Balla—Project for a dress, 1928–1929.

32 Giacomo Balla—Project for a swimming suit, ca. 1930.

33 Giacomo Balla—*The Conversation*, 1934.

34 Giacomo Balla—Projects for scarves, 1918–1925.

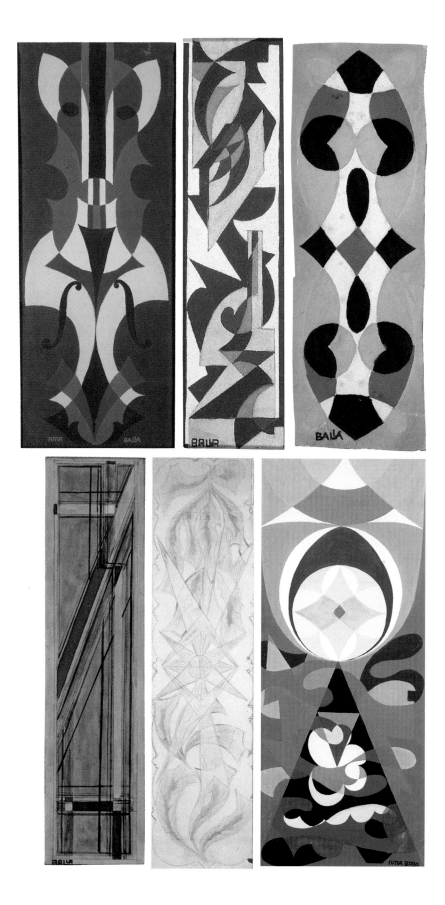

35 Tullio Crali—Projects for men's clothes, 1932.

36 Tullio Crali—Projects for men's suit and shirt, 1932.

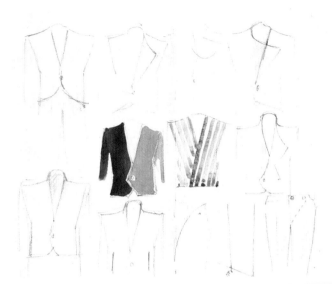

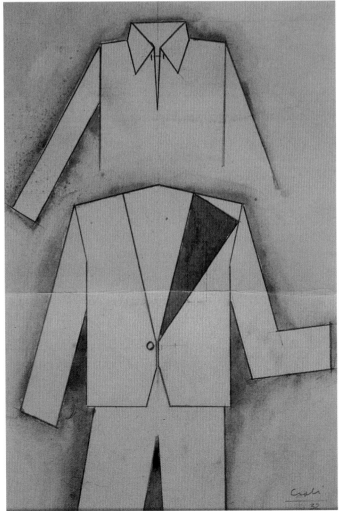

37 Tullio Crali—Projects for a dress, 1932.

38 Tullio Crali—Projects for men's suits, 1932.

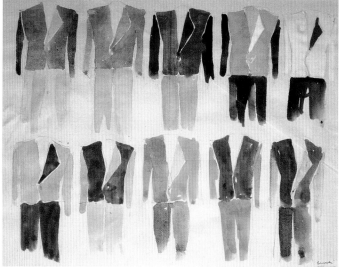

40–41 Tullio Crali—Projects for dresses, 1932–1933.

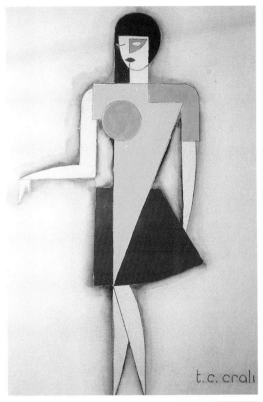

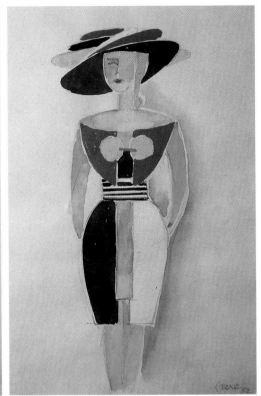

"abito soleombra"   t.c.crali 1933

"abito pila"   t.c.crali 1933

42 Sonia Delaunay—Jacket, 1923.

43 Sonia Delaunay—Coat "Autumn Leaves," later transformed into a curtain, 1924.

This garment is in the first place of almost any length from the short or curtailed dalmatica reaching little lower than the knee to the long dress which trailed some yards upon the ground.

The sleeves were sometimes long and sometimes short. But a common form of the super-tunic was the sleeveless dalmatica which after the reign of Henry III was so cut as to become not only sleeveless but sideless from the shoulder to the waist.

In the exquisite drawings of Queen Mary's Psalter, the manuscript marked 2.B. VII in the British Museum, we constantly meet with examples of the short super-tunic. From this and other sources we learn that the skirt was sometimes open in front and sometimes at the back and sometimes on both sides as high as the hip, that there was a great variety of sleeves and that it was only ladies of high rank who appear to have worn the sleeveless surcoat or the pendant sleeve.

The neck of the super-tunic was generally cut like that of the tunic, open in front and laced or buttoned, the hood being sometimes attached to it and sometimes worn as a distinct article of dress with a small cape. But with the reign of the second Edward and the fopperies and fooleries which were encouraged by the favourites of the Court the cut of the neck piece grew lower and lower.

The mantle, super-totus or overall was a particularly elegant part of the 13th and 14th century costume if we except one kind as a travelling dress sometimes called *balandrana* and which possessed long, full, and shapeless sleeves. The collar or neck-piece of the mantle in its simplest form was concentric with the neck: as the tunic and super-tunic fell more upon the shoulders so too the other garment was gradually allowed to fall lower.

The fastenings were of three or four kinds. First we have the fibula or brooch, buckle or clasp in front and on the right shoulder, in the latter case the mantle being twisted round, then we have the broad band or link often richly embroidered; then the long cord, and last the button fastening when the upper part of shoulder piece of the mantle had developed into a kind of small cape. The fibula and cord fastenings appear to be the earliest; and it was probably for the decoration of these cords that the mercer whose wares I have enumerated supplied the "Fine tassels for fixing with great buttons of gold or silk."

Such then being the character of the dress and its fastenings it remains for me to tell you how it was ornamented, or, in modern language, what were its trimmings.

The first point of interest is the manner in which ornament was used. In the 13th century the ornaments of every-day dress were as a rule restricted to that form which we now express by the word trimmings. During the preceding century Court-fashion had run riot with embroidery and other forms of decoration, garments were literally *covered* with gold and silver and even precious stones were freely used. The queen of Henry II wore a robe bespangled with crescents of gold and Richard I's mantle was over-spread with half moons and shining orbs of *solid* silver; but with the reign of the third Henry came a reign of greater simplicity. Thus ornament retired from the general surface of the garment to its border, and, instead of concealing the fabric with a redundancy which was formless and without any order or method, adorned it within the compass of narrow bands of great beauty and really good workmanship around all its margins.

At the neck of the super-tunic or dalmatica worn by great officials was a stiff bordering of considerable beauty often enriched with valuable jewels. This was the type of the modern collar. The margins of the sleeves of both tunic and super-tunic were encircled by similar bands which laid the foundation for a modern cuff and wristband. The lower margins or skirt-hems of these garments as well as the edge of the mantle were similarly enriched. It is important to notice that in this method of ornamenting the costume the lines or bands of decorations were horizontal, thus opposing, and therefore heightening, the effect and beauty of the natural form.

Early in the 14th century this principle of decoration received an increased development. The horizontal bands formed by the enriched margins of the tunic, the super-tunic and the mantle were found so valuable in an art point of view that they were produced in the fabric itself, sometimes in excess, as is particularly observable on some of the figures which illustrate a missal of this period, No 17006 in the British Museum.

The proper use of these bands is, however, well shown in the illustrations I have taken from the Arundel Psalter and the missal I have just mentioned.

We now come to consider the character of these borders.

First in order is *fringe,* the use of which was at this period almost confined to England. We have seen how a Pope was fascinated by the golden fringe worn by an Englishman and forthwith contrived to compass the thing he coveted.

Fringe is, as you are all aware, a very old, perhaps the oldest form of border trimming. Thirteenth century fringes were of gold and other rich materials and formed a bordering peculiarly soft, flexible and delicate. Appliqué work and embroidery on fine linen, silk, etc: were used by themselves and possibly in combination with the fringes.

The appliqué work, which is not only very beautiful but easy to execute, was made as follows.

Having secured your design, which, by the way, is a slight preliminary matter in all art processes, you proceed to cut out the patterns or figures in the various colours of the design, taking care to keep them a little larger than the drawing to allow for sewing down the edges upon the ground colour. In the simplest work where it is only the placing of one colour upon another nothing more is required than an edging of cord to the pattern or figure, covering the line of stitching and secured to it by being worked over with coloured silk or thread. But where the design involves more than two colours the colours are not cut out as they appear in the design but are superimposed: for example in the cross of the specimen here exhibited the blue is not cut out in small pieces and joined to the white on the same plane as in modern patch-work but is shaped to the full size of the cross and actually underlines the white.

The *embroidery* of the 13th century must be examined to be understood. It would be useless for me to attempt to describe this evening as it ought to be described the glorious needlework of that most artistic age.

Between the richly embroidered and jewelled borders and such as were made by a single line of coloured silk or thread which was literally the stitching of the hem of the garment there were two distinct varieties, thus making four, all other forms being more or less combinations of these processes.

Next in point of magnificence to the jewel border was the silk embroidery of the late example of which we have so many specimens. This process was more commonly used in combination with gold and gems, hence the term *orfrays*. This also was worked upon a foundation of canvass, vellum or linen and sometimes silk and then sewn upon the dress.

Third in order of richness is what I may call the cord work; where the border, or ribaning as Chaucer calls it, is of uniform colour and the pattern entirely formed by raised lines of cord or common twine. This was a process very commonly employed with cloth of gold and gold lace, the cord being sewn or whipped over and completely covered with gold thread. The effigy of Richard I supplies us with four examples of this class of border work.

But this kind, like the last mentioned, was not infrequently used in combination with jewels as illustrated by the effigies and illuminations of the 13th and latter part of the 12th centuries. Nor must it be imagined that these enrichments were confined to the official robes of king or priest. There were of course distinctions of dress according with the social rank of the wearer; the labourer had to be content with a short tunic, the burgess might have in addition a super-tunic and like Dogberry bring forward the fact of his having *two* gowns to his back as evidence of his respectability, but all above this class might be possessed of tunic, super-tunic and mantle, the material, wool, silk or velvet, and the quality of border being the distinguishing marks.

Nor must it be forgotten that between the male and female costume as well as between the civil and ecclesiastical there was not the difference which is popularly supposed to have existed. A nun, for example, is to this day dressed as a widow or elderly lady of the beginning of the 13th century would have been dressed except that the nun is forbidden the use of ornament and rich or costly *material*.

So again if we had worn the everyday costume of the reign of Henry III with long tunics, short hanging or open sleeves to the super-tunic and a cowl or hood no one would have seen anything very remarkable in the costume of the Norwich Benedictines for the monks' dress, except in material and colour, had little to distinguish it from that of the lawyer or the architect, whilst the clerical dress in 1237 was so unclerical that at the council held by the Pope's Legate Otto in St. Paul's, London in that year it was decreed that "whereas, with regard to the dress of the clerks which appears to be not clerical, but rather military, a great scandal has arisen among the laity" they, the clerks, shall under penalty of a deprivation of their benefices "wear garments of becoming measure and shall wear close hoods when appointed to holy orders especially in this Church, before their prelates at the assemblies of the clergy, and everywhere in their parishes" "following the rule of clerical property in their garments, spurs, bridles and saddles."

Thus far my task has been mainly archeological. I propose now to enquire into the nature of those features in modern costume which correspond to those I have already endeavoured to describe.

The main things to be observed are: 1st, the variableness of modern fashion; 2nd the wide difference between the male and female costume, and 3rd the absence of colour. The changeableness of 19th century fashion is perhaps not only the greatest evil, but the parent of all other evils in modern costume with which we have to contend. There is no such thing now-a-days as contentment in dress, for is [sic] perchance a becoming hat, a graceful mantle or an artistic serviceable coat be approved by the world this season it must be given up next season. No amount of gracefulness or appropriateness being powerful enough to stay the restless hand of fickle fashion. The rule seems to be that directly a thing becomes vulgar in the old and true sense of the world it must needs be despised as vulgar in the modern and erroneous sense of the world.

There are only three ways . . . one or other we must select . . . to account for this changeableness.

In the first place Fashion, like the true artist, may be unsatisfied by her best efforts and may be even seeking to do better; or she may be desirous to keep those social distinctions which many hold to be necessary to the well-being of the state; or she may be after all only a pander to the pride and the deformity of the world.

When lordes and ladies ever do devise
Themselves to setten forth to strangers sight
Some frounce their curled hair in courtly guise
Some prancke their ruffes and other trimly dight
Their gay attire: each others greater pride does spight.[1]

Again the great difference which exists between male and female costume is another characteristic defect of the age in which we live. All natural relative proportion is ignored: the man is deprived of every vestige of drapery in the artistic sense of the word, and his limbs are disguised in bag-like coverings, whilst the woman copies the conventional short-skirted school-girl *or* clothes herself in a wasteful amplitude of skirt.

The difference between male and female costume is not, however, confined to form but extends even to material. We know how linen, wool, silk, satin, velvet, were used in old times for the clothing of men as well as for that of women; but, (as in the matter of drapery) the men have been forced by fashion to give up all claim to the richer materials and to encase themselves in gloomy monotony of broad-cloth.

The general absence of colour is another important characteristic of our costume. An English crowd, (no matter how brightly coloured certain of its *details* may be), always resolves itself into a dull grey owing to the preponderance of black and white.

In old times everyone had a wholesome horror of black and consequently we never find it employed except as the national colour of the Danes in religious habits and in heraldry. It was not till the reign of Edward III that black was used even for mourning, and then only as a cloak with a hood over ordinary coloured garments. But now, as far as gentlemen are concerned, the evening dress at least of one half of the world is black and a man who would dare to sit down at dinner in any other colour would be deemed

1. *Fairy Queen* 1, 4, 14.

guilty of a breach of etiquette, or, at the best, be smiled as the victim of a weak and harmless eccentricity.

There are, however, two little bits of light flickering amidst this almost universal gloom. One of these is the coloured scarf now so frequently worn by gentlemen, and the other the scarlet tunic, to use a mediaeval name, worn by ladies, which is always visible when worn with the walking dress or short super-tunic and it is occasionally revealed with admirable effect when worn under a long or trailing robe.

The general shape of modern dress happily presents us with more hopeful signs than it did a few years back. Crinoline has vanished from the drawing room, and is gradually disappearing from the streets. Costume, more especially that adopted in the country houses, is decidedly looking up. For instance, ladies' walking dress just now, consisting of tunic, super-tunic with high neck, tight fitting fur jacket and velvet hat with brilliant leather would be perfectly pleasing and picturesque if it were not for the short proportions obtained by the use of coarse trimming, extravagantly high boots and cut edges.

A few years ago the male costume was equally hopeful; coloured stockings and knickerbockers with the short coat or Norfolk shirt and felt hat or cap were felt to be appropriate and artistic.

What has become of this most artistic costume? A costume which only wanted a slight alteration in the sleeve to make it worthy to rank with the 14th and 15th century dresses. For the cut of the sleeve is the only point of difference between the cut of a modern Norfolk shirt and the very picturesque jacket or doublet introduced early in the reign of Edward IV.

It is some satisfaction to know that tight-fitting sleeves or hanging sleeves over them are being at last adopted by ladies. Will gentlemen see the advantage and follow suit?

But good form in shape or cut is of little avail unless we can get rid of the present system of trimming with all its higgledy-piggledy of furious exaggeration of band and button and bow. There can be no excuse for such trimmings as those exhibited in the modern examples before us marked 2, 3, and 4B.

One of the best modern braid borders I have seen was spoilt by an excessive use of little bits of jet. I have had a diagram made of this specimen work enlarged sixteen times to enable you to compare it with an example of old work which I have enlarged in the same ratio. If, however, we could get rid of braid altogether and adopt a closely-made silk or gold cord there would be much more chance for good plain designs. Indeed, very many of the best borders of the middle ages may be easily reproduced by sewing down cord in the manner shown in the specimen of appliqué work before you, whilst the difficulty of treating braid in other than straight and continuous lines is manifested whenever anything else is attempted.

Nor is there any difficulty in securing artistic trimmings if ladies are so minded. I have seen some most exquisite little borders at Hellbronner's in Regent street. But the most glorious border the world ever saw would have no chance so long as there exists that passionate longing for mere novelty which is one of the great curses of modern society in each and all its phases.

As regards our evening dress perhaps the least said is better. It is true the revival of the turn-down collar, by showing the neck, was one step towards that right development of the human form which is characteristic of all good costume. The Prince of Wales,[2] too, may be thanked for the revival of white waistcoats, for any relief to the dreary conventionalism of black cloth may be fairly regarded as a blessing; these are unfortunately the only exceptions to the corrupt taste which prescribes the usual evening dress of a gentleman of the present period.

Of a lady's dress I will not trust myself to speak, its indecency of cut being, as a rule, unequalled even by its ugliness of trimming.

Time will not permit me to enter upon the subject of our official costume which, from the royal crown to the policeman's helmet, is utterly debased; nor can I now trespass any further on your patience to set forth the present promising aspect of children's dress or the uncompromising aspect of church vestments.

But before I conclude I feel tempted to express a hope that it is from lack of positive art instruction rather than from willfulness of choice that in this question of dress as in many other branches of art we moderns possess so little discrimination. If this be so, and if we in our better moments, deeming all things visible to have their varying degrees of power for good or for evil, elect to labour for the good through the action of the Beautiful, our likeness in the habit as we live may yet be handled by poet and painter, sculptor and architect, without fear of their being ridiculous.

Lastly, let me revert for a moment to the questions I put at the commencement of this paper: . . . what has archeology to do with dress? and, are the fashions of today capable of being raised to the dignity of art?

As regards the first question I think you will admit that the study of costume constitutes one important branch of it. Archeology fills in the details of every picture of the past, it forges the links of the chain which binds together all time; it brings into stronger light all those great events which have contributed to build up those blessings we now enjoy. It clothes with vivid reality all those noble ones whose figures would otherwise have but a shadowy indistinctness in the mighty procession of the world's issue. It tells us among many other things how the decoration of dress was once as much an art as the decoration of a temple. It tells us how both ladies' and gentlemen's dresses were once under the direction of artists many of whose names are recorded; as, for example, Adam de Basinges, Adam de Bakering, John de Colonia, Thomas Chenier, John Blaton, William Courtenay and Stephen Vyne, under whose superintendence women worked sometimes for their amusement and sometimes for their profit. It helps us to a better appreciation of the wonderful picturings of such poets as Chaucer and Dante, and illustrates every page of our early literature.

The other question, viz., are the fashions of today capable of being raised to the dignity of art? is one which I have already answered in the affirmative; for in spite of the many gross absurdities which mark the conventionalities of our present costume, in spite of the swallow-tails and chimney pots, of bastard embroidery and big buttons, I am satisfied we possess sufficient elements of beauty and appropriateness from which a costume

2. Afterwards King Edward VII.

might be developed equal to any of past times; and were such a development to take place our architects, sculptors, painters and poets would not have to seek, (as they now do), in ages long gone by for subjects fit for the artist, but would be content to be the chroniclers of their own age.

Of this much I am satisfied: that no art is possible to us unless we take a broad and comprehensive view of the power and purpose of art. If you really desire noble buildings, strange as it may sound you must have an eye to your boots. It is idle to talk of art at the rate we do now-a-days unless we can feel it to be a reality to ourselves. We must be drenched through and through with it, not merely put it on now and then. We must have it in its proper degree in our servants' hall and our scullery maids' dormitory as in our drawing rooms and best bedrooms: we must see it in the back offices as well as in the front elevation; in the table as well as in the front-door jamb, in the table-cloth as in the table. And finally we must have it in lay vestments as well as in clerical vestments if we desire to have art present with us a growing, developing, living, joyous reality.

GEORGE H. DARWIN DEVELOPMENT IN DRESS *Macmillan's Magazine* 26
(September 1872)

The development of dress presents a strong analogy to that of organisms, as explained by the modern theories of evolution; and in this article I propose to illustrate some of the features which they have in common. We shall see that the truth expressed by the proverb "Natura non facit saltum" is applicable in the one case as in the other; the law of progress holds good in dress, and forms blend into one another with almost complete continuity. In both cases a form yields to a succeeding form, which is better adapted to the then surrounding conditions; thus, when it ceased to be requisite that men in active life should be ready to ride at any moment, and when riding had for some time ceased to be the ordinary method of travelling, knee breeches and boots yielded to trousers. The "Ulster Coat," now so much in vogue, is evidently largely fostered by railway travelling, and could hardly have flourished in the last century, when man either rode or travelled in coaches, where there was no spare room for any very bulky garment.

A new invention bears a kind of analogy to a new variation in animals; there are many such inventions, and many such variations; those that are not really beneficial die away, and those that are really good become incorporated by "natural selection," as a new item in our system. I may illustrate this by pointing out how mackintosh-coats and crush hats have become somewhat important items in our dress.

Then, again, the degree of advancement in the scale of dress may be pretty accurately estimated by the extent to which various "organs" are specialized. For example, about sixty years ago, our present evening-dress was the ordinary dress for gentlemen; top-boots, always worn by old-fashioned "John Bull" in *Punch*'s cartoons, are now reserved for the hunting field; and that the red coat was formerly only a best coat appears from the following observations of "a Lawyer of the Middle Temple" in No. 129 of the *Spectator:*—"Here (in Cornwall) we fancied ourselves in Charles II.'s reign,—the people having made little variations in their dress since that time. The smartest of the country squires appear still in the Monmouth cock; and when they go awooing (whether they have any post in the militia or not) they put on a red coat."[1]

But besides the general adaptation of dress above referred to, there is another influence which has perhaps a still more important bearing on the development of dress, and that is fashion. The love of novelty, and the extraordinary tendency which men have to exaggerate any peculiarity, for the time being considered a mark of good station in life, or handsome in itself, give rise I suppose to fashion. This influence bears no distant analogy to the "sexual selection," on which so much stress has recently been laid in the "Descent of Man." Both in animals and dress, remnants of former stages of development survive to a later age, and thus preserve a tattered record of the history of their evolution.

These remnants may be observed in two different stages or forms. 1st. Some parts of the dress have been fostered and exaggerated by the selection of fashion, and are then retained and crystallized, as it were, as part of our dress, notwithstanding that their

1. See p. 356 of Fairholt's *Costume in England,* London, 1846.

use is entirely gone (*e.g.* the embroidered pocket-flaps in a court uniform, now sewn fast to the coat). 2ndly. Parts originally useful have ceased to be of any service, and have been handed down in an atrophied condition.

The first class of cases have their analogue in the peacock's tail, as explained by sexual selection; and the second in the wing of the apteryx, as explained by the effects of disuse.

Of the second kind of remnant, Mr. Tylor gives very good instances when he says:[2] "The ridiculous little tails of the German postilion's coat show of themselves how they come to dwindle to such absurd rudiments; but the English clergyman's bands no longer convey their history to the eye, and look unaccountable enough till one has seen the intermediate stages through which they came down from the more serviceable wide collars, such as Milton wears in his portraits, and which gave their name to the 'band-box' they used to be kept in." These collars are curiously enough worn to this day by the choristers of Jesus College, Cambridge.

According to such ideas as these it becomes interesting to try to discover the mark of descent in our dresses, and in making this attempt many things apparently meaningless may be shown to be full of meaning.

Women's dress retains a general similarity from age to age, together with a great instability in details, and therefore does not afford too much subject for remark as does men's dress. I propose, therefore, to confine myself almost entirely to the latter, and to begin at the top of the body, and to work downwards through the principal articles of clothing.

HATS.—Hats were originally made of some soft material, probably of cloth or leather, and in order to make them fit the head, a cord was fastened round them, so as to form a sort of contraction. This is illustrated on 524 of Fairholt's "Costume in England," in the figure of the head of an Anglo-Saxon woman, wearing a hood bound on with a head-band; and on p. 530 are figures of several hats worn during the fourteenth century, which were bound to the head by rolls of cloth, and all the early hats seem provided with some sort of band. We may trace the remnants of this cord or band in the present hat-band. A similar survival may be observed in the strings of the Scotch-cap and even in the mitre of the bishop.[3] It is probable that the hat-band would long ago have disappeared had it not been made use of for the purpose of hiding the seam joining the crown to the brim. If this explanation of the retention of the hat-band is the true one, we have here a part originally of use for one purpose applied to a new one, and so changing its function; a case which has an analogy to that of the development of the swimming-bladders of fishes, used to give them lightness in the water, into the lungs of mammals and birds, used as the furnace for supporting animal heat. The duties of the hat-band have been taken in modern hats by two running strings fastened to the lining, and these again have in their turn become obsolete, for they are now generally represented by a small piece of string, by means of which it is no longer possible to make the hat fit the head more closely.

2. P. 16, vol. 1 of *Primitive Culture,* London, 1871.

3. For the origin of this curious head-dress, see Fairholt, p. 564.

The ancestor from which our chimney-pot hat takes most of its characteristics is the broad-brimmed low-crowned hat, with an immense plume falling down on the shoulder, which was worn during the reign of Charles II.[4] At the end of the seventeenth, and during the eighteenth century, this hat was varied by the omission of the plume and by giving to the brim various "cocks." That these "cocks" were former merely temporary is shown by Hogarth's picture of Hudibras beating Sidropel and his man Whacum, where there is a hat, the brim of which is buttoned up in front to the crown with three buttons. This would be a hat of the seventeenth century. Afterwards, during the eighteenth century, the brim was bent up in two or three places, and notwithstanding that these "cocks" become permanent, yet the hats still retained the marks of their origin in the button and strap on the right side. The cockade, I imagine, took its named from its being a badge worn on one of the "cocks."

The modern cocked-hat, apparently of such an anomalous shape, proves, on examination, to be merely a hat of the shape above referred to; it appears further that the right side was bent up at an earlier date than the left, for the hat is not symmetrical, and the "cock" on the right side forms a straight crease in the (quondam) brim, and that on the left is bent rather over the crown, thus making the right side of the hat rather straighter than the left. The hat-band here remains in the shape of two gold tassels, which are just visible within the two points of the cocked-hat.

A bishop's hat shows the transition from the three-cocked hat to our present chimney-pot; and because sixty years ago beaver-fur was the fashionable material for hats, we must now need wear a silken imitation, which would deceive no one into thinking it fur, and which is bad to resist the effects of weather. Even in a lady's bonnet the elements of brim, crown and hat-band may be traced.

The "busby" of our hussars affords a curious instance of survival. It would now appear to be merely a fancy head-dress, but on inspection it proves not to be so. The hussar was originally a Hungarian soldier, and he brought his hat with him to our country. I found the clue to the meaning of the hat in a picture of a Hungarian peasant. He wore a red night-cap, something like that worn by our brewers' men, or by a Sicilian peasant, but the cap was edged with so broad a band of fur, that it made in fact a low "busby." And now in our hussars the fur has grown enormously, and the bag has dwindled into a flapping ornament, which may be detached at pleasure. Lastly, in the new "busby" of the Royal Engineers the bag has vanished, although the top of the cap (which is made of cloth and not of fur) is still blue, as was the bag formerly; the top cannot, however, be seen, except from a bird's eye point of view.

It appears that all cockades and plumes are worn on the left side of the hat, and this may, I think, be explained by the fact that a large plume, such as that worn in the time of Charles II., or that of the modern Italian Bersaglieri, would impede the free use of the sword; and this same explanation would also serve to show how it was that the right side of the hat was the first to receive a "cock." A London servant would be little inclined to think that he wears his cockade on the left side to give his sword-arm full liberty.

4. See Fairholt, p. 540.

COATS.—Everyone must have noticed the nick in the folded collar of the coat and of waistcoat; this is of course made to allow for the buttoning round the neck, but it is in the condition of a rudimentary organ, for the nick would probably not come into the right place, and in the waistcoat at least there are usually neither the requisite button nor button-holes.

"The modern gentleman's coat may be said to take its origin from the *vest,* or long outer garment, worn towards the end of the reign of Charles II."[5] This vest seems to have had no gathering at the waist, and to have been buttoned all down the front, and in the shape rather like a loose bag; to facilitate riding it was furnished with a slit behind, which could be buttoned up at pleasure; the button-holes were embroidered, and in order to secure similarity of embroidery on each slide of the slit, the buttons were sewn on a strip of lace matching the corresponding button-hole on the other side. These buttons and button-holes left their marks in the coats of a century later in the form of gold lacing on either side of the slit of the tails.

In about the year 1700, it began to be the fashion to gather in the vest or coat at the waist, and it seems that this was first done by two buttons near the hips being buttoned to loops rather nearer to the edge of the coat, and situated at about the level of the waist. Our soldiers much in the same manner now make a waist in their loose overcoats, by buttoning a short strap to two buttons, placed a considerable distance apart on the back.

This old fashion is illustrated in a figure dressed in the costume of 1696, in an old illustration of the "Tale of the Tub," and also in the figure of a dandy smelling a nosegay, in Hogarth's picture entitled "Here Justice triumphs in his Easy Chair," as well as elsewhere. Engravings of this transition period of dress are, however, somewhat rare, and it is naturally not common to be able to get a good view of the part of the coat under arms. This habit of gathering in the waist will, I think, explain how it was that, although the buttons and button-holes were retained down the front edges, the coat came to be worn somewhat open in front.

The coat naturally fell in a number of plaits or folds below these hip buttons: but in most of Hogarth's pictures, although the buttons and plaits remain, yet the creases above the buttons disappear, and seams appear to run from the buttons up under the arms. It may be worth mentioning that in all such matters of detail Hogarth's accuracy is notorious, and that therefore his engravings are most valuable for the study of the dress of the period. At the end of the seventeenth, and at the beginning of the eighteenth centuries, coats seem very commonly to have been furnished with slits running from the edge of the skirt, up under the arms, and these were made to button up, in a manner similar in all respects to the slit of the tails. The sword was usually worn under the coat, and the sword-hilt came through the slit on the left side. Later on these slits appear to have been sewed up, and the buttons and button-holes died away, with the exception of two or three buttons just at the tops of the slits; thus in coats of about the year 1705, it is not uncommon to see several buttons clustered about the tops of all three slits. The buttons at the top of the centre slit entirely disappeared, but the buttons now on the back of our coats

5. Fairholt, p. 479.

trace their pedigree up to those on the hips. Thus it is not improbable that although our present buttons represent those used for making the waist, as above explained, yet that they in part represent the buttons for fastening up these side slits.

The fold which we now wear below the buttons on the back are the descendants of the falling plaits, notwithstanding they appear as though they were made for, and that they are in fact commonly used as the recesses for the tail-pockets; but that this was not their original object is proved by the fact that during the last century the pockets were either vertical or horizontal, placed a little in front of the two hip buttons (which have since moved round towards the back), and had highly embroidered flaps, buttons, and button-holes. The horizontal pockets may now be traced in the pocket-flaps of court dress before alluded to; and the vertical pocket is represented by some curious braiding and a row of buttons, which may be observed on the tails of the tunic of the foot-guards. The detail of the manner in which this last rudiment became reduced to its present shape may be traced in books of uniforms, and one of the stages may now be frequently seen in the livery of servants, in the form of a row of three or four buttons running down near the edge of the tail, sewn on to a scalloped patch of cloth (the pocket flap), which is itself sewed to the coat.

In the last century, when the coats had large flapping skirts, it became the custom (as may be seen in Hogarth's pictures) to button back the two corners of the coat, and also to button forward the inner corners, so as to separate the tails for convenience in riding.[6] This custom left its traces in the uniform of our soldiers down to the introduction of the modern tunic, and such traces may still be seen in some uniforms, for example, those of a Lord Lieutenant of the French gensdarmerie. In the uniforms of which I speak, the coats have swallow-tails, and these are broadly edged with a light-coloured border, tapering upwards and getting broader downwards; at the bottom of the tail, below where the borders join (at which joining there is usually a button), there is a small triangle of the same colour as the coat, with its apex at this button. This curious appearance is explained thus:—the two corners, one of which is buttoned forwards and the other backwards, could not be buttoned actually to the edge of the coat, but had to be fastened a little inland as it were; and thus part of the coat was visible at the bottom of the tail: the light-coloured border, although sewn to the coat, evidently now represents the lining, which was shown by the corners being turned back.

It was not until the reign of George III. that coats were cut back at the waist, as are our present evening coats, but since, before that fashion was introduced, the coats had become swallow-tailed in the manner explained, it seems likely that this form of coat was suggested by the previous fashion. And, indeed, stages of development of somewhat intermediate character may be observed in old engravings. In the uniforms of the last century the coats were double-breasted, but were generally worn open, with the flaps thrown back and buttoned to rows of buttons on the coat. These flaps, of course, showed the lining of the coat, and were of the same colour as the tails; the button-holes were usually embroidered, and thus the whole of the front of the coat become richly laced. Towards the end of the century the coats were made tight, and were fastened together in front by

6. It seems to have been in actual use in 1760, although not in 1794. See Cannon's *Hist. Rec. of Brit. Army*, London, 1837, the 2nd Dragoon Guards.

hooks, but the vestiges of the flaps remained in a double line of buttons, and in the front of the coat being of a different colour from that of the rest, and being richly laced. A uniform of this nature is still retained in some foreign armies. This seems also to explain the use of the term "facings" as applied to the collar and cuffs of a uniform, since, as we shall see hereafter, they would be of the same colour as these flaps. It may also explain the habit of braiding the front of a coat, as is it done in our Hussar and other regiments.

In a "History of Male Fashions," published in the *London Chronicle* in 1762, we find that "surtouts have now four laps on each side, which are called 'dog's ears;' when these pieces are unbuttoned, they flap backwards and forwards, like so many supernumerary patches just tacked on at one end, and the wearer seems to have been playing at backswords till his coat was cut to pieces. . . . Very spruce *smarts* have no buttons nor holes upon the breast of these their surtouts, save what are upon the ears, and their garments only wrap over their bodies like a morning gown." These dog's ears may now be seen in a very meaningless state on the breasts of the patrol-jackets of our officers, and this is confirmed by the fact that their jackets are not buttoned, but fastened by hooks.

In early times, when coats were of silk or velvet, and enormously expensive, it was no doubt customarily to turn up the cuffs, so as not to soil the coat, and thus the custom of having the cuffs turned back came in. During the latter part of the seventeenth and during the eighteenth century, the cuffs were very widely turned back, and the sleeves consequently very short, and this led to dandies wearing large lace cuffs to their shirts.

The pictures of Hogarth and of others show that the coat cuffs were buttoned back to a row of buttons running round the wrist. These buttons still exist in the sleeves of a Queen's Counsel, although the cuffs are sewed back and the button-holes only exist in the form of pieces of braid. This habit explains why our soldiers now have their cuffs of different colours from that of their coats; the colour of the linings was probably determined for each regiment by the colonel for the time being, since he formerly supplied the clothing; and we know that the colour of the facings was by no means fixed until recently. The shape of the cuff has been recently altered in the line regiments, so that all the original meaning is gone.

In order to allow of turning back with ease, the sleeve was generally split on the outer side, and this split could be fastened together with a line of buttons and embroidered holes. In Hogarth's pictures some two or three of these buttons may be commonly seen above the reversed cuff; and notwithstanding that at first the buttons were out of sight (as they ought to be) in the reversed part of the cuff, yet after the turning back had become quite a fixed habit, and when sleeves were made tight again, it seems to have been usual to have the button for the cuff sewed on to the proper inside, that is to say, the real outside of the sleeve.

The early stage may be seen in Hogarth's picture of the "Guards marching to Finley," and the present rudiment is excellently illustrated in the cuffs of the same regiment now. The curious buttons and gold lace on the cuffs and collars of the tunics of the Life Guards have the like explanation, but this is hardly intelligible without reference to a book of uniforms, as for example Cannon's "History of the 2nd Dragoon Guards."

The collar of a coat would in ordinary weather be turned down and the lining shown; hence the collar has commonly a different colour from that of the coat, and in uniforms the same colour as have the cuffs, which form, with the collars, the so-called "facings." A picture of Lucien Bonaparte in Lacroix's work on Costume shows a collar so immense that were it turned up it would be as high as the top of his head. This drawing indicates that even the very broad stand-up collars worn in uniforms in the early part of this century, and of a different colour from that of the coat, were merely survivals of an older form of turn-down collar. In these days, notwithstanding that the same difference in colour indicated that the collar was originally turned down, yet in all uniforms it is made to stand up.

The pieces of braid or seams which run around the wrist in ordinary coats are clearly the last remains of the inversion of the cuffs.

TROUSERS.—I will merely observe that we find an intermediate stage between trousers and breeches in the pantaloon, in which the knee-buttons of the breeches have walked down the ankle. I have seen also a German servant who wore a row of buttons running from the knee to the angle of his trousers.

BOOTS.—One of the most perfect rudiments is presented by top-boots. These boots were originally meant to come above the knee; and, as may be observed in old pictures, it became customary to turn the upper part down, so that the lining was visible all around the top. The lining being of unblacked leather formed the brown top which is now worn. The original boot-tag may be observed in the form of a mere wisp of leather sewn fast to the top, whilst the real acting tag is sewn to the inside of the boot. The back of the top is also fastened up, so that it could not by any ingenuity be turned up again into its original position.

Again, why do we black and polish our boots? The key is found in the French *cirage,* or blacking. We black our boots because brown leather would, with wet and use, naturally get discoloured with dark patches, and thus boots to look well should be coloured black. Now, shooting boots are usually greased, and that it was formerly customary to treat ordinary boots in the same manner is shown by the following verse in the ballad of "Argentile and Curan:"

He borrowed on the working daies
    His holy russets oft,
And of the bacon's fat to make
    His startops black and soft.

Startops were a kind of rustic high shoes. Fairholt in his work states that "the oldest kind of blacking for boots and shoes appears to have been a thick, viscid, oily substance." But for neat boots a cleaner substance than grease would be required, and thus wax would be thought of; and that this was the case is shown by the French word *cire,* which means indifferently to "wax" or to "polish boots." Boots are of course polished because wax takes so good a polish. Lastly, patent-leather is an imitation of common blacking.

I have now gone through the principal articles of men's clothing, and have shown how numerous and curious are the rudiments or "survivals" as Mr. Tylor calls them; a more thorough search proves the existence of many more. For instance, the various gowns worn at the Universities and elsewhere, afford examples. These gowns were, as late as the reign of Queen Elizabeth, simply upper garments,[7] but have survived into this age as mere badges. Their chief peculiarities consist in the sleeves, and it is curious that nearly all of such peculiarities point to various devices by which the wearing of the sleeves has been eluded or rendered less burdensome. Thus the plaits and buttons in a barrister's gown, and the slit in front of the sleeve of the B.A.'s gown, are for this purpose. In an M.A. gown, the sleeves extend below the knees, but there is a hole in the side through which the arm is passed; the end of the sleeve is sewed up, but there is a kind of scollop at the lower part, which represents the narrowing for the waist. A barrister's gown has a small hood sewed to the left shoulder, which would hardly go on to the head of an infant, even if it could be opened out into a hood shape.

It is not, however, in our dress alone that these survivals exist; they are to be found in all the things of our every-day life. For instance, anyone who has experienced a drive on the road so bad that leaning back in the carriage is impossible, will understand the full benefit to be derived from arm-slings such as are placed in first-class railway carriages, and will agree that in such carriages they are mere survivals. The rounded tracery on the outsides of railway carriages show the remnants of the idea that a coach was the proper pattern on which to build them; and the word "guard" is derived from the man who sat behind the coach and defended the passengers and mails with his blunderbuss.

In the early trains (1838–1839) of the Birmingham Railway there were special "mail" carriages, which were made very narrow, and to hold only four in each compartment (two and two), so as to be like the coach they had just superseded. The words *dele, stet,* used in correcting proof-sheets, the words *sed vide* or *s.v., ubi sup., ibid., loc. cit.* used in foot-notes, the sign "&" which is merely a corruption of the word *et,* the word *finis* until recently placed at the end of books, are all doubtless survivals from the day when all books were in Latin, The mark ^ used in writing for interpolations appears to be the remains of an arrow pointing to the sentence to be included. The royal "broad-arrow" mark is a survival of the head of "a barbed javelin, carried by serjeants-at-arms in the king's presence as early as Richard the First's time."[8] Then again we probably mount horses from the left side lest our swords should impede us. The small saddle on the surcingle of a horse, the seams in the backs of cloth-bound books, and those at the back of gloves are rudiments,—but to give the catalogue of such things would be almost endless. I have said enough, however, to show that by remembering that there is *nihil sine causa,* the observation of even common things of every-day life may be less trivial than it might at first sight appear

It seems a general rule that on solemn or ceremonial occasions men retain archaic forms; thus is it that court dress is a survival of the every-day dress of the last

---

7. See figures, pp. 254, 311, Fairholt.
8. Fairholt, p. 580.

century; that uniforms in general are richer in rudiments than common dress; that a carriage with a postilion is *de rigueur* at a wedding; and that (as mentioned by Sir John Lubbock) the priests of a savage nation, acquainted with the use of metals, still use a stone knife for their sacrifices—just as Anglican priests still prefer candles to gas.

The details given in this article, although merely curious, and perhaps insignificant in themselves, show that the study of dress from an evolutional standpoint serves as yet one further illustrations of the almost infinite ramification to which natural selections and its associated doctrines of development may be applied.

WALTER CRANE OF THE PROGRESS OF TASTE IN DRESS IN RELATION TO
ART EDUCATION   *Aglaia,*[1] no. 3 (1894)

If taste in dress could be traced to, or its cultivation and exercise were solely due to, the influence of the constant study of beautiful forms and fine historical models in design, as well as of the living human figure, we might be justified in looking to our schools of art to give us the best types and standards in costume. There are, however, too many missing links between the ordinary art student and the practical designer, between the tasteful person and the leader of fashion, to enable us to prove a close connection of cause and effect in the matter.

No doubt the general and extended cultivation of a knowledge of art even on the ordinary art-school lines has contributed not a little to the general interest in artistic questions, and quickened the average eye to some extent; but it must be said that we have not yet succeeded in making our schools remarkable as sources of invention, of initiative, or, on the whole, distinguished for capacity of artistic selection. We should be expecting too much, perhaps, to look for those things from training grounds. We ought to be satisfied if they ultimately turn out a fair average of capable artists, or, rather, enable students to become capable artists.

Even if all schools were equally well equipped in respect of models and teaching staff, under the present system there is practically but little margin left by the regime of the Board of Education for individual experiment and the inquiry off the main line of the prescribed courses of study in which passes or honours are obtainable.

The courses and classes of study are arranged in certain stereotyped ways, so that it becomes an object to attain a certain mechanical proficiency on certain methods of drawing, and the representation of a certain range of forms, in order to obtain certificates, rather than to cultivate the sense of beauty in individuals with a view to the public benefit and the raising of the standards of taste.

These defects are, it seems to me, inseparable from any attempt to teach art and taste in schools (that is to say by precept and principle rather than by practice), and upon a uniform system directed from a central department. Such an organization must necessarily tend to become rigid and work according to routine, and its administrators' best faculties are apt to be too much absorbed in mastering the details and rules of the system itself, and in the working of it, to be able to think out, much less to adopt, vivifying changes from time to time.

At certain changes, no doubt, by its command of expert opinion, such a Department may be of service to the schools of the country collectively in setting up a standard of taste, and advancing from time to time by means of the national competitions, which are the means of instituting instructive comparisons between the work of different schools.

But the real educating after influences; the inspiring and refining sources of artistic inventions in design must be found in the splendid array of examples of ancient arts of all kinds in our museums and galleries—which are mines of artistic wealth to the student and the designer.

1. *Aglaia* was the journal of The Healthy and Artistic Dress Union *[Ed.].*

Yet the most ordinary art-school training cannot be without its effect, even if only negative. The mere practice of cultivating the observation and uniting it with a certain power of depicting form is an education in itself, and gives people fresh eyes for nature and life.

The mere effect upon the eye and feeling of following the pure lines and forms of antique Greek sculpture, and the severe and expressive lines of drapery can hardly be without a practical influence to some degree even upon the least impressionable.

At all events, we have living artists, many of whom have survived the usual art-school or Academic training, and who through their works have certainly influenced contemporary taste in dress, at least as far as the costume of women is concerned.

I think there can be no doubt, for instance, of the influence in our time of what is commonly known as pre-Raphaelite school, and its later representatives in this direction; from the influence of Rossetti (which lately, indeed, seems to have revived and renewed itself in various ways) to the influence of William Morris and Edward Burne-Jones: But it is an influence which never owed anything to Academic teaching.

Under the new impulse—the new inspiration of the mid-century from the purer and simpler lines, forms, and colours of early medieval art, the dress of women in our time may be said to have been quite transformed for a while, and though the pendulum of fashion swings to and from, it does not much affect, except in some small details, a distinct type of dress which has become associated with artistic people—those who seriously study and consider of the highest value and importance beautiful and harmonious surroundings in daily life.

Beginning in the households of the artists themselves, the type of dress to which I allude, by imitation (which is the sincerest form of flattery—or insult, as some will have it) it soon became spread abroad until, in the seventies and early eighties, we saw the fashionable world and the stage aping, with more or less grotesque vulgarity, what it was fain to think were the fashions of the inner and most refined artistic cult. Commerce, ever ready to dot the i's and cross the t's of anything that spells increased profits, was not slow to flood the market with what were labelled "art colours" and "aesthetic" fabric of all kinds; but whatever vulgarity, absurdity, and insincerity might have been mixed up by its enemies with what was known as the aesthetic movement, it undoubtedly did indicate a general desire for greater beauty in ordinary life and gave us many charming materials and colours which, in combination with genuine taste, produced some very beautiful as well as simple dresses: while its main effect is seen, and continues to be seen upon the domestic background of interior fittings, furniture, furniture-fabrics and wall-paper. The giddy, aimless masquerade of fashion continues, however, perhaps not without a sort of secret alliance with the exigencies of the factory and the market, and it has lately revived, in part, the modes of the grandmothers of the present generation, but, as is often the fate of revivals, has somewhat vulgarized them in the process.

Modern dress seems to be much in the same position as modern architecture. In both it looks as if the period of organic style and spontaneous growth has been passed, and that we can only attempt, pending important and drastic social changes, to revive certain types, and endeavour as best we can to adapt them to modern requirements.

Yet architects are bolder than dressmakers. They think nothing of going back to classic or medieval times for models, while the modiste generally does not venture much farther than fifty or a hundred years back, and somewhat timidly at that. Small modifications, small changes and adaptations are always taking place, but it generally takes a decade to change the type of dress.

Regarding dress as a department of design, like design, we may consciously bring to bear upon it the result of artistic experience and knowledge of form.

Now a study of the human figure teaches one to respect it. It does not induce a wish to ignore its lines in clothing it, to contradict its proportions, or to misrepresent its character.

It seems curious, then, that the courses of study from the antique and the life usual at our art schools do not have a greater effect upon taste and choice in costume they appear to have.

We must remember, however, the many crossing influences that come in, the many motives and hidden causes that bear, in the complexity of modern existence, upon the question, and the stronger social motive powers which determine the forms of modern dress.

Fundamentally, we may say dress is more or less a question of climate.

Pure utility would be satisfied if the warmth is fairly distributed, and the actions of the body and limbs is free. The child with a loose tunic, leaving arms and legs bare and free, still represents primitive and classic man; and he also often satisfies the artist.

But the child is free to grow, to get as much joy out of life as it can. It does not feel under the necessity of pleasing Mrs. Grundy, except perhaps when mud-pies are "off."

Primitive, again, and picturesque is the dress of the labourer, ploughman, fisherman, navy; though purely adapted to use and service. Concessions to aestheticism, if any, only come in by a way of a coloured neckerchief, the broidery of a smock frock, or the pattern of a knitted jersey.

Yet each and all are constant and favourite subjects of the modern painter. Why?

Fundamentally, I think, because their dress is expressive of their occupation and character, as may be said of the dress of all working people.

The peasantry in all European countries alone has preserved anywhere national and local picturesqueness and character in their dress; often, too, where it still lingers unspoiled, as in Greece, and in Hungary and Bohemia, adorned with beautiful embroidery worked by the women themselves.

The last relics of historic and traditional costumes must be sought therefore among the people, and for the picturesqueness we must still seek the labourer.

This seems a strange commentary upon all modern painstaking, conscious efforts to attain the natural, simply beautiful, and suitable in dress, to be at once healthy and artistic. There really ought not to be so much difficulty about it.

If we lived simple, useful, and beautiful lives, we could not help being picturesque in the highest sense.

There is the modern difficulty.

We are driven back from every point to the ever-present social question.

Therefore, it seems to me that, though highly valuable and educational, we must not rely entirely upon conscious cultivation and conscious effort to lift the question of dress above vulgarity and affectation.

Modern society encourages the ideal of donothingness, so that it becomes an object to get rid of the outward signs of your particular occupation as soon as you cease work, if you are a worker, and to look as if you never did any if you are not.

This notion, combined perhaps with the gradual degradation of all manual labour under the modern system, has combined with business habits and English love of neatness, and perhaps prosaic and puritan plainness to produce the conventional costume of the modern "gentleman"—really the business man or bourgeois citizen.

The ruling type always prevails and stamps its image and superscription upon life everywhere.

Thus the outward and visible signs of the prosperous and respectable, the powerful and important, have come to be the frock-coat and tall hat—gradually evolved from the broad-brim and square cut jerkin of the Puritan of the seventeenth century.

Even the modern gentleman, when he takes to actually doing something, or playing at something, becomes at once more or less picturesque.

The flannels of the cricketer, and the boating man, the parti-coloured jerseys of our football teams—the modern equivalent, I suppose, of the knightly coat heraldry of the lists—all have a certain character and expressiveness. The costume of the cyclist again is another instance of adaptation to pursuit allied to picturesqueness, since it acknowledges at least the form of figure, and especially the legs, lost in ordinary civilian costume. In the various forms of riding-dress, again, we get a certain freedom and variety in costume through adaptation, both in men's and women's dress.

What modern costume really lacks is not so much character and picturesqueness, as beauty and romance—a general indictment which might be brought against modern life. We are really ruled by the dead weight of the prosaic, the prudent, the timid, the respectable, over and above the specializing adaptive necessities of utility before mentioned.

When we turn from the prosaic picturesqueness of such specialized dresses to the region of pure ornament, as in the modern full or evening dress of men and women, what do we find?

As far as men are concerned pure convention, the severest simplicity, without beauty, and almost without ornament, and, except in the case of those entitled to wear orders, confined to studs, watch-chain, etc. The clothes, the negation of colour—black, enlivened only by the white linen and white waistcoat, and patent leather.

I have here drawn a contrast between a gentleman's dress of the present time and one of the fourteenth century.

Both are extremely simple in design; but the medieval one alone can claim beauty of design, as it is true to the lines of the figure, and does not cut it up by sharp divisions and contrasts.

In the repression of ornament, we may detect another influence, that of monarchical and aristocratic institutions. Since if ornaments were freely worn by ordinary citizens, what would become of the doubtful distinction of ribbon and stars. The ordinary citizen, in the exercise of his individual taste, might have finer jewellery and better design upon him than the courtier and the diplomatist. That would never do, of course.

The same rock ahead will be found, I think, in the case of trousers.

Knee breeches, silk stockings, and buckled shoes are obviously more elegant and becoming than tubes of black cloth; but if the ordinary citizen takes to them what becomes of the official dignity of the golden footman, or of the cabinet minister at court, my Lord Mayor, Mr. Speaker, and other notabilities?

Men's dress having been reduced to the extreme of plainness in ordinary life, any relics of antiquity are used to denote official position, and the very plainness of evening dress is made use of to set off the decorations of courtly persons.

These are a few of complexities which attend any serious attempt to reform men's dress. They serve to convince one that costume is really controlled by the forms of social life, condition, occupation, rank, general tradition, sentiment, and sense of fitness, so that we can only reasonably expect great changes in the outsides of life when corresponding changes are affecting the inside—the economic foundations, constitution, and moral tone of society.

But let us look at the ladies.

Here at all events appear to be a field for the cultivation and display of taste and beauty alone. Mere convenience and utility in a lady's evening dress does not appear to be consulted at all. It often loses much of its primal covering capacity, and takes the form of a floral dressing to set off the head and bust and arms of the fair wearer. Most delicate materials and colours are used—white samite, mystic, wonderful; trailing clouds of glory in tulle and gauze; Eastern embroidery, and Chinese and Indian silks, gold, coral, pearl, diamonds and precious stones and flowers both real and (alas!) artificial, are some of the materials which contribute to the modern lady's evening toilette.

In the choice and use of these beautiful materials there is evidently abundant room for the exercise of the nicest judgement and the most refined and delicate individual taste. There can be no doubt, too, that these qualities are often met with, and that they are invariably found with a love and considerable knowledge of art. I do not say that a knowledge of art alone will enable people to dress tastefully. That is not always the case. The power of expression of taste or individuality in dress is no doubt like other gifts of expression, innate.

But a study of art, the training of the eye to appreciate the delicacies of beautiful line and quality of colour, and beauty of design in pattern, even without much executive power, must act upon the selective capacity generally. I think there is no doubt that we do see the signs of artistic culture, over and above natural distinction of choice, more frequently in the dress of refined and cultured women in our days than at any former period, perhaps, since the first half of the sixteenth century. There is more variety, more individuality, signs of that increasing independence of thought and action which distinguish our countrywomen.

The immense range of choice, both in simple and costly materials in women's dress, may be put down to increased commercial activity and the modern command of the markets of the world, no doubt. The taste and discrimination which selects and combines them in an artistic dress, is, to begin with, instinctive, but is largely aided and guided by the conscious cultivation and the study of art and the works of artists, I think.

We may, indeed, detect certain distinct influences in certain leading types of women's dress, even in that comparatively narrow region left to individual choice by the dictates of fashion or the milliner, dressmaker, and draper, and comparatively few feel themselves at liberty to move much beyond this.

If then our dictators for the mass, must at present be sought principally in these professional or trade directions we are thrown back again upon the quality and effectiveness of our artistic and technical education.

The great municipalities are busy spending large sums upon technical institutes, where the artistic lamb is expected to lie down with the manufacturing and commercial lion, where science and art are to become inseparable, if not undistinguishable, and inventive design is expected to keep pace with the labour or wage-saving ingenuities, and mechanical economics forced upon the manufacturer by competition. Among other things millinery and dressmaking will be taught, so that one may suppose the technical school will have a direct bearing upon taste in dress.

The same difficulty arises here as in the case of art-school teaching. You may lead a horse in the water but you cannot make him drink. Rather, perhaps, we are providing patent buckets before securing a water supply. What I mean is that, ultimately, in all the arts, in all matters of taste and beauty we must go back to life and nature. Beauty is inseparably associated with love, and cannot be produced without it: and unless the conditions of ordinary life admit of beauty we must not expect the reproduction of beautiful things. We cannot expect that science, or mechanical principles, or commercial demand will enable us to produce it in any direction to order. We cannot expect to get beauty at any price, if while arranging an elaborate system of art education on the one hand we allow ourselves to destroy its sources in nature, in the beauty of our own land, by ruthless destruction or vulgarization now too common. Beauty and taste can only spring out of the conditions of the materials which go to the making of a harmonious life. They must have opportunities of germinating and growing up in minds with leisure to think, with capacity to feel, with freedom and opportunity to select, with materials and margin for experiment, and above all with a centralizing social ideal—a key-note of love hope or faith.

Let us ask ourselves how far we are, individually or collectively, from the attainment of such conditions.

OSCAR WILDE SLAVES OF FASHION *Art and Decoration* (London, 1920)

Miss Leffler-Arnim's statement, in a lecture delivered recently at St. Saviour's Hospital, that "she had heard of instances where ladies were so determined not to exceed the fashionable measurement that they had actually held on to a cross-bar while their maids fastened the fifteen-inch corset," has excited a good deal of incredulity, but there is nothing really improbable in it. From the sixteenth century to our own day there is hardly any form of torture that has not been inflicted on girls, and endured by women, in obedience to the dictates of an unreasonable and monstrous Fashion. "In order to obtain a real Spanish figure," says Montaigne, "what a Gehenna of suffering will not women endure, drawn in and compressed by great coches entering the flesh; nay, sometimes they even die thereof!" "A few days after my arrival at school," Mrs. Somerville tells us in her memoirs, "although perfectly straight and well made, I was enclosed in stiff stays, with a steel busk in front; while above my frock, bands drew my shoulders back till the shoulder-blades met. Then a steel rod with a semi-circle, which went under my chin, was clasped to the steel busk in my stays. In this constrained state I and most of the younger girls had to prepare our lessons"; and in the life of Miss Edgeworth we read that, being sent to a certain fashionable establishment, "she underwent all the usual tortures of back-boards, iron collars and dumbs, and also (because she was a very tiny person) the unusual one of being hung by the neck to draw out the muscles and increase the growth," a signal failure in her case. Indeed, instances of absolute mutilation and misery are so common in the past that it is unnecessary to multiply them; but it is really sad to think that in our own day a civilized woman can hang on to a cross-bar while her maid laces her waist into a fifteen-inch circle. To begin with, the waist is not a circle at all, but an oval; nor can there be any greater error than to imagine that an unnaturally small waist gives an air of grace, or even of slightness, to the whole figure. Its effect, as a rule, is simply to exaggerate the width of the shoulders and the hips; and those whose figures possess that stateliness which is called stoutness by the vulgar, convert what is a quality into a defect by yielding to the silly edicts of Fashion on the subject of tight-lacing. The fashionable English waist, also, is not merely far too small, and consequently quite out of proportion to the rest of the figure, but it is worn far too low down. I use the expression "worn" advisedly, for a waist nowadays seems to be regarded as an article of apparel to be put on when and where one likes. A long waist always implies shortness of the lower limbs, and, from the artistic point of view, has the effect of diminishing the height; and I am glad to see that many of the most charming women in Paris are returning to the idea of the Directoire style of dress. This style is not by any means perfect, but at least it has the merit of indicating the proper position of the waist. I feel quite sure that all English women of culture and position will set their faces against such stupid and dangerous practices as are related by Miss Leffler-Arnim. Fashion's motto is: *Il faut souffrir pour être belle;* but the motto of art and of common-sense is: *Il faut être bête pour souffrir.*

Talking of Fashion, a critic in the *Pall Mall Gazette* expresses his surprise that I should have allowed an illustration of a hat, covered with "the bodies of dead birds," to appear in the first number of the *Woman's World;* and as I have received many letters on the subject, it is only right that I should state my exact position in the matter. Fashion is such an essential part of the mundus muliebris of our day, that it seems to me absolutely necessary that its growth, development, and phases should be duly chronicled; and the historical and practical value of such a record depends entirely upon its perfect fidelity to fact. Besides, it is quite easy for the children of light to adapt almost any fashionable form of dress to the requirements of utility and the demands of good taste. The Sarah Bernhardt tea-gown, for instance, figured in the present issue, has many good points about it, and the gigantic dress-improver does not appear to me to be really essential to the mode; and though the Postillion costume of the fancy dress ball is absolutely detestable in its silliness and vulgarity, the so-called Late Georgian costume in the same plate is rather pleasing. I must, however, protest against the idea that to chronicle the development of Fashion implies any approval of the particular forms that Fashion may adopt.

OSCAR WILDE WOMAN'S DRESS *Pall Mall Gazette* 40, no. 6114 (14 October 1884)

Mr. Oscar Wilde, who asks us to permit him "that most charming of all pleasures, the pleasure of answering one's critics," sends us the following remarks:—

The "Girl Graduate" must of course have precedence, not merely for her sex but for her sanity: her letter is extremely sensible. She makes two points: that high heels are a necessity for any lady who wishes to keep her dress clean from the Stygian mud of our streets, and that without a tight corset "the ordinary number of petticoats and etceteras" cannot be properly or conveniently held up. Now, it is quite true that as long as the lower garments are suspended from the hips a corset is an absolute necessity; the mistake lies in not suspending all apparel from the shoulders. In the latter case a corset becomes useless, the body is left free and unconfined for respiration and motion, there is more health, and consequently more beauty. Indeed all the most ungainly and uncomfortable articles of dress that fashion has ever in her folly prescribed, not the tight corset merely, but the farthingale, the vertugadin, the hoop, the crinoline, and that modern monstrosity the so-called "dress improver" also, all of them have owed their origin to the same error, the error of not seeing that it is from the shoulders, and from the shoulders only, that all garments should be hung.

And as regards high heels, I quite admit that some additional height to the shoe or boot is necessary if long gowns are to be worn in the street; but what I object to is that the height should be given to the heel only, and not to the sole of the foot also. The modern high-heeled boot is, in fact, merely the clog of the time of Henry VI., with the front prop left out, and its inevitable effect is to throw the body forward, to shorten the steps, and consequently to produce that want of grace which always follows want of freedom.

Why should clogs be despised? Much art has been expended on clogs. They have been made of lovely woods, and delicately inlaid with ivory, and with mother-of-pearl. A clog might be a dream of beauty, and, if not too high or too heavy, most comfortable also. But if there be any who do not like clogs, let them try some adaptation of the trouser of the Turkish lady, which is loose round the limb and tight at the ankle.

The "Girl Graduate," with a pathos to which I am not insensible, entreats me not to apotheosize "that awful, befringed, beflounced, and bekilted divided skirt." Well, I will acknowledge that the fringes, the flounces, and the kilting do certainly defeat the whole object of the dress, which is that of ease and liberty; but I regard these things as mere wicked superfluities, tragic proofs that the divided skirt is ashamed of its own division. The principle of the dress is good, and, though it is not by any means perfection, it is a step towards it.

Here I leave the "Girl Graduate," with much regret, for Mr. Wentworth Huyshe. Mr. Huyshe makes the old criticism that Greek dress is unsuited to our climate, and, to me the somewhat new assertion, that the men's dress of a hundred years ago was preferable to that of the second part of the seventeenth century, which I consider to have been the exquisite period of English costume.

Now, as regards the first of these two statements, I will say, to begin with, that the warmth of apparel does not depend really on the number of garments worn, but on the material of which they are made. One of the chief faults of modern dress is that it is composed of far too many articles of clothing, most of which are of the wrong substance; but over a substratum of pure wool, such as is supplied by Dr. Jaeger under the modern German system, some modification of Greek costume is perfectly applicable to our climate, our country and our century. This important fact has already been pointed out by Mr. E. W. Godwin in his excellent, though too brief handbook on Dress, contributed to the Health Exhibition. I call it an important fact because it makes almost any form of lovely costume perfectly practicable in our cold climate. Mr. Godwin, it is true, points out that the English ladies of the thirteenth century abandoned after some time the flowing garments of the early Renaissance in favour of a tighter mode, such as Northern Europe seems to demand. This I quite admit, and its significance; but what I contend, and what I am sure Mr. Godwin would agree with me in, is that the principles, the laws of Greek dress may be perfectly realized, even in a moderately tight gown with sleeves: I mean the principle of suspending all apparel from the shoulders, and of relying for beauty of effect not on the stiff ready-made ornaments of the modern milliner—the bows where there should be no bows, and the flounces where there should be no flounces—but on the exquisite play of light and line that one gets from rich and rippling folds. I am not proposing any antiquarian revival of an ancient costume, but trying merely to point out the right laws of dress, laws which are dictated by art and not by archaeology, by science and not by fashion; and just as the best work of art in our days is that which combines classic grace with absolute reality, so from a continuation of the Greek principles of beauty with the German principles of health will come, I feel certain, the costume of the future.

And now to the question of men's dress, or rather to Mr. Huyshe's claim of the superiority, in point of costume, of the last quarter of the eighteenth century over the second quarter of the seventeenth. The broad-brimmed hat of 1640 kept the rain of winter and the glare of summer from the face; the same cannot be said of the hat of one hundred years ago, which, with its comparatively narrow brim and high crown, was the precursor of the modern "chimney-pot": a wide turned-down collar is a healthier thing than a strangling stock, and a short cloak much more comfortable than a sleeved overcoat, even though the latter may have had "three capes"; a cloak is easier to put on and off, lies lightly on the shoulder in summer, and wrapped round one in winter keeps one perfectly warm. A doublet, again, is simpler than a coat and waistcoat; instead of two garments one has one; by not being open also it protects the chest better.

Short loose trousers are in every way to be preferred to the tight knee-breeches which often impede the proper circulation of the blood; and finally, the soft leather boots which could be worn above or below the knee, are more supple, and give consequently more freedom, than the stiff Hessian which Mr. Huyshe so praises. I say nothing about the question of grace and picturesqueness, for I suppose that no one, not even Mr. Huyshe, would prefer a macaroni to a cavalier, a Lawrence to a Vandyke, or the third George to the first Charles; but for ease, warmth and comfort this seventeenth-century dress is infinitely superior to anything that came after it, and I do not think it is excelled by any preceding form of costume. I sincerely trust that we may soon see in England some national revival of it.

OSCAR WILDE   MORE RADICAL IDEAS UPON DRESS REFORM   *Pall Mall Gazette* 40, no. 6224 (11 November 1884).

I have been much interested at reading the large amount of correspondence that has been called forth by my recent lecture on Dress. It shows me that the subject of dress reform is one that is occupying many wise and charming people, who have at heart the principles of health, freedom, and beauty in costume, and I hope that "H.B.T." and "Materfamilias" will have all the real influence which their letters—excellent letters both of them—certainly deserve

I turn first to Mr. Huyshe's second letter, and the drawing that accompanies it; but before entering into any examination of the theory contained in each, I think I should state at once that I have absolutely no idea whether this gentleman wears his hair long or short, or his cuffs back or forward, or indeed what he is like at all. I hope he consults his own comfort and wishes in everything which has to do with his dress, and is allowed to enjoy that individualism in apparel which he so eloquently claims for himself, and so foolishly tries to deny to others; but I really could not take Mr. Wentworth Huyshe's personal appearance as any intellectual basis for an investigation of the principles which should guide the costume of a nation. I am not denying the force, or even the popularity, of the "'Eave arf a brick" school of criticism, but I acknowledge it does not interest me. The gamin in the gutter may be a necessity, but the gamin in discussion is a nuisance. So I will proceed at once to the real point at issue, the value of the late eighteenth-century costume over that worn in the second quarter of the seventeenth: the relative merits, that is, of the principles contained in each. Now, as regards the eighteenth-century costume, Mr. Wentworth Huyshe acknowledges that he has had no practical experience of it at all; in fact he makes a pathetic appeal to his friends to corroborate him in his assertion, which I do not question for a moment, that he has never been "guilty of the eccentricity" of wearing himself the dress which he proposes for general adoption by others. There is something so naive and so amusing about this last passage in Mr. Huyshe's letter that I am really in doubt whether I am not doing him a wrong in regarding him as having any serious, or sincere, views on the question of a possible reform in dress; still, as irrespective of any attitude of Mr. Huyshe's in the matter, the subject is in itself an interesting one, I think it is worth continuing, particularly as I have myself worn this late eighteenth-century dress many times, both in public and in private, and so may claim to have a very positive right to speak on its comfort and suitability. The particular form of the dress I wore was very similar to that given in Mr. Godwin's handbook, from a print of Northcote's, and had a certain elegance and grace about it which was very charming; still, I gave it up for these reasons:—After a further consideration of the laws of dress I saw that a doublet is a far simpler and easier garment than a coat and waistcoat, and, if buttoned from the shoulder, far warmer also, and that tails have no place in costume, except on some Darwinian theory of heredity; from absolute experience in the matter I found that the excessive tightness of knee-breeches is not really comfortable if one wears them constantly; and, in fact, I satisfied myself that the dress is not one founded on any real principles. The broad-brimmed hat and loose cloak, which, as my object was not, of course, historical accuracy but modern ease, I had always worn with the costume in question, I have still retained, and find them most comfortable.

Well, although Mr. Huyshe has no real experience of the dress he proposes, he gives us a drawing of it, which he labels, somewhat prematurely, "An ideal dress." An ideal dress of course it is not; "passably picturesque," he says I may possibly think it; well, passably picturesque it may be, but not beautiful, certainly, simply because it is not founded on right principles, or, indeed, on any principles at all. Picturesqueness one may get in a variety of ways; ugly things that are strange, or unfamiliar to us, for instance, may be picturesque, such as a late sixteenth-century costume, or a Georgian house. Ruins, again, may be picturesque, but beautiful they never can be, because their lines are meaningless. Beauty, in fact, is to be got only from the perfection of principles; and in "the ideal dress" of Mr. Huyshe there are no ideas or principles at all, much less the perfection of either. Let us examine it, and see its faults; they are obvious to any one who desires more than a "Fancy-dress ball" basis for costume. To begin with, the hat and boots are all wrong. Whatever one wears on the extremities, such as the feet and head, should, for the sake of comfort, be made of a soft material, and for the sake of freedom should take its shape from the way one chooses to wear it, and not from any stiff, stereotyped design of hat or boot maker. In a hat made on right principles one should be able to turn the brim up or down according as the day is dark or fair, dry or wet; but the hat brim of Mr. Huyshe's drawing is perfectly stiff, and does not give much protection to the face, or the possibility of any at all to the back of the head or the ears, in case of a cold east wind; whereas the bycocket, a hat made in accordance with the right laws, can be turned down behind and at the sides, and so give the same warmth as a hood. The crown, again, of Mr. Huyshe's hat is far too high; a high crown diminishes the stature of a small person, and in the case of any one who is tall is a great inconvenience when one is getting in and out of hansoms and railway carriages, or passing under a street awning: in no case is it of any value whatsoever, and being useless it is of course against the principles of dress.

As regards the boots, they are not quite so ugly or so uncomfortable as the hat; still they are evidently made of stiff leather, as otherwise they would fall down to the ankle, whereas the boot should be made of soft leather always, and if worn high at all must be either laced up the front or carried well over the knee: in the latter case one combines perfect freedom for walking together with perfect protection against rain, neither of which advantages a short stiff boot will ever give one, and when one is resting in the house the long soft boot can be turned down as the boot of 1640 was. Then there is the overcoat: now, what are the right principles of an overcoat? To begin with, it should be capable of being easily put on or off, and worn over any kind of dress; consequently it should never have narrow sleeves, such as are shown in Mr. Huyshe's drawing. If an opening or slit for the arm is required it should be made quite wide, and may be protected by a flap, as in that excellent overall the modern Inverness cape; secondly, it should not be too tight, as otherwise all freedom of walking is impeded. If the young gentleman in the drawing buttons his overcoat he may succeed in being statuesque, though that I doubt very strongly, but he will never succeed in being swift; his super-totus is made for him on no principle whatsoever; a super-totus, or overall, should be capable of being worn long or short, quite loose or moderately tight, just as the wearer wishes; he should be able to have one arm free and one arm covered or both arms free or both arms covered, just as he chooses for his convenience in riding, walking, or driving; an overall again should never be heavy, and should always be warm: lastly, it should be capable of being easily carried if one wants to take it off; in fact, its principles are those of freedom and comfort, and a cloak realizes them all, just as much as an overcoat of the pattern suggested by Mr. Huyshe violates them.

The knee-breeches are of course far too tight; any one who has worn them for any length of time—any one, in fact, whose views on the subject are not purely theoretical—will agree with me there; like everything else in the dress, they are a great mistake. The substitution of the jacket for the coat and waistcoat of the period is a step in the right direction, which I am glad to see; it is, however, far too tight over the hips for any possible comfort. Whenever a jacket or doublet comes below the waist it should be slit at each side. In the seventeenth century the skirt of the jacket was sometimes laced on by points and tags, so that it could be removed at will, sometimes it was merely left open at the sides: in each case it exemplified what are always the true principles of dress, I mean freedom and adaptability to circumstances.

Finally, as regards drawings of this kind, I would point out that there is absolutely no limit at all to the amount of "passably picturesque" costumes which can be either revived or invented for us; but that unless a costume is founded on principles and exemplified laws, it never can be of any real value to us in the reform of dress. This particular drawing of Mr. Huyshe's, for instance, proves absolutely nothing, except that our grandfathers did not understand the proper laws of dress. There is not a single rule of right costume which is not violated in it, for it gives us stiffness, tightness and discomfort instead of comfort, freedom and ease.

Now here, on the other hand, is a dress which, being founded on principles, can serve us as an excellent guide and model; it has been drawn for me, most kindly, by Mr. Godwin from the Duke of Newcastle's delightful book on horsemanship, a book which is one of our best authorities on our best era of costume. I do not of course propose it necessarily for absolute imitation; that is not the way in which one should regard it; it is not, I mean, a revival of a dead costume, but a realization of living laws. I give it as an example of a particular application of principles which are universally right. This rationally dressed young man can turn his hat brim down if it rains, and his loose trousers and boots down if he is tired—that is, he can adapt his costume to circumstances; then he enjoys perfect freedom, the arms and legs are not made awkward or uncomfortable by the excessive tightness of narrow sleeves and knee-breeches, and the hips are left quite untrammelled, always an important point; and as regards comfort, his jacket is not too loose for warmth, nor too close for respiration; his neck is well protected without being strangled, and even his ostrich feathers, if any Philistine should object to them, are not merely dandyism, but fan him very pleasantly, I am sure, in summer, and when the weather is bad they are no doubt left at home, and his cloak taken out. *The value of the dress is simply that every separate article of it expresses a law.* My young man is consequently apparelled with ideas, while Mr. Huyshe's young man is stiffened with facts; the latter teaches one nothing; from the former one learns everything. I need hardly say that this dress is good, not because it is seventeenth century, but because it is constructed on the true principles of costume, just as a square lintel or pointed arch is good, not because one may be Greek and the other Gothic, but because each of them is the best method of spanning a certain-sized opening, or resisting a certain weight. The fact, however, that this dress was generally worn in England two centuries and a half ago shows at least this, that the right laws of dress have been understood and realized in our country, and so in our country may be realized and understood again. As regards the absolute beauty of this dress and its meaning, I should like to say a few words more. Mr. Wentworth Huyshe solemnly announces that "he and those who think with him" cannot permit this question of beauty to be imported into the question of dress; that he and those who think with him take "practical views on the subject," and so on. Well, I will not enter here into a discussion as to how far any one who does not take beauty and the value of beauty into account can claim to be practical at all. The word practical is nearly always the last refuge of the uncivilized. Of all misused words it is the most evilly treated. But what I want to point out is that beauty is essentially organic; that is, it comes, not from without, but from within, not from any added prettiness, but from the perfection of its own being; and that consequently, as the body is beautiful, so all apparel that rightly clothes it must be beautiful also in its construction and in its lines.

I have no more desire to define ugliness than I have daring to define beauty; but still I would like to remind those who mock at beauty as being an unpractical thing of this fact, that an ugly thing is merely a thing that is badly made, or a thing that does not serve its purpose; that ugliness is want of fitness; that ugliness is failure; that ugliness is uselessness, such as ornament in the wrong place, while beauty, as some one finely said, is the purgation of all superfluities. There is a divine economy about beauty; it gives us just what is needful and no more, whereas ugliness is always extravagant; ugliness is a spendthrift and wastes its material; in fine, ugliness—and I would commend this remark to Mr. Wentworth Huyshe—ugliness, as much in costume as in anything else, is always the sign that somebody has been unpractical. So the costume of the future in England, if it is founded on the true laws of freedom, comfort, and adaptability to circumstances, cannot fail to be most beautiful also, because beauty is the sign always of the rightness of principles, the mystical seal that is set upon what is perfect, and upon what is perfect only.

As for your other correspondent, the first principle of dress that all garments should be hung from the shoulders and not from the waist seems to me to be generally approved of, although an "Old Sailor" declares that no sailors or athletes ever suspend their clothes from the shoulders, but always from the hips. My own recollection of the river and running ground at Oxford—those two homes of Hellenism in our little Gothic town—is that the best runners and rowers (and my own college turned out many) wore always a tight jersey, with short drawers attached to it, the whole costume being woven in one piece. As for sailors, it is true, I admit, and the bad custom seems to involve that constant "hitching up" of the lower garments which, however popular in transpontine dramas, cannot, I think, but be considered an extremely awkward habit; and as all awkwardness comes from discomfort of some kind, I trust that this point in our sailor's dress will be looked to in the coming reform of our navy, for, in spite of all protests, I hope we are about to reform everything, from torpedoes to top-hats, and from crinolettes to cruises.

Then as regards clogs, my suggestion of them seems to have aroused a great deal of terror. Fashion in her high-heeled boots has screamed, and the dreadful word "anachronism" has been used. Now, whatever is useful cannot be an anachronism. Such a word is applicable only to the revival of some folly; and, besides, in the England of our own day clogs are still worn in many of our manufacturing towns, such as Oldham. I fear that in Oldham they may not be dreams of beauty; in Oldham the art of inlaying them with ivory and with pearl may possibly be unknown; yet in Oldham they serve their purpose. Nor is it so long since they were worn by the upper classes of this country generally. Only a few days ago I had the pleasure of talking to a lady who remembered with affectionate regret the clogs of her girlhood; they were, according to her, not too high nor too heavy, and were provided, besides, with some kind of spring in the sole so as to make them the more supple for the foot in walking. Personally, I object to all additional height being given to a boot or shoe; it is really against the proper principles of dress, although, if any such height is to be given it should be by means of two props; not one; but what I should prefer to see is some adaptation of the divided skirt or long and moderately loose knickerbockers. If, however, the divided skirt is to be of any positive value, it must give up all idea of "being identical in appearance with an ordinary skirt"; it must diminish the moderate width of each of its divisions, and sacrifice its foolish frills and flounces; the moment it imitates a dress it is lost; but let it visibly announce itself as what it actually is, and it will go far towards solving a real difficulty. I feel sure that there will be found many graceful and charming girls ready to adopt a costume founded on these principles, in spite of Mr. Wentworth Huyshe's terrible threat that he will not propose to them as long as they wear it, for all charges of a want of womanly character in these forms of dress are really meaningless; every right article of apparel belongs equally to both sexes, and there is absolutely no such thing as a definitely feminine garment. One word of warning I should like to be allowed to give: The over-tunic should be made full and moderately loose; it may, if desired, be shaped more or less to the figure, but in no case should it be confined at the waist by any straight band or belt; on the contrary, it should fall from the shoulder to the knee, or below it, in fine curves and vertical lines, giving more freedom and consequently more grace. Few garments are so absolutely unbecoming as a belted tunic that reaches to the knees, a fact which I wish some of our Rosalinds would consider when they don doublet and hose; indeed, to the disregard of this artistic principle is due the ugliness, the want of proportion, in the Bloomer costume, a costume which in other respects is sensible.

"How can you possibly paint these ugly three-cornered hats?" asked a reckless critic once of Sir Joshua Reynolds. "I see light and shade in them," answered the artist. *"Les grands coloristes,"* says Baudelaire in a charming article on the artistic value of frock coats, *"les grands coloristes savent faire de la couleur avec un habit noir, une cravate blanche, et un fond gris."*

"Art seeks and finds the beautiful in all times, as did her high priest Rembrandt, when he saw the picturesque grandeur of the Jews' quarter of Amsterdam, and lamented not that its inhabitants were not Greeks," were the fine and simple words used by Mr Whistler in one of the most valuable passages of his lecture. The most valuable, that is, to the painter: for there is nothing of which the ordinary English painter needs more to be reminded than that the true artist does not wait for life to be made picturesque for him, but sees life under picturesque conditions always—under conditions, that is to say, which are at once new and delightful. But between the attitude of the painter towards the public and the attitude of a people towards art, there is a wide difference. That, under certain conditions of light and shade, what is ugly in fact may in its effect become beautiful, is true; and this, indeed, is the real *modernité* of art, but these conditions are exactly what we cannot be always sure of, as we stroll down Picadilly in the glaring vulgarity of the noonday, or lounge in the park with a foolish sunset as a background. Were we able to carry our *chiaroscuro* about with us, as we do our umbrellas, all would be well; but this being impossible, I hardly think that pretty and delightful people will continue to wear a style of dress as ugly as it is useless and as meaningless as it is monstrous, even on the chance of such a master as Mr Whistler spiritualizing them into a symphony or refining them into a mist. For the arts are made for life, and not life for arts.

Nor do I feel quite sure that Mr Whistler has been himself always true to the dogma he seems to lay down, that a painter should paint only the dress of his age and of his actual surroundings; far be it from me to burden a butterfly with the heavy responsibility of its past: I have always been of the opinion that consistency is the last refuge of the unimaginative: but have we not all seen, and most of us admired, a picture from his hand of dresses of Japan? has not Tite Street been thrilled with the tidings that the models of Chelsea were posing to the master, in peplums, for pastels?

Whatever comes from Mr Whistler's brush is far too perfect in its loveliness to stand or fall by any intellectual dogma on art, even by its own: for Beauty is justified of all her children, and cares nothing for explanations, but it is impossible to look through any collection of modern pictures in London, from Burlington House to the Grosvenor Gallery, without feeling that the professional model is ruining painting and reducing it to a collection of mere pose and *pastiche.*

Are we not all weary of him, that venerable impostor fresh from the steps of the Piazza di Spagna, who, in the leisure moments that he can spare from his customary organ, makes the round of the studios and it is waited for in Holland Park? Do we not all recognize him, when, with the gay *insouciance* of his nation, he reappears on the walls of our summer exhibitions as everything that he is not, and nothing that he is, glaring at us here as a patriarch of Canaan, here beaming as a brigand from Abruzzi? Popular is he, this poor peripatetic professor of posing, with those whose joy it is to paint the posthumous portrait of the last philanthropist who in his lifetime had neglected to be photographed—yet he is the sign of decadence, the symbol of decay.

For all costumes are caricatures. The basis of art is not the Fancy Ball. Where there is a loveliness of dress, there is no dressing up. And so, were our national attire delightful in color and in constructions simple and sincere; were dress the expression of the loveliness that it shields and of the swiftness and motion that it does not impede; did its lines break from the shoulder instead of bulging from the waist; did the inverted wineglass cease to be the ideal of form; were these things brought about, as brought about they will be, then would painting be no longer an artificial reaction against the ugliness of life, but become, as it should be, the natural's expression of life's beauty. Now would painting merely, but other arts also, be the gainers by a change such as that which I propose; the gainers, I mean, through the increased atmosphere of Beauty by which the artists would be surrounded and in which they would grow up. For Art is not to be taught in Academies. Is it what one looks at, not what one listens to, that makes the artist. The real schools should be the streets. There is not, for instance, a single delicate line, or delightful proportion, in the dress of Greeks, which is not echoed exquisitely in their architecture. A nation arrayed in stove-pipe hats and dress-improvers might have built the Pantechnichon possibly, but the Parthenon never. And finally, there is this to be said: art, it is true, can never have any other claim but her own perfection, and it may be that the artist, desiring merely to contemplate and to create, is wise in not busying himself about change in others: yet wisdom is not always the best; there are times when she sinks to the level of commmon sense; and from the passionate folly of those—and there are so many—who desire that Beauty shall be confined no longer to the *bric-à-brac* of the collector and the dust of the museum, but shall be, as it should be, the natural and national inheritance of all—from all this noble unwisdom, I say, who knows what new loveliness shall be given to life, and, under these more exquisite conditions, what perfect artist born? *Le milieu se renouvelant, l'art se renouvelle.*

Speaking, however, from his own passionless pedestal, Mr Whistler, in pointing out that the power of a painter is to be found in his power of vision, not in his cleverness of hand, has expressed a truth which needed expression, and which, coming from the lord of form and colour, cannot fail to have its influence. His lecture, the Apocrypha though it be for the people, yet remains from this time as the Bible for the painter, the masterpiece of masterpieces, the songs of songs. It is true he has pronounced the panegyric of the Philistine, but I fancy Ariel praising Caliban for a jest: and, in that he has read the Commination Service over the critics, let all men thank him, the critics themselves, indeed, most of all, for he has now relieved them from the necessity of a tedious existence. Considered, again, merely as an orator, Mr Whistler seems to me to stand almost alone. Indeed, among all our public speakers I know but few who can combine so felicitously as he does the mirth and malice of Puck with the style of the minor prophets.

JOSEF HOFFMANN   THE INDIVIDUAL DRESS   "Das individuelle Kleid," *Die Waage* 1, no. 15 (9 April 1898)

It is astonishing that at a time when one wants to be absolutely original and remarkable, in fact very few people are really original. Moreover, even those who are compelled by their professions to appear original, and those who want to be not just original but extravagant, openly submit to fashion in their exterior appearance.

One would very much like to discover the reasons for this. Is it that they are too shy to be peculiar, or are they afraid of risking their position in society and of being considered mad? Certainly not. What is most likely is that it is the modern trend of always being en masse that is the decisive factor.

The reasons mentioned above are not accepted by people who are truly original. They act in a completely naive and spontaneous way. If there is a difference between them and others, this is due neither to a mania of being conspicuous nor to bizarrerie, but is a result of inner development. It is the need to create harmony that is being expressed unconsciously. This expression was absent when the principles of education compelled people to be uniform and when their inner necessity was repressed while they were still young. By such repression, one could paralyze any creative impulse, even in minds that were original and full of fantasy.

One could demonstrate how strong the impulse toward uniformity is in human beings by examining several examples of savages who adopt a uniform appearance according to their tribe, especially in how they style their hair or beards. However, this is part of a chapter on the national costumes that should be treated separately. People who belonged to the great cultures of antiquity and who were influenced by strong minds (the Greeks, the Italians, and the Arabs) adopted an individual style for their hair and beards.

At the beginning of the Middle Ages, people wore the chiton and the mantle. The mantle that we Germans still wore twenty or thirty years ago is worn today by the Italians, and not only by peasants or by shepherds, who use it in an individual way, but also by the bourgeoisie, who all wear it in the same way. In contrast, ordinary people wear it according their desires and needs. This garment has lost a great deal because it is now worn around the neck and closed at the chest. Horsemen have already abandoned it in favor of the overcoat. The further that men's dress has moved from the mantle and the simple shirt, long or short, the less original it has become, because of the characteristic way clothes are worn. It is this, and not the way in which clothing is cut, that is the essential element, as can be seen now only among oriental and East Asian peoples.

Over the following centuries, clothing degenerated into the grotesque and the bizarre, and it was only in the fifteenth and sixteenth centuries that the dress of men and women gained something that is worthy of our attention and did not exclude grace or charm.

In the seventeenth century, when almost everything adopted the cut of military dress, clothes managed to maintain an impressive appearance. The same is true of the Baroque that followed, with its long wigs. But the next period, with its hairnets, was completely bizarre. People had three-cornered hats that were totally useless, offering no protection from the rain or the sun, and that often had to be held in the hand because their hair was powdered. The only advantage was that the metabolic processes of the head were not at all hindered. Nevertheless, when dress was used to officially express something significant, such as freedom, convictions, or elegance, the attempt failed. One can find examples of such failure in the period from the end of the eighteenth and the beginning of the nineteenth century. If today one sees images of that time, they seem ridiculous rather then giving the impression of individual freedom. Moreover, it is ironic that the type of dress that was then thought to be a symbol of freedom has since become a symbol of servitude. Even if wearing tails is useful in a salon, this is the dress of servants and prototypical of submission.

Tailors can certainly help ordinary people, but not men who wish to make a lasting impression. As we have seen, dress can give someone dignity or make a fool of him.

As it aspires to see the new thing coming, taste will always go to from one extreme to another: it has gone from a graciously arranged tower of hair to the distressing haircut known as the "Fiesco." For a prisoner, perhaps also for a soldier or a worker, who often has to work in the dust and in humid conditions, this haircut might have been practical. However, it could never be beautiful or individual. As one cannot make another face for oneself, choosing other ears or a different nose, one should make do with what is available. This means keeping whatever is typical and differentiates oneself from others—as should be done with hair and beards. From this, everything else will follow. Imagine a man with a lot of hair and a big beard wearing a tiny hat on his head: the lack of harmony will be obvious.

One can recognize someone from far away by their personal way of walking or by their movements; a voice is so specific that the first sound is enough to know whose voice it is; one eye hiding behind a mask can be enough to identify a person. In the same way, we would like an element of dress and the way in which dress is worn to be as familiar as the elements mentioned above so that we can recognize it as being in accord with the wearer's character.

For modern people like ourselves, there are few elements remaining in male dress that make it more original. First, there is the selection of what is worn. The way in which a garment is worn already takes second place, because the cut has been previously adapted to the male form. When the only questions are those of length and width, or the way in which the outfit is adapted to the proportions of the body, then one has to take color into consideration. This allows a certain degree of variation and the expression of personal taste—even in male clothes, where only halftones are used.

With women's clothing there is far greater freedom in using characteristic elements, but their use is comparatively less common than in male clothing. In women's dress, the possibilities in cut and color are greater, and very beautiful colors—in other words, colors that a painter would consider beautiful—might become fashionable. But, then one could hardly choose really complimentary or harmonious colors to match them. That would be unheard of! Unlively or bland color harmonies are always used. Although the cut of women's clothing has many advantages, it does not prevent these garments from being often unhealthy and unaesthetic. The greater freedom is usually counterbalanced by a lack of concern for hygiene, a factor that is never present in male clothing. Therefore, a sensible eye, as well as common sense, is often shocked by women's clothing.

In India and in most of the Orient, clothes are worn that are not only healthier but also give extraordinary freedom to individual taste in their form and color. The form and even the principles according to which the garment is made are fixed. However, I have seen thousands of people wearing their clothes in constantly new ways; and this is the most beautiful thing I have ever seen, as far as women's appearance is concerned.

How could one then integrate such diversity into our anonymous modern clothing? How could one individualize modern dress? Such action should not be the result of a comprehensive study; everyone should instead just follow their own tastes and needs. If this happens, then we will see real harmony with individual predispositions. The vain person will remain vain, and the dignified person will remain dignified. The aesthetically educated and emotionally mature woman will not tolerate a single mistake in her appearance. A modest girl will express charming simplicity when compared to a lady who is conscious of clothes and neatness. The serious lady will wrap herself in dark folds; the prompt and energetic person will wear a practical outfit that allows freedom of movement. The person with simple tastes will choose simple, discreet clothing in accordance with their character. The housewife will wear garments that are appropriate to her status. The impression made by dress, which is often so shocking, will change into its opposite; dress will be noticed only because of its agreement with the character of its wearer. Then, man will be the superior to the dressmaker, unlike the present situation, in which the dressmaker dominates man. Only in this way can one overthrow the tyranny of fashion so that individuals can express their rights.

It is incredible that certain people get together to determine what sort of dress, hats, or color will be fashionable, and that millions of people obey the decrees of the few. They are not aware they could cause incalculable damage to their health by accepting what the few have decided is decent or useful for them and what is not.

To avoid any misunderstanding, we want to make it clear that we do not want to return to an old type of clothing or to multicolored and brocaded dress. No: we want free, light attire that allows all kind of movements, that can be worn open or closed, that fits well, and that can be put on and taken off without any help. First of all, away with all linen that is starched to the point of being unpleasant. In this way, any resemblance to a doll will disappear, especially in male dress.

The unimaginatively uniform haircut is related to this. Once this tyranny has been broken and rights have been returned to individuals, the conventional way of bowing, of turning one's head to a one-quarter or three-quarters angle for a curtsy, will be replaced by a natural, rich, and pleasant appearance. It will then only be fair if the thick-headed appear lacking in substance in comparison with those who behave naturally.

At another time, we may present, with clear examples, how to put into practice the ideas that have been expressed above.

*I dedicate the publication of this lecture to Dr. Deneken, the director of the
Kaiser Wilhelm-Museum in Krefeld. I know very well, however, that I can only
pay a tiny part of my debt toward someone who enabled me to realize an old
dream. I am deeply indebted to him, as are all those interested in the promotion
of women's clothing, for organizing the first exhibition of artistic dress and for
the consequences that this brought about. I have a particularly happy recollection of the days spent in Krefeld when we together launched our attack on fashion and I gave the following lecture. I often think of the encouragement I
received then, which helped me so much in my efforts.*

Berlin, October 1900   Henry van de Velde

It is in the nature of things that artists will be interested in women's clothing. Their right
to trespass on this field may be contested less than their contribution to furniture or interior design. Yet it would have been impossible, four or five years ago, to prepare a reform
of women's clothing, like that of furniture, jewelry, carpet design, wallpaper, and books.
We could never have imagined that the prophetic vision of ours would be realized so soon.

Dress seemed infinitely far from art, and we had accepted the idea that the gap
that lies between them would never be bridged. We were wrong. To bring them together,
we just had to apply the same logic we used to reform other fields of the applied arts. It is
only recently that artists have become aware of their real task. They have discovered that
limiting beauty to painting or monumental sculpture neglects vast fields, as varied and fer-
tile as life itself. Consequently, their aim was to ennoble craft by reviving the meaning it
had in the past. Without knowing it, they have behaved like our primitive ancestors who,
after obtaining their food, thought about finding a roof, then about adorning themselves
in order to attract a woman, and finally about clothing, to protect themselves from bad
weather. In the same way, the modern renaissance of the applied arts began with architecture, before being extended to furniture and to everything that touches ordinary, decorative objects. Finally, it has approached its last conquest—that of dress.

This new renaissance has occurred at just the right time. By the natural chronol-
ogy of its evolution, I am convinced that it is nothing other than the wonderful blossom-
ing of seeds planted by life itself manifesting its eternal renewal in this way.

We live in enviable times. When I think I might have been alive around 1830, I
get goose bumps! You may tell me that I could as well have stood up for the same principles in 1830, because today I am one of the main activists in this renaissance. This would
mean, however, that we are the sole agents of this development, as if Morris and Ruskin
had not existed before us or that they could have decided to launch this revival of the
applied arts on the spur of the moment, simply because they considered it to be a good
idea. You do not think this and neither do I. You know very well that anything that happens is inevitably preceded by favorable circumstances. You also know that events,

inventions, or transformations depend on inexorable conditions, in the same way that the forces of nature cause ripe fruit to fall from the tree or drag the child away from his mother's breast because his development requires it. I will announce the first exhibition of artistic dress in Krefeld, in August 1900. This exhibition consecrates for the first time many individual efforts. It is an important event, as it will call into being other demonstrations of the same kind. From now on, shows of women's clothing will take their place among art exhibitions. Undoubtedly, we will begin to see clothing exhibited sometimes next to paintings and sculptures, as has recently been the case with other works of applied art.

The first of us to take on dress design wanted solely to dress women in the smartest possible way. We were rebelling against fashion and its representatives, who had other ambitions and had forgotten this simple yet natural aim. Every year, they seem compelled to invent a style so different from that of the previous season that fashion's slaves are forced to replace their wardrobes. Some time ago, a number of men and women rose up against this despotism and had the courage to free themselves from it. Artists were among these adversaries of fashion. Nonetheless, their opposition was not a joint endeavor—it did not offer anything new and it did not propose an alternative ideal. Their reaction would have been wholly unproductive had it not contributed to supporting and spreading a feeling of revolt. Today, artists are not alone in thinking that the perpetual changes in fashion are motivated by purely commercial goals. Many women also have understood that for a long time they have played a ridiculous role by giving so much importance to the arbitrary decisions of a few great, mainly Parisian, couturiers. These people have imposed dresses on them that were loose at first, then tight, then bell-shaped, then very close-fitting, for no reason other than whim or personal interest.

I would like to express my admiration for those women who, aware of how ridiculous this situation was, refused to submit to it and dared to dress in a way different from others in their circle. I know how much courage was needed; I know the harassment, the indiscreet curiosity, the rude remarks they were exposed to in the street, at the theater, or even in their own homes when they dressed according to their feelings and personal taste. I have often wondered if public taste has become so corrupt that it is no longer able to acknowledge what is right and beautiful in a woman dressed as she pleases. I have concluded that the strangeness of personalized dress is sufficient to create a scandal. Let us suppose that several people adopt a dress that, for the time being, is unique. The public will accept this without thinking of it as a manifestation of fashion that escapes any criticism or judgment, whether good or bad. The public cannot express a well-considered judgment, and all novelties suffer from being unique.

In fact, it has not been so long that these changes in fashion have reigned with such punctual regularity. Until the end of the eighteenth century, modifications in dress obeyed traditional laws. They had their own logic and were valid for a whole era. The periods of the Revolution, the Directoire, the Empire expressed themselves in dress. Under those circumstances, the notion of "fashion" does not apply. It was only half a century ago that fashion as it exists now became part of the history of dress. From 1840 on, there has been a permanent need to renovate dress. Despite its frantic pursuit of novelty, however, fashion does not evolve. Its transformations only decree that dresses should be tight, adorned with flounces or pleats, and so on. Imposed by shrewd professionals motivated by their personal interests, these ridiculous details have been given a great deal of importance.

The beginnings of fashion and its reign coincided with a tremendous development of submissive feelings. The lack of taste was rarely so obvious as under the Restoration and until the recent renaissance—in other words, until 1892. A total upheaval of the personality annihilated what remained of the will. A generalized slavish passivity in all fields of creation and thinking made men and women give up all concern for how they looked. Until then, it was usual for people of the same social standing to dress in the same way in the same circumstances. Individuality dissolved in this uniform code of dress. This was not the mark of a couturier's imagination but expressed the general will, which, from time immemorial, was defined by the living conditions of the whole race—by the same education, the same material life, and the same religion. Differences existed from one country to another, from one province to another, whereas nowadays they can be observed from one house to another in the same country or province. Will we ever experience such unity again?

The present movement is mainly concerned with women's clothing, because men's clothing is less dependent on merchants' opportunism. I think this is so because men try less to please and want to be comfortable in their clothes. They do not want to be hampered in their movements or their occupations. We men have less patience, and this character trait has prevented tailors from exaggerating their inventions. The same is not true of women. A lady who does not have any occupation other than being attractive is able to bear physical discomfort in order to please; her patience and passivity are unlimited. This material (because I do not believe that couturiers consider women otherwise) is docile and malleable. The couturière's best argument—that "this is fashion"—does not arouse the slightest protest or complaint. Fashion is the eye of Argus that surveys its own world of show. It is the great enemy that has generated the decline of all the decorative arts and even the degeneration of "grand" art.

In the Middle Ages, people were uniquely concerned with logic. Logic was the mighty, unequivocal force that manifested itself in all acts and needs. People were satisfied with the successes gained owing to this consistent attitude. In all fields, whether technical or scientific, an organic and timeless beauty was obtained that can be found today in the shapes of old tools, furniture, and costumes. Nowadays, the beauty of structures is so deeply hidden, concealed by the aberrant excesses of misplaced ornamentation, that is extremely difficult to perceive. If one wants to do so, one has to study the complete anthology of this decorative imagination. A simple cupboard, which should just be a well-conceived piece of furniture in keeping with its function, becomes a heap of allegorical sculptures, in this case representing the four seasons, with their diverse tasks and pleasures. No one would be able to decipher such a form, realize that it is a cupboard, or imagine what it contained. One would see only naked men and women, caryatids carrying fruit and sheaves of wheat, agricultural tools, piles of weapons, birds, and game. In the field of women's clothing, the same errors have led to these extremely illogical constructions that, lacking any visible structure, superimpose on all sorts of bodies a cloud of bows and flounces and small pleats. They alter the body, transforming it into a formless mass of flesh, concealing limbs and joints, and completely hiding the beauty of the human figure.

From 1840 on, women's clothing has floundered in extravagance. In 1890, it reached a summit of irrationality, having gone so far that it was no longer possible to see how a dress was made. The slightest trace of a seam had disappeared. As with the cupboard or lamp we discussed earlier, the elements used for its making were concealed. They tried to make us believe that the dresses were made of anything but needle and cloth. These "masterpieces" were greatly appreciated and admired. People were amazed by this "French virtuosity" that was able to realize a dress from a thousand mere nothings, held together God knows how, wrapping up one knows not what, probably a woman, because a head emerged from the creation and one could see the odd arm and hand. In every field, the same failure of imagination is evident. During the whole *Kunstgewerbe* period, this aberration did not spare any daily objects, which never resembled their true nature and were never suited to their purpose. Today, this period is finished and logic, that powerful releaser of artistic sense, has reasserted its rights. It incites us to banish the furniture of the past even when it is not so old, as is the case if it originates in an authentic source. Logic is renewing all aspects of architecture and all interior design. It also guides those concerned by dress.

Several years ago, fashion had already suffered a real attack. The first organized belligerents were recruited in Germany; they raised the flag of Dress Reform but the enemy retaliated victoriously. Today, fashion reigns as freely as ever. Yet while Dress Reform was based on health principles, its representatives ignored beauty, thereby proving their ignorance of feminine psychology. To be successful, they should have set another fashion against the old one and pretended that it was a new "German" fashion rather than a French one. In addition to this excessive honesty, they made another error, which, as we said before, was a lack of concern with beauty. Dress Reform contained a puritanical element, somewhat dry and frozen, which was rather disheartening. The pamphlets prosaically advocating the new dogma held opinions that were far too orthodox. Nevertheless, this movement left many marks.

In any case, it had the honor of liberating us from the corset, that instrument of torture, which deserves to be exhibited in a museum of antiques between the thumbscrew and the chastity belt. The corset is well and truly finished, at least as required by the couturiers, whose aim was purely and simply to adapt women to the dress they invented, instead of flattering women's figures or helping them to move in their clothes. Nowadays, the corset has developed into a logical and positive form; it has become a framework that is not opposed to the forms of the body and that enables dresses to be designed according to regular principles. Women can once again decide to wear clothes composed of several parts. Until now, those who refused to submit to fashion were compelled to choose dresses in one piece, of the kind that is used at home when having tea, or in the garden. To close them, they had to wear belts with metal buckles. Nevertheless, the contradiction with fashion was so obvious that we had to wait for a long time to see this type of dress in our region. In England, women wore them tight under the breast, following the model of Pre-Raphaelite paintings and the fashion of the first Empire, which was quickly adopted in that country. But on the Continent people still looked to Paris, and it was up to men to show their companions the way to more freedom. They chose English fashion, whose rational principles then also affected women's clothing.

One can admit that reason is as contagious as madness. One proof of this is that the whole of the younger generation is striving to achieve the same goal in all fields of the applied arts. One can see signs everywhere demonstrating that we are beginning to reestablish the logic of things. This awareness is characteristic of the prelude to a new renaissance and promises a development of the modern style, which will be as marvelous as the styles of the past that honored reason and trusted logic. The principles of Greek art are eternal and inalienable, as are those of Roman or Gothic art. It is on these eternal and inalienable foundations that we have to found the modern style. However, its expression will be different from what preceded it inasmuch as contemporary materials and conditions of life are also different from those of the past.

These new emergent styles influence artists who are attempting to work in the field of dress. By what means can they achieve their goal? They have to do exactly the same thing for women's clothing as they did for the other objects of industrial arts they have already mastered. They must have a clear and simple image of what attire should be. This, however, is not easy. What is proper for clothing is often so deeply hidden nowadays that a complete reordering is necessary in order to develop clear ideas about it. One has to begin by getting rid of everything that is purely ornamental. Then dress will pass through a transitional period, as was the case with furniture and lamps. This phase would already be over so far as artists are concerned if it were not indispensable for the public to see and get used to the healthy forms that are destined to replace those condemned to oblivion. Besides, the public is so used to an excess of ornamentation and furbelows that it will be quite a long time before complaints about their absence cease. However, it is impossible to improve things if we do not fight to abolish this kind of decoration and leave it behind with the other elements of its evolution that, from now on, belong to history.

Contemporary dress has many more degenerate elements that can be seen at first glance, many more survivals of cuts adapted to the needs of the past that are superfluous today. Some years ago, George H. Darwin, Charles Darwin's son, had the idea of applying his father's theory of evolution to dress. His research led from one discovery to the next, and his findings are as convincing as those that led Charles Darwin to his conclusions on the origin of species and of humans. His study was published in 1872 in *Macmillan's Magazine*. It begins with the following words:

The development of dress presents a strong analogy to that of organisms, as explained by the modern theories of evolution[.] . . . We shall see that the truth expressed by the proverb "Natura non facit saltum" is applicable in the one case as in the other; the law of progress holds good in dress, and forms blend into one another with almost complete

continuity. In both cases a form yields to a succeeding form, which is better adapted to the then surrounding conditions.[1]

With the patience of a scientific researcher, George Darwin observed the history of clothing. He showed how the elements that had become useless because of changes in our way of life progressively disappeared. He compared a new discovery to modifications in animal life.

Discoveries and modifications disappear when they are no longer useful, and those that survive are integrated into the general conditions of existence favored by natural selection. Among other inventions in the field of clothing, he mentions the "Ulster Coat" and the "mackintosh-coat," whose development was fostered by the new means of transport. Besides the general adaptation of clothes to the living conditions of the time, Darwin names an influence that is even more important. This is a love of novelty and a generalized tendency to exaggerate what is becoming, or what is momentarily recognized as, the distinctive mark of a certain social elite. This factor bears a close analogy with the selection of species as described by Darwin in his work on the origin of humanity. Another analogy to which he draws our attention is that in both animals and dress, one can see remnants of former stages of development that survive in a later age. These remnants appear in two different ways: sometimes, parts of the dress are selected and retained even though their utility has entirely disappeared; at other times, elements of the past are maintained in an atrophied form.

I refer people who are interested in this new conception of the history of clothes to the works of Darwin. Our task should be only to distinguish the superfluous elements and the remnants of the ancient parts in dress. The more clearly we realize that these forms developed from circumstances that are no longer present, the easier it will be to get rid of them.

I think I can assert that we will witness the radical rout of all these degenerated and useless elements. On the one hand, if this aberration lasts and we do not decide to adopt a rigorously logical approach, there is a real risk of losing any notion of the organic element in dress. On the other hand, the gap between our clothes and the culture of our time will become so great that we will no longer be able to identify which modifications are necessary for dress to correspond harmoniously with our way of life. Fortunately, all this does not depend only on the logic of reason. Certain technical novelties have so strongly affected our existence that we cannot escape their formative influence. Thus, the railway has rendered the horse-riding costume obsolete; in the same way, bicycles and automobiles have generated garments adapted to these means of transport. Just think of everything that distinguishes us from our fathers. Think of people who spend their lives surrounded by machines and who are no longer interested in stone houses but in steel bridges and towers. Think of those who, after five days' traveling, reach places so far away that it would have taken our fathers more than half of their lives to get to. Then tell me if such people can continue to dress in the same way as when swords were worn at one's side. Can one really dress in the same way as people did at the time of the stagecoach or wear shirts with old-fashioned cuffs with oversleeves?

1. George H. Darwin, "Development in Dress," *Macmillan's Magazine* 26 (September 1872); reprinted in this volume, p. 96 *[Ed.]*.

Artists should be imbued with the atmosphere and the conditions of modern life if they want to create something that will last. By limiting themselves to advocating beauty, they will find themselves as ill thought of as those who privileged only utilitarian demands in their attempts to reform dress. Naturally, not all dress should be designed with the bicycle or the automobile in mind or, even less, people working in factories and among machines. One could design garments especially adapted to these functions. Meanwhile, it is not impossible that while developing dress designed for contemporary activities, one might discover the general principle of dress, which could later be adapted to attire for going out or for the city as well as to dress for working or traveling. The construction of a farm and of a cathedral obeys the same principles. One also has to design dress according to general tectonic principles. In this field, our creations should express a logical structure that clearly shows both the goal and the means used in their fabrication.

In designing dress, it is easier to show the component parts than to hide the way in which a piece of clothing is made. One cannot work cloth in the same way as stone, wood, or metal, which, when they are shaped by a skilled but foolish hand, can be so thoroughly transformed that they resemble anything but stone, wood, or metal. In practice, however, it will be as difficult to emphasize dress seams as it has been to show the skeleton of our houses, the joints of our furniture, or the welds of metal objects. Yet one should not believe that everything has been done in dress design when seams and joints are shown. I know village dressmakers who have never given up this healthy practice, but I would not consider entrusting the reform of our dress to them. We have to concentrate our efforts on the emergence of a rational conception of dress and must strive hard to rediscover the secret of ancient clothes, which were properly made.

What I expect from visible seams is honesty in bringing out how a dress was made, and I would like to broaden this approach as much as possible.

This will give rise to appropriate ornamentation of dress and will condition its very existence. The effect of decoration will thus be to emphasize the way in which the dress is made; at the same time, it will provide space for the expression of intrinsic organic life, either in abstract forms or in naturalistic motifs. Artistic taste and a personal preference for this or that type of ornament will compete here. There will be the same confrontation in the field of dress between abstract linear decoration and naturalistic motifs as there has been in other branches of industrial arts.

Personally, I think that abstract ornament will win. I could further justify my preference for this style; I could develop and explain the nature, origin, and significance of this type of decoration, to which so many different and absurd names have been given; but this is not the time to do so. Simply allow me to briefly draw your attention to the following point. With naturalistic decoration, the choice of motifs depends on the hazards of taste and feeling. With the decoration I have developed and that I wish to justify, these elements are the results of understanding, of logical necessity. Whereas a naturalistic artist chooses an animal, a flower, or a naked woman according to his desire or his inspiration of the moment, I insert decoration for which there is no other choice, which is generated by inner necessity. In such cases, the artist's inspiration consists in finding the germ of what is hidden in the space that is to be decorated. It is an endeavor that requires careful examination and precise thought. In contrast, the naturalistic artist is satisfied as soon as he manages to create a nice motif; and the more absurd it is, the more poetic he finds it. The irrational has done more damage to poetry than narrow-mindedness has to poets. Whose fault is it that poetry remains unknown in the superior, rational, and eternal spheres of mathematics, astronomy, and all abstract sciences? Until now, women's clothing has been dominated by floral decoration—that is very close to the most banal sort of sentimentality! Women and flowers, that is the eternal connection! Unfortunately, those who become ecstatic over a floral motif forget that natural flowers have a life and decorative laws of their own, and that is better not to touch them. In dressmaking, floral decoration is and remains an arbitrary choice, whereas abstract ornament, which arises from its own inner necessity, is submitted to precise rules conditioned by the form of the garment. These are the free play of the relationships, articulations, and movements of all parts of the body that dress covers but should not hide. Present-day dress is far from fulfilling these demands. Couturiers seem to completely ignore feminine forms, though these are not a matter of indifference either to women or to men.

Customarily, clothing is required in order to protect women not only from bad weather but also from the concupiscent glances of men. Yet this does not mean that the body should be intentionally hidden to the point that one cannot see the figure at all. We demand that the dress should just veil what one could call the physical individuality. Moreover, women would readily agree to let their figures and their forms be appreciated.

A dress designed in this way can only be moral. Fashion sins much more and is immoral when it demands the exposure first of the breasts, and then of other parts of the body. Fashion often goes to this kind of extreme when it does not have anything else to offer in terms of novelty.

I have still to answer the question I asked at the beginning: to what extent should a dress be individual and how far should artists go in imagining personalized garments for every woman? Furthermore, is it conceivable that our women should all dress in the same way, as is the case in areas that have maintained the use of traditional regional costume? These questions may seem to be contradictory. Indeed, how can one achieve both an individual look and uniformity at the same time? How can one harmonize these two contrasting ambitions: that every woman dress suitably for her figure and that all women wear the same dress?

The contradiction is more apparent than real. What is important is that the diverging demands of individuality and community come together today in our efforts to establish a readjustment of social conditions. I will not express myself on this subject now. If I were asked to do so, I admit I would not consent, as I do not have a formula that would not have to be modified tomorrow. Concerning dress, however, I think I can convince you that these two demands are not mutually exclusive. There are circumstances in human life in which everyone's dress should be different—indoors, for example. There are others, mainly in the street, in which dress should be alike. A third circumstance, celebrations and great events, requires uniform dress. Everything we do to express our personality will strengthen the units of force that we represent, which will then converge to elevate the level of community life as a result of our individual efforts. Therefore, anything we do to embellish our home is also useful to the community. People will be aware of the beauty of our home. Publicizing individual successes will therefore be profitable to others.

If the masses lack beauty, that is because of an accumulation of isolated instances of ugliness. An individual who consciously makes an effort to propagate beauty in his home learns immediately what to do and think to achieve his goal. His efforts will then be widely acknowledged, and he will thus be contributing to the restoration of beauty in every field of life and for all humanity.

The ugliness of a crowd dressed in a heterogeneous way provokes repugnance. One would like this feeling to disappear and be replaced by a more agreeable sensation. I do not feel this repugnance when I see a population dressed in a homogeneous way. In Zeeland, it is beautiful to see this similarity on the dunes or on the beach. In the shady alleys of Scheveningen, every one dresses like the local fishermen; no discord troubles the harmony of the whole. I find the same beauty in some regions of Westphalia or Bavaria; and, undoubtedly, one could find it in many other places where I have not had the opportunity of meeting the population. I do not wish to assert the absolute beauty of these costumes. On the contrary, I am ready to criticize them quite severely. I simply mean that in a crowd, in church, in public places or markets, uniformity of dress incontestably produces an impression of harmony.

The same is true of men's tailcoats. For a great event, a dinner, or an evening event, men contribute more to beauty, though this is certainly not owing to their personality but rather because of the similarity of their costume. If women allowed themselves to be persuaded, they might be willing to accept the idea of a "toilette obligée." Would it be possible to design this, or to decide that such and such dress will be the expected attire for all women? In any case, we should strive to find a dress for any circumstance, and we will then see if what I have dared to assert is truly confirmed. Yet this type of research will not have any real consequences. In fact, a long process of crystallization, which has already been accomplished for masculine dress, should precede the achievement of such attire. One instant is enough to appreciate the essential beauty of any uniform and to realize how many future social gatherings will gain in dignity if they ceased being an arena for the absurd competition of women using the senseless and deceptive means given them by their couturiers. One might answer that the same garment could be just as advantageous for Mrs. X as for Mrs. Z. Nevertheless, one could object that at least one of the two ladies will never be advantageously dressed and that the same objection can be applied to men. Actually, I almost think that all women could wear a really well-designed dress. If its beauty is based on the principles of its design and its ornamentation, then it will not lose anything if it is worn by Mrs. A rather than Mrs. B.

As for fashion, what does it do but invent dresses, mantles, hats for all sort of bodies and all heads? As this does not in the least weaken its prestige, why should our conception of dress be considered unproductive when our creations are based on the organic principles of logical construction while fashion just follows its own fantasies?

Henry van de Velde—Street dress.

Henry van de Velde—Afternoon dress.

Alfred Mohrbutter—Town dress.

We have said enough about the idea of a uniform for women in society. It is enough for us to mention it as a possibility. There will be time to go back to the subject and to approve the idea when it seems that it is likely to develop, as it has been the case for masculine dress. For the moment, we ought to direct our forces toward those who intend to dress according to their personal tastes. Concerning women's clothing, we have to rediscover the moral value that is the common philosophical goal of all our research in the other branches of industrial arts. It should be an honor for an artist to help women once again find morality in the activities that occupy most of their lives and that, unfortunately, are marked by immorality nowadays. The artist's ascendancy will probably be temporary, as women are sufficiently inventive not to need our help forever. They will need us just to design the ornament used to decorate the cloth they cut and sew themselves. In

fact, not every woman, even when she has good taste, is able to find the appropriate ornaments. Women should make it a point of honor, however, to succeed in cutting cloth without our help. If a woman decides to wear a self-designed dress outside her home, she has to assume responsibility for the consequences. When she has overcome the difficulties inherent in carefully choosing a piece of cloth and a pattern adapted to her specifications, she will have to estimate the time necessary to produce something attractive, then consider the conflicts with her suppliers who, for their convenience, will be delighted to refuse her demands. Finally, after going through all these steps, such a woman will realize that her determination will necessarily lead her to a genuine existential revolution in the sense of a better quality of life. She will free herself from the stunning tyranny of fashion.

If her example will be followed and her woman friends also discover that clothing is a serious business and not just a game, then fashion will be in a bad position. It will lose some of its obedient subjects, and its propaganda will be less and less effective. Women will be ready to defend their efforts; they will no longer be willing to throw a garment away at the end of every season, without any chance to wear it again. In fact, all their work and their efforts would not justify such brief usage. We will then see women discover the spirit of the good old days, when clothes were highly esteemed and respected for the beauty of their fabric and for the quantity of work they embodied. Once more, the message of the past announces our victory. The past serves us as a guide so that we meet the future with complete confidence.

HENRY VAN DE VELDE A NEW ART PRINCIPLE IN MODERN WOMEN'S CLOTHING "Das neue Kunst-Prinzip in der modernen Frauen-Kleidung," *Deutsche Kunst und Dekoration* 5, no. 8 (May 1902)

I am particularly happy to have been invited by Mr. Alexander Koch, the editor of this review, to write a text for this special supplement devoted to dress. So many misconceptions have developed in this area since women became aware of their responsibilities in a field where they have lost their dominant role and have been reduced to a state of slavery—mainly as a result of their own passivity, but also because of a number of other factors. I am eager to take advantage of this opportunity both to correct certain misconceptions and to give a brief overview of the history of this movement.

The imprint left by facts and dates fades very quickly, as I realized when I started working on my book *The Renaissance of the Applied Arts,* in which I attempt to establish facts and dates going back no more than ten years. My perception of the events and people that played a part in this renaissance of the industrial arts had already become clouded. Will the same be true of the efforts made to raise the artistic level of clothing and will our pioneering role in this field be contested?

In this case, the events date back to the year 1890 and there are only a few documents that establish the facts. At the beginning of 1900, Dr. Deneken, the director of the Krefeld Museum, had the idea of organizing an exhibition of clothes made from artists' designs. He courageously turned this idea into reality, seizing the opportunity presented by a retrospective exhibition of garments being organized at the time by the Union of German Tailors and Dressmakers.

Deneken approached all the artists he knew of who had been involved in designing clothes for women, and the following responded enthusiastically to his invitation: Alfred Mohrbutter, Margarete von Brauchitsch, Richard Riemerschmid, Bernard Pankok, Professor F. A. Kruger, Curt Hermann, the director Paul Schulze of Krefeld, the late Hugo van der Woude, and myself. The exhibition opened on 4 April 1900, and lasted until the 13th. There were enough clothes made according to artists' designs to fill a large gallery in the Krefeld City Hall, in addition to a room devoted to six of my own costumes. The artists exhibited forty items—twenty-four costumes and sixteen original designs by Mohrbutter and myself.

The great merit of the exhibition was to give form to an as yet latent, vague idea that artists had something to say concerning the question of dress and that women had submitted for too long to the despotism of professionals who had exploited their passivity less in the interests of beauty than for purely materialistic reasons. The exhibition thus affected not only those who visited it but also those who read about it in the newspapers. Like a young horseman recently knighted by his peers, this idea was thereby empowered to confront life and its tribulations. Some saw this young knight as a direct descendant of Don Quixote, but they were soon obliged to take him seriously.

An album was published in connection with this first exhibition with reproductions of some of the costumes and a preface by Maria van de Velde explaining the importance of the event and of the publication. Concerning the costumes that were exhibited, she wrote: "These garments were not conceived as exhibition pieces but were designed by artists for individual women in accordance with their wishes." Further on, she continues: "An event such as this will reinforce the determination of committed artists to persevere on their chosen paths." About the exhibition itself, she says: "Regular exhibitions would support and guide women who wish to break with the world of fashion. And by showing the very best in fashion, these exhibitions would not fail to exert a strong artistic influence on tailors and dressmakers." In the beginning, we had a clear vision—nowadays apparently forgotten—of what we hoped to achieve. From the moment that fashion began to exert its domination, clothing no longer expressed an individual sense of beauty or any artistic value in general.

During the exhibition, I gave a talk in Krefeld on the development of artistic dress for women [reprinted above], in which I thanked the director of the Krefeld Museum for having turned a long-standing dream of mine into reality. I added that all those of us who had been involved in creating garments with the sole purpose of dressing women as well as possible have experienced a feeling of revolt against fashion and its representatives, who have turned their backs on this simple, natural aim in pursuit of another—namely, the development of a new style for each season, so different from the previous one that the slaves of fashion feel obliged to replace their wardrobes every six months.

Some time ago, a number of courageous men and women rebelled against this situation and freed themselves from the tyranny of these outrageous directives. From that time on, artists have been the enemies of fashion. Their opposition, however, was not methodical; it brought about nothing new and formulated no ideal that could be opposed to that of fashion. It would have been completely fruitless if it hadn't spread and maintained the feeling of revolt so that nowadays, artists are not alone in thinking that the perpetual changes in fashion are motivated by purely commercial aims. Many women have understood the ridiculous role they have been playing for so long. They have realized that they had surrendered to the despotism of a few major, mainly Parisian, clothing firms that imposed on them first loose dresses, then tight dresses for no other reason than to manipulate fantasy to serve their own profit. I can hardly express my admiration for the women who, having understood how ridiculous the situation was, refused to submit to it any longer and decided to dress differently from others in their circle. In the talk, I then developed three proposals: first, when at home, a woman should only be concerned with expressing her personality; second, in the street, she should rein in the expression of her personality since the streets are public and her clothes should therefore blend in, like those of men; third, on special occasions women, like men, should wear compulsory formal dress.

I would like to emphasize that I didn't forget to mention the Dress Reform movement, a development parallel to our own, though it had taken on a precise form before ours. In some respects, its concerns merge with our own, but it is different in that it is not concerned with the expression of beauty, which is our main aim. Some years ago, fashion had already suffered a major assault. It was in Germany that the first troops were organized under the banner of Dress Reform. Fashion resisted victoriously and reigns today as freely as ever. The Dress Reform movement, however, was based solely on the principles of health; its representatives were not interested in beauty at all, proving how little they understood feminine psychology. In order to succeed, they should have opposed a different fashion to the dominant tendency, presenting it as the latest innovation—a "German" style, for example, rather than a French one. It would then have been at least as successful as the English or American styles that have brought us so many remarkable innovations over the last few years.

In addition to their excessive honesty, German Dress Reform activists committed a second error, as I mentioned before, of not taking beauty into consideration. Dress Reform was somewhat puritanical, rather dry, plain, and off-putting. The point of view outlined in the dull principles of the new dogma was much too orthodox. But the movement left its mark and can take credit for liberating us from that modern instrument of torture—the corset, which should take its place in a museum for antiquities between the thumbscrew and the chastity belt.

Meanwhile, my three proposals were being vigorously debated—especially after the lectures I gave in Dresden, Berlin and Vienna in the winter of 1900–1901. Willful misunderstandings were added to those that were not; I had to justify myself for having conceived of "feminine tails" (my third proposal) and I was forced to go deeply into the first two proposals.

Dress is a battle subject to the same laws as the rest of social life, with some striving to establish generalities while others prefer to deal with individual cases. However, these factors are easier to distinguish in relation to dress than in social life. Dress is determined by where it is worn, whether in a private or a public space. The atmosphere in one's own home is different from that on the street, which is itself different from that of special occasions, and it is clear that dress must adapt to these essential differences. Men—or their tailors (both deserve praise)—have grasped these differences, expressing their personalities more or less strongly in the clothes they wear at work or at home, resembling one another in public, and looking identical at special celebrations. Today, I will limit myself to briefly drawing your attention to these three points in relation to women's dress by suggesting a basis on which to work in order to promote their artistic development.

During my lecture in Krefeld, I stated that this kind of exhibition was viable and that its example would be followed.

This exhibition consecrates for the first time many individual efforts. It is an important event, as it will call into being other demonstrations of the same kind. From now on, shows of women's clothing will take their place among art exhibitions. Undoubtedly, we will begin to see clothing exhibited sometimes next to paintings and sculpture, as has recently been the case with other works of applied art.

In fact, a similar exhibition took place in Leipzig in 1901 under the direction of Mr. Thiel; another was organized in Berlin at the beginning of winter by Mr. Schultze-Naumburg. The public's interest was thus kept alive. These exhibitions as well as other individual efforts continued to attract the public's attention. In my opinion, these later shows were more fruitful and better designed to affect a large number of women and to incite them to free themselves from a foreign and self-interested dependency. I will not deal with the role of women who are dependent on fashion, nor with the immorality of this institution, but I do want to underline individual efforts and draw attention to those who have persevered in their struggle to everything that has not yet been accomplished. Above all, I have to admit that we are far from having attained the level of elegance of Parisian couturiers. This is sad but true. It is intentionally, therefore, that a number of new costumes from Paris are shown alongside the artistic experiments that followed the first outfits of 1900. I realize that one may object that one of the main and most obvious advantages of these costumes is the perfection of their cut and manufacture, and that these qualities put them far above our work.

This necessarily leads us to the obvious conclusion that until influential couturiers become interested in our efforts, our movement will not attain the scope we hoped for. I know a number of women who would willingly participate but who are prevented from doing so by an insurmountable repugnance for badly made clothes. In addition, they are not self-confident enough to entrust their instructions to a second- or third-rate tailor. I fully understand their revulsion, since the charm of a well-cut dress is too great for a feminine woman to resist, and we have to admit that we haven't attained the elegance of these garments. The design of these dresses is extremely ordinary and their charm lies solely in the beauty of their execution. There is no doubt that one day the major dressmaking firms will become interested in our research; already, they no longer ignore it. The *soutache* decoration of the dress reproduced here clearly shows the influence of our movement, unless the couturier simply wished to exploit the curiosity of certain customers. Haute couture would be running too great a risk if it were not to follow our movement. It will, of course, borrow what is easiest to assimilate, the most obvious characteristics, without doing justice to their essential nature. I do not believe that a lack of clarity explains why haute couture ignores precisely the main element in our research: namely, the original design and totally new cut of our clothes. Rather than using our ornamentation, which loses its effect in their hands, these firms would have much to gain by putting their extraordinary skills to the service of our designs.

There is a world of difference between the clothes designed for Miss Oppler by Professor Behrens or van de Velde and those reproduced in this book. The costume developed from a project by Dr. E. B. shows what can be achieved when a woman allows her artistic sensitivity rather than her dressmaker to guide her. One cannot imagine an outfit that would better suit her personality, her figure, or her beauty. It is extremely stylish and has been made to last. It is as if women from two different worlds—two worlds that actually do exist—wore these garments. The habits, accommodation, furniture, decoration, and kitchens of these two universes are diametrically opposed. However, both are deeply concerned with beauty. Hardly anything distinguishes them, but the little that does is at the same time infinite. Our world, in which we are trying to resurrect beauty, has revealed two completely forgotten principles. The first consists of conceiving an object in relation to its intended function. It requires that we abandon anything that conceals this aim and that we bring out whatever can help make it visible. The second principle asserts that each material has its own intrinsic beauty through which it expresses its existence. Each material aspires to life, and it is the artist's task to awaken its dormant life in order to enlarge its properties and its effects on mankind.

These principles also govern dress. The illustrations show that the aims pursued in the structure of these garments are clearly expressed in the provocative way the cloth falls. What is even more striking, however, is the ice-cold feeling that overcomes one when looking at the French garments. The cloth used is not alive: the silk, the material, has been treated as if it were metal or leather. It is worth noting, in passing, that we have chosen to reproduce only the best of what is available. One might say that our rational principles are not reconcilable with qualities such as charm and elegance and never will be. To counter this objection, we have confronted the Parisian models with garments that have qualities other than charm and elegance and that nevertheless are governed by rational principles. Our vigilance, however, was not enough to suppress all arbitrary incursions, though these were not significant enough to give rise to criticism. All our efforts are directed toward logic, and beauty will certainly follow.

I think I can assert that these efforts, together with those of American and English artists who design clothes, have forced the large Parisian firms to take into consideration the principle of "sensible" dress. We have opened their eyes to the appalling taste of some of their creations, full of innumerable useless bits, vestiges of elements that were necessary or justified in the past. In his first article in *Dokumente der Frauen,* Professor Alfred Roller of Vienna castigated these as follows:

There are buttons that don't button, fasteners and buckles that close nothing, ribbons that tie nothing, knots and stitches that don't bring anything together, lace and fringes that in the past were used as borders but that don't border anything, yokes that aren't yokes, bodices and sleeves whose only function is to be visible, printed patterns of cross-stitches and woven embroidery, baubles, pompons carefully stuffed over wooden shells, gloves that have been made to look like Swedish leather, shoes with laces that have to be buttoned and shoes with buttons that are closed with elastic straps, bow ties, scarves, hatbands, rosettes, belts that are strapped or buckled, flowers made of cloth or plush that look real, plastic combs and pins that imitate shell, ivory, coral or mother-of-pearl. . . . Plus everything else that is clearly presented as false! False skirts, false hems, false sleeves, false collars, false pockets—I don't think there is a single element of feminine dress that doesn't have its "false" counterpart.

The reign of this sort of aberration seems to be over nowadays, but who knows if the danger of a "renaissance" has been completely eliminated? Supposing that we are spared this and that good sense prevails, limiting the despotism of the Parisian dress firms, we could hope to teach them even more—above all, that the real beauty of cloth lies in the play of its folds, in how it falls. This is what one should start from when creating a design. It is necessary to make the folds stand out, bring the cloth alive—something that disappeared from French designs a long time ago.

We don't experience life in only one material. All materials reveal the secret of their beauty—cloth is beautiful when it is alive. Color in painting, bronze and marble in sculpture, words in literature—all express a particular beauty that stimulates the senses and the imagination. I remember something said to me by Dr. Deneken, the director of the Krefeld Museum, at the time of the first exhibition: "It seems to me that we are heading toward a style based on folds." In fact, that is precisely what distinguishes ours from Parisian designs that are based on charm and elegance. At the heart of the movement we launched is the struggle for the true life of material and the desire to create clothing with deep, gentle folds that move and reflect the contrasts of light and shade; whereas the only justification for the parallel tendency, with which we do not want to be confused, is its war on the corset. For us, this is just an accessory element about which people can decide for themselves; the others consider opposition to it an article of their faith. The *Dokumente der Frauen* shows how shaky this belief is. In her report, Marie Lang, the Viennese director, sets out the opinions of doctors whose knowledge is supposed to be beyond criticism. How else can one explain why she approached them for their opinions, for each one contradicts the other. Professor Richard von Krafft-Ebing declares, "I consider the use of the corset to be one of the worst aberrations of female dress. One only has to see a corseted liver on the dissecting table to realize this." Dr. Siddy Pal begins his answer in the following manner: "It is a mistake to claim that the use of a corset is bad and unhealthy. A large number of women could undoubtedly do without one, but for others it should not only be recommended but deliberately prescribed." The university professor Dr. Friedrich Schauta curtly states: "As far as the corset is concerned, no doctor could do anything but condemn it categorically." Another university professor, Dr. C. Breus, asserts to the contrary: "From the point of view of health, the corset should not be discarded lightly as it so often is."

The Dress Reform movement will long remain caught up in its own contradictions, during which time we will have made real progress toward the conquest of beauty. In the meantime, we will have grasped many of the secrets of the styles and designs of Parisian dress, which will contribute in no small way to our future triumph.

FRIEDRICH DENEKEN ARTISTIC DRESS AND PERSONALIZED DRESS

"Künstlerkleid und Eigenkleid," in *Zweiter Bericht des Stadtischen Kaiser Wilhelm Museum* (Krefeld, 1904)

The principle of artistic dress has become very important in contemporary clothing for women. Over the last four years, the idea of a reform of women's clothing, in the sense of personalized and artistic dress, has gained wide acceptance among German women, and many artists and talented women have found fulfillment in this new area. We have every reason to follow this movement closely since it began with the exhibition of women's clothing by artists that was held in Krefeld in 1900.

It is absolutely natural that this evolution was initiated in Krefeld. This German "Center of Silk" obviously takes particular interest in a development that should generate an increased demand for the fine cloth produced by its silk and velvet industry. Moreover, the city possesses other conditions favorable to such a development. The women of Krefeld, whatever their background, have a striking personal sense of dress and color that is not common in Germany—qualities that without doubt are the result of a long familiarity, going back over several generations, with the products of local industry.

Before the exhibition of 1900, an artistic performance of tableaux vivants was presented at the city hall in November 1899 that left a strong impression on the minds of its participants and spectators. Alfred Mohrbutter had composed seven pictures on the theme of "Work and Festivals" and for his production had created several beautiful women's garments inspired by English Pre-Raphaelite painting, the costumes of ancient Greece, and the French Empire style. The ideal costume that resulted aroused women's interest in the advantages of one-piece clothing; many of them, without depending on the dominant trends of fashion, thought up their own designs, which were then carried out according to their instructions.

At the time of the tableaux vivants performance, the prospect of an exhibition of ordinary clothing had already been raised, but it seemed necessary to wait for an appropriate moment for such an enterprise. This came more quickly than expected. In the summer of 1900, a day dedicated to the tailors and dressmakers of Germany was due to take place in Krefeld. A major exhibition of the profession was planned in conjunction with this celebration, and someone thought of linking it with a special exhibition of women's clothing designed by artists. The directorate of the museum presented a proposal to this effect that was enthusiastically taken up by the organizing committee and its president, Mr. Th. Wormanns, head of the Corporation of Tailors and Dressmakers of Krefeld. Since the guild had no misgivings about the project and was willing to contribute significantly to it, there was no longer anything blocking the plan's realization.

It was known that several of the artists who were trying to integrate art and life were already involved with women's dress. The experience of his "living images" had also inspired A. Mohrbutter to attempt to design evening clothes himself. Other artists, who had established their own styles, were stimulated to do the same. As well as designing furniture for their own homes, they wanted to create garments for their young wives. Otto

Eckmann, a universal genius, was one of these artists. By that time, he had not only created several dresses for his wife, but he was also thinking deeply about the question of an artistic reform of women's dress and he therefore fully supported the Krefeld project. Unfortunately, his participation in the exhibition was prevented by a cruise that he was obliged to undertake for health reasons. In addition to Alfred Mohrbutter, whose help we could once again count on, the participation of Henry van de Velde, who at that time was still living in Uccle near Brussels, was particularly welcome. Six of his magnificent dresses, made up under his wife's supervision, were exhibited in a special room illuminated by electric lights; they represented one of the high points of the whole exhibition.

Several Krefeld ladies gave important support to the project by having garments made up according to A. Mohrbutter's designs (and under his supervision) by local dressmakers; they then lent these to the exhibition. The firms Kirschgens and Heider, J. W.Koppenburg, and the successors of Madame Sakrzewski (Hermine Wolters) thus shared the task of making up eight costumes for everyday or formal wear. One of these dresses, created by Paul Schulze of Krefeld, included decoration and embroidery done at the city's Royal School of Weaving. Artists from Munich—F. A. Kruger, B. Pankok, and R. Riemerschmid—had sent in dresses with embroidery created at the United Workshops for Art in Crafts, in Munich. Aside from the artists already mentioned, the participation of Margarete von Brauchitsch from Munich, as well as that of Curt Hoffmann and H. van der Woude from Berlin, left its mark on the event. The clothes exhibited were reproduced in an album devoted to modern women's dress designed by artists and containing thirty-two illustrations, which was published by Friedr. Wolfrum of Dusseldorf and printed by J. B. Klein. Maria van der Velde wrote an introduction that took the form of a personal expression of faith. Her ideas were presented energetically and forcefully in a talk given by Henry van de Velde to participants in the German Dressmakers' Day and members of the Association of Krefeld Museum in the Hall of the Oil Press, titled "The Artistic Improvement of Women's Clothing." From among the many valuable ideas in this talk, which as I mentioned has been published by Kramer and Baum, allow me here to point out some of the most important.

The speaker began by denouncing the fact that contemporary women's clothing is subject to a fascination with fashion and the arbitrary decisions of a few Parisian haute couture firms. This spell has developed to such a degree that women are often considered ridiculous if they try to dress according to their personal tastes. The Dress Reform movement, with its motives of health, is itself powerless against such slavery, although it can take credit for freeing us from the corset, that modern instrument of torture, which should take its place in a museum for antiques alongside the thumbscrew and the chastity belt. It is up to artists to accomplish what the reformers failed to do. It is up to them to create clothes that respect the canons of beauty while at the same time taking into consideration the principles of health. It is necessary above all to get rid of useless decoration and to achieve the desired effects by the cut and quality of the materials used, and by careful craftsmanship. Decoration should arise from the elements used to make the dress. It is particularly important not to conceal seams but, on the contrary, to make use of them as natural decorative elements. Artists will help women free themselves from fashion, but their contribution will be temporary. Women should consider it a point of honor to do without artists, to learn to create for themselves their own formal and casual clothing, choosing the material and shapes appropriate for each type. In this way, they will rediscover the spirit of the past, when clothes were held in high esteem for the beauty of their fabric and out of respect for the work lavished on them by skillful hands.

Like the ripples caused by dropping a stone into water, the effects of the Krefeld exhibition will continue to spread and renew themselves. First, we took up clothes made up from independent designs, preferably one-piece bag-shaped dresses. This style also developed elsewhere and is thought to typify an "artist's dress." Because newspapers from all over the world mentioned the Krefeld exhibition, these new ideas quickly gained supporters almost everywhere, who then took it upon themselves to spread the ideas further. Exhibitions of women's dress were soon being organized in other German cities; in the following year, they were held in at least six—Leipzig, Dresden, Darmstadt, Berlin, Altona, and Hamburg—and, somewhat later, in Munich, Karlsruhe, and Bremen. Enlightening talks on the subject were given in Dresden and Vienna by H. van der Velde, and by A. Mohrbutter in Altona, Berlin, and Hamburg. In this way, the principles behind the Krefeld exhibition gave rise to a general movement. The questions involved were discussed in daily papers, specialized publications, art reviews, and family magazines. Pamphlets and books relying on van der Velde's arguments in favor of artistic women's dress soon went a step further, encouraging readers to make their own clothes and providing patterns or illustrations to help them do so.

In his talk in Krefeld, H. van de Velde had emphasized that the aim of his campaign was not "artistic dress" but rather the creation of authentic, personal clothing. However, our exhibition was of a sort that implied that the participation of artists was an essential, indispensable condition for the creation of "reformed clothing." To counterbalance this position, there was apparently felt to be a need for a complementary exhibition that would emphasize the ideas and personal tastes of women themselves. The women of the Dilettantenverein in Krefeld experienced this need with particular intensity. It was decided that it would be especially desirable for one of these women to give a talk to convince her colleagues about this aspect of the question. The group therefore invited Anna Muthesius, who was then living in London, to take on this responsibility. In January 1903, she gave a talk at the Krefeld Chamber of Commerce on "Personalized Dress for Women." She made her arguments even more convincing by giving practical information drawn from her long experience of making her own clothes. In a subtle, lively, and humorous way, she described the elements that have to be taken into consideration if a woman hopes to be satisfied with her appearance: her hairstyle, the shape of the hat that frames her face, the type of clothing that suits the individual proportions of her figure (especially the size of her head and shoulders). She discussed the color of cloth in relation to dyes and hair color. She treated the subject of jewelry—in short, it was a complete encyclopedia on the art of clothing. This talk was published by Kramer and Baun. It is a charming little book, which must be urgently recommended as reading for all women.

The talk given by Mrs. Muthesius helped spread the notion that a positive evolution of women's clothing required the active contribution of women themselves. It is likewise encouraging that in some of the largest German cities, workshops have sprung up where women and young girls can learn the very useful feminine activity of making their own clothes, guided on certain occasions by artists. But meanwhile, there is no shortage of obstacles to progress. Among these is the widespread misconception that considers one-piece dresses to be the only form for the future.

In any case, the bag-shaped dress embodies the most vigorous protest against two-piece outfits, with a waistline made tight by a corset. It has two main advantages in terms of formal attire. On the one hand, it creates a fine impression by lengthening the figure, whereas a dress broken at the waist shortens it. On the other hand, it is ideal for creating the beautiful effects of drapery. However, it is not at all suitable for many occasions or for some of the uses to which it has recently been put. For work and sport, for instance, a different style should be adopted that more or less follows the free and natural contours of the body. Those who raise objections against this reform of dress too often forget that it is at the very beginning of its evolution. The artists who exhibited in Krefeld are very well aware that their work cannot be used as models. Just as the ancient Greeks did not develop overnight the clothing we admire in their work from the fifth and fourth centuries b.c., Romulus and Remus did not enter history proudly draped in the sort of togas worn by Caesar or Anthony. One cannot expect women to change their appearance at the drop of a hat either. This will take time and the coming together of several factors. It is even possible to foresee that the evolution will be slow, as it will depend on the gradual development of personal taste among women. For a time, it seemed that one-piece dresses were going to become the new fashion. The fact that nowadays this trend has somewhat moved into the background is in no way a worrying symptom. It is of no importance, for instance, whether the new forms are triumphantly celebrated at the Berlin Press Ball or not. The foundations of a constant and regular evolution are much deeper than the whims of fashion.

The innermost essence of our culture depends on the principles of health, nationality, individuality, and finally beauty (which should affect all aspects of our lives) being applied to women's dress. This discovery and the application of natural laws are characteristic of our times. The lessons drawn from them have born fruit in the care we take of our bodies, in therapeutic gymnastics, in children's games, in sports, and in our living conditions. Is it possible to imagine that the elements that have proved so favorable for our general welfare should be neglected when it comes to women's dress? Should women continue to dress in a way that contradicts the forms and functions of their bodies? What Dr. Lahmann makes clear in his short text "The Reform of Clothing" should convince even the most incorrigible defenders of the corset. In addition, is not the French influence on women's dress in our country a humiliating sign of intellectual poverty? While we strive to eradicate gallicisms from the German language and to reinforce a feeling of national pride in all areas, the very idea of imitating Parisian women makes our wives feel superior. They get themselves up in all that shoddy French stuff, in cloth trimmings and spangles: in other words, in innumerable elements that are as tasteless as they are anti-German! Moreover, the impact of Parisian fashions is an anachronism. It is short-sighted and completely contradicts our own cultural evolution, as we have just seen. All our ideas about national identity and personal initiative lead to the same conclusion. Just as in the field of interior decoration we are no longer interested in the "know-how" of a designer but appreciate the artistic flair of the owner instead, so in a woman's dress we hope to discover an expression of the wearer's taste and skill, something that automatically implies a quest for beauty. Our heightened aesthetic requirements will not stop short of women's dress—good taste will also attempt to express itself in this field. Even though women's dress is not one of the most elevated aspects of our lives, it nevertheless embodies an important facet of our culture; and by ennobling their appearance, women will become one of the manifestations of beauty that illuminate our lives as do the kindly stars.

EDUARD JOSEF WIMMER-WISGRILL ON THE BECOMING OF FASHION

"Über das Werden der Mode" (lecture, 1930)

Dear ladies, I am sure you will be able to recollect without any difficulty the period around 1925, after the exhibition *Arts décoratifs* in Paris. It was the time of the first postwar cultural consciousness, the first official sighs of relief. Once again it was possible to travel to Paris without offending national pride. For the first time, it was clearly evident that Le Corbusier was the leading modern French architect, and even the leading architect of our time. It was also when Parisian haute couture was displaying its capacities in the most opulent way, carefully guarding the secrets of its creations, revealing them only to its most trusted clients. It was then, and only as a result of this opportunity, that everyone was able to see with astonishment how much fashion had advanced—and how stuck it had become! Certainly, it had taken three steps forward, but then it had to take one or two (certainly not all three!) back again.

It was a time when women's shift- or cloaklike dresses were being abbreviated in innumerable versions, going from short to shorter to so short that it was impossible to get any shorter. Aside from that, these dresses were mostly sleeveless and were cut like shifts for young girls. In order to turn these last remnants of covering into evening dresses, it was necessary to use the heaviest brocade and the most luxurious embroidery with paste jewelry and semiprecious stones, since the simple shape of the dress itself had to be retained. The whole thing always looked wretched and was wearable only on the dainty bodies of young girls. It was a trend that had gone to its utmost limits—a sort of "Thus far, but no further!"

You will remember that at the same time hair was worn very short, cut in a masculine "Eton school" style. It was the peak moment in the emancipation of women's clothing. One more step, the normally forbidden fourth step forward, and women would have been obliged to wear shorts. This, however, did not occur—for the time being! The curtain then fell and a new game began, though it was not exactly like the previous one. Women's dresses and women's hair got longer and you, who went through this period of the past, witnessed "a becoming of fashion" such as you cannot experience every year. It was particularly interesting to be present at a time when such a tremendous event was taking place, of an intensity that we will probably only observe once in our lives. I believe that for you, your experience and participation in this was like that of our contemporaries who lived through the great revolution after the war. You were too close, too involved personally, to have been able to correctly evaluate the scale of the process. I mean that you immediately had to take a personal position regarding these innovations, from an aesthetic point of view—deciding whether these novelties clothed you sufficiently and, on a purely material level, how to cover the extra expense of the increased use of fabric. You were undoubtedly so preoccupied with these troubling circumstances that the great metamorphosis took place before you were able to become fully aware of what was happening.

If I have emphasized this extreme example, it is in the conviction that doing so will enable us to understand what fashion is really about.

This period, whose end we thus experienced, started at the beginning of the century and lasted for about twenty-five years. It commenced with the downfall of the corset and with the first clothing of the Dress Reform movement. This dress (repulsively ugly, terrifying to men, but a gift to the cartoonists of *Simplizissimus*) marked a radical departure from wasplike waistlines. It was a sort of pyramid-shaped sack that hung from a woman's shoulders and was usually decorated with an abundant supply of Art Nouveau motifs. This dress weighed down the shoulders of most of the suffragettes of the day in Germany and Austria, but nowadays, from a historical perspective, one can fully appreciate these courageous women for their idealism, self-abnegation, and foresight. Something had been born that went far beyond fashion and can be considered to be the female costume of the century, as far as we can see. It is important to note that the foundations of this cultural evolution were laid in Germany. This discovery, tasteless though it was at first, was sufficiently esteemed in Paris for competent artists, most notably Paul Poiret, to elaborate on it and, with French know-how, to adapt it for the whole civilized world.

What occurred later was a logical and coherent development. After liberation from the corset, liberation from the hatpin, which rightfully was dreaded as a public danger, became important. Women's hats, pulled down over the head to really protect it, no longer needed any external means of fastening. Helene Odilon, in Vienna, was the first to demonstrate on stage how to use the hatpin-free hat. Then came the liberation at home from dresses with fabric training behind them and from dust-sweeping skirts. Short hair came much later—real liberation from a monstrous bondage.

The trend toward shortening women's skirts was the most significant achievement and, with all the movement forward and back, a full twenty-five years was needed for the undertaking. It was during this period that women, fighting for their liberation in so many areas, attained most of their successes. That women at the time expressed this process in their clothing seems natural to us today. That's why the results of so much arduous and constant struggle no longer have anything to do with fashion, but should be considered as dress and the expression of culture. And yet!

And yet. From 1925, after the *Arts décoratifs* exhibition in Paris, a break occurred: waists returned, as did something very similar to the rejected corset. Nowadays, the latest hat styles from Paris are worn so far back that it is worrying—will they be able to stand up to the Viennese wind on their own? Afternoon clothes are once again worn loose and long; evening dresses again have swaths of fabric trailing behind them; and women's hair, long once more, is often piled up elaborately. Every day we can see such facts with amazement and wonder how this has happened. How is it possible to lose overnight the victories won through so much suffering and over such a long time? Was it not dress after all, but just fashion—capricious, ephemeral, and unpredictable fashion? I do not believe this is the case—the changes have affected women in their womanhood. It is certainly the mark of Eros: eroticism opposing its most dangerous enemy. There was a danger that women had revealed too much—nakedness does not stimulate erotic fantasies and habit leads to indifference. There was a danger that women had become too masculine and had lost their means of attraction. It was a moment of real danger; it was the twelfth hour; the roof was on fire!

So what happened then? What brought help, salvation, deliverance? Fashion, so often criticized and condemned, is what once again established an agreeable balance. The process we have been describing, this striving for a more highly developed culture, this rather intellectual struggle, was paralyzed at just the right time by something reasonable, healthy, and down-to-earth that we could call "Fashion in the Making." In this constantly renewed combat between the two factions, Dress and Fashion, we can follow Weininger and attribute the letter M (masculine) to the struggle and the letter F (feminine) to Fashion, seeing in this mutual influence the expression of a happy marriage. So despite the apparent retreat on all fronts, the conquered terrain is not entirely lost.

Dear ladies, you know very well that you would not drive your car in a hoop skirt but would do so in a short dress or, later, probably in trousers. On the other hand, nor will you forget so soon that men did not maintain for very long their interest in your bare legs, your shirt-dresses, and your masculine haircuts. However, dear ladies, in your new flowing garments that conceal your limbs while revealing them at the same time, you experience something that feels absolutely right. It is the equilibrium, the balance, the rediscovered harmony between Dress and Fashion unifying what has been regained with what has not been lost. Unifying what will be lost again? That's life—real life; and that's the way things go.

LILLY REICH QUESTIONS OF FASHION "Modefragen," *Die Form* 5 (1922)

From the perspective of the international fashion scene, the development of the German fashion industry and the increase in its production capacities over the last few years have been extraordinary. Exports of both ready-to-wear goods and high-quality made-to-measure clothes have never been so great. Intense activity reigns in all dressmaking workshops, and the feverish atmosphere of this work pulls everything into its rhythm. There are very few other fields of work that are so productive, so technically inventive, that deal with so much dazzling new material, and that waste so much taste and skill in such a short time. However, the end result of all this activity, the overall picture, is unsatisfactory and draws criticism.

For whom is this industry working? Who are the clients of these luxury workshops? What has this endless capacity of production, this unlimited investment of material and money, achieved? From a socioeconomic point of view, perhaps it is gratifying that these reserves of wealth and this capacity for production should be active and engaged beyond the boundaries of this country. That, however, is not an argument that will be developed here. What is important here is the concept embodied in these products and the question of whether they reflect and express our times.

Fashion is international; and though it is not my intention to question this fact, it is also true that in terms both of production processes and of form, national characteristics must be taken into consideration. Our industry's dependence on Parisian fashion has always been obvious, and it is the same today as it was before the war. All our efforts to work with our own nature, to use our own ideas and materials, were abandoned by the fashion scene as soon as it once again had access to Paris. Over the last few years, in addition to this dependency on imported ideas, a dependency on exports has developed. The functioning of the industry is determined by a variety of economic factors, and it is entirely dependent on the laws of supply and demand.

Because of the impoverishment of the last few years, the group of those responsible for the best creations within the country is very small. In our country, the conditions for this work are fixed by a handful of upper-class ladies, some actresses and film stars, and a large circle of middle-class women, who all respond favorably to these ideas from abroad. Everyone else is excluded. They are offered ready-made mass-produced goods that imitate designs conceived in the circumstances mentioned above.

Postwar economic development and the increase in exports have speeded up production to such an extent that it has led to rash increases in production, usually motivated by purely short-term commercial considerations at the expense of stability, calm, and natural development. This hastiness often leads to neglect of problems in the manufacturing and design of made-to-measure clothes. Any design that gives free rein to the decorative and ornamental imagination gets reduced to an empty schema even in the workshops of our finest firms. The organic unity of the design is ignored, and the firms pretend to solve the problems of construction by using snap buttons and false seams that gather up the cloth. The impression is always astonishing and the value and beauty of the material seductive. The aesthete is satisfied, the snob even more so, but all that remains is an empty outer skin.

There is hardly any other field in which effort and material are wasted so lightly and with so little consideration, or where ideas are pillaged and ruined so freely. The appeal of a little lace used to particular effect in a good design is lost in a few weeks as a result of thousands of "new" mechanical lace designs, "à la Vénétienne," industrially produced in a great rush and just as rapidly and unnaturally applied to clothing. The same happens to good-quality, carefully designed embroidery as to printed textiles. Senseless and thoughtless copies are made, and the following day hundreds of variations on good textile designs from the past or the present are on the market. Not only clothing but everything related to appearance is standardized and reproduced. Every other woman plagiarizes someone else who herself has copied an Asta Nielsen. The Procrustean bed of fashion shortens and lengthens women's bodies every few months and not, as in the past, every few years. Fashion in the past had style as it was produced by stable life conditions and social conventions. It was always national and, at the same time, international in its general outlines. It developed slowly and naturally. Contemporary fashion has no style—it is always just "fashion."

A design taken out of context and rapidly reproduced quickly becomes a fad. It is just decorative, and its emptiness soon leads to a weariness that requires a new disguise. It reveals agitation, greed, and passing vanity. All that remains is a stunning and momentarily enticing shell. It responds to the worst instincts of our times and generates impulses that are even worse. It does not burden itself with the poverty of the times, or concern itself with the problems of the day. The culture of its supporters is solely concerned with physical appearance. Its cultural environment, its spiritual life, is empty and banal—its taste, the highest snobbery. Its lack of tradition leads to a feeling of insecurity, and the signs of the times are likewise chaotic.

It is not my intention to present fashion as the affair of the petit bourgeoisie or as a playground for moral or individual experiments. It must remain what it is—a charming, attractive lady full of humor and elegance. All dogma is foreign to it. Fortunately, it is not possible to establish any laws or standards for fashion, as it is probably the most vital area of activity and the liveliest means of expression of a person, a class, or a race. Clothes are utilitarian objects and not works of art. They are subject to the conventions of the day. However, clothes can also have metaphysical effects through their inner laws, their calm and restraint, their cheerful coquetry and vivacity, their playful grace, healthy simplicity, and dignity. Clothes can and should combine to form an inseparable, organic unity with the person wearing them. They should be an image of the wearer's spirit, heightening the expression of his soul and his feeling of being alive. The work that fashion is based on, however, must follow the prerequisite conditions of life, correspond with the demands of the time, and show discipline.

An example of this discipline is available in street clothes, which apart from some minor variations have been the same for years. Sports clothes are another example, although they have begun to be subject to the influence of theatricality and snobbery. Both are good examples of natural solutions to standardized clothing that everywhere is based on the same practical constraints.

Our epoch cannot avoid standardization, mass-produced goods, or industrial work. Our poverty and our lack of time push us in that direction. But it is also important to determine the particularity of this production so that it can develop organically and not conceal itself by imitating handmade work. Certainly, we cannot do without handwork, the high quality of craftsmanship that, especially in this area, gives the best results. It should not, however, be considered the sole means of creating happiness for sentimental reasons.

Who knows where the path to new forms will be discovered? Certainly it will not be found by following in the footsteps of those who are influential today. Good things take time, and what is important is that the spirit of women can be expressed and that a woman want to be what she is and not pretend to be what she is not.

Manifesto futurista
del vestito da uomo

BISOGNA DISTRUGGERE IL VESTITO PASSATISTA

BISOGNA INVENTARE IL VESTITO FUTURISTA

ADOPERARE nelle stoffe i colori: MUSCOLARI ... OPPATURA

FUTURISTA

nel nuovo manifesto

Giacomo Balla—Manuscript of the
"Futurist Manifesto of Male Dress,"
1913–1914.

GIACOMO BALLA MALE FUTURIST DRESS A Manifesto "Le Vêtement
masculin futuriste manifeste" (Milan, 20 May 1914)

Humanity always wore mourning clothes, or the heavy armor, or the priestly mantle, or
the cape. The man's body was always saddened by the black color, imprisoned by belts,
or overburdened by draperies.

During the Middle Ages and the Renaissance, clothes almost always had static,
heavy, draped or puffed-out, solemn, grave, sacerdotal, uncomfortable, and cumbersome
colors and forms. They were expressions of melancholy, slavery, or terror, the negation of
the muscular life, which suffocated in an antihygienic passéisme of weighty fabrics and
boring, effeminate, or decadent halftones.

This is why, today or in the past, the crowded streets, the theaters, and the salons have depressing, distressing, and funerary rhythms and moods.

We want to abolish:

1. Mourning clothes that even the pallbearers themselves should refuse.

2. All nice, shaded, neutral, fancy, and dark colors.

3. All striped, checked, or dotted fabric designs.

4. The so-called good taste and harmony of hues and forms, which weaken our nerves and
slow us down.

5. The symmetrical cut and the static line that tire, depress, grieve, and chain the muscles,
the uniformity of lapels and all ornamental oddness.

6. The useless buttons.

7. The detachable collars and the starched cuffs.

We want to liberate humanity from slow Romantic nostalgia and from the difficulty of life.

We want to color and rejuvenate in a Futurist way the crowds in our streets.

Finally, we want to give people beautiful festive clothes.

Futurist clothing will therefore be:

1. Dynamic, with the dynamic colors and patterns of fabrics (triangles, cones, ellipses, spirals, circles).

2. Asymmetrical. For example, the tips of sleeves and fronts of jackets will be round on the
left side and square on the right side. The same for waistcoats, trousers, and cardigans.

3. Nimble; that is, able to increase the flexibility of the body and encourage its energy.

4. Simple and comfortable; that is, easy to put on and off. Some essential buttons.

5. Hygienic; that is, cut in such a way that every pore of the skin can easily breathe. In order to achieve this, avoid any tight-fitting part and any tight belt.

6. Joyful. Very joyful iridescent fabrics. Fabrics with muscular colors, wildly violet, very, very, very, very red, 300,000 times green, 20,000 times blue, yellow, oraaange, scaaaaaarlet.

7. Illuminating. Phosphorescent fabrics that can spread light around when it rains and improve the melancholic dullness of twilight.

8. Strong-willed. Violent, aggressive, imperative, and impetuous colors.

9. Flying and aerial; that is, linked to the atmosphere through the grading of tones and the momentum of the dynamic lines.

10. Short-lived, so that we may incessantly renew the pleasure and liveliness of our body and patronize the fabric industry.

11. Variable, by means of *modifiers*. I call *modifiers* appliqué pieces of cloth (of different size, thickness, or color) that can be attached at will to any part of the dress with pneumatic buttons. Thus, anyone can not only modify but also invent a new dress for a new mood at any instant. The modifier might be imperative, loving, caressing, persuasive, diplomatic, one-tone, multitone, shocking, discordant, decisive, perfumed, etc.

An astounding variety of clothes will emerge from all this, which will without cease brighten up the cities, even if their population absolutely lacks imagination and color sensibility.

This dynamic joy of dresses moving in the noisy streets among the climbing Futurist architecture will multiply everywhere the prismatic spark of a gigantic jeweler's front. We will without cease have, in us and around us, three-dimensional color acrobatics, which will generate innumerable new abstractions of dynamic rhythms in the growing Futurist sensibility.

GIACOMO BALLA THE ANTINEUTRAL DRESS A Futurist Manifesto

"Il vestito antineutrale: manifesto futurista" (Milan: Direzione del Movimento Futurista, 11 September 1914)

> *We will glorify war, the world's only hygiene.*
> **Marinetti (First Futurist Manifesto, 20 February 20 1909)**
>
> *Long live Asinari di Bernezzo!*
> **Marinetti (First Futurist Evening, Teatro Lirico, February 1910)**

Humanity always dressed itself with calm, fear, caution, and indecision, wearing forever the mourning dress, the mantle, or the cape. The man's body was always diminished by neutral hues and shades, debased by wearing black, stifled by belts, imprisoned by draperies.

Until now, men wore clothes of static color and forms—that is, solemnly draped, heavy, uncomfortable, and sacerdotal. They were expressions of timidity, melancholy, and slavery, the negation of the muscular life, which suffocated in an antihygienic passéisme of weighty fabrics and boring, effeminate, or decadent halftones. Moods and rhythms of depressing, distressing, and funereal peace.

TODAY, we want to abolish:

1. All of the neutral, "soft," shaded, fancy, gray, and humiliating colors.

2. All pedantic, professorial, and Teutonic hues and forms. Stripes, checks, and diplomatic little dots.

3. The mourning clothes, which are not adapted even for the pallbearers. The heroic dead should not be wept over but celebrated by wearing red clothes

4. The mediocrity of equilibrium, the so-called good taste and the so-called harmony of hues and forms that check our enthusiasm and slow us down.

5. The symmetrical cut and the static line that tire, depress, grieve, and chain the muscles, the uniformity of lapels. The useless buttons. The starched collars and cuffs.

We Futurists want to liberate our race from any neutrality, from fearful and quietist indecision, from nihilist pessimism, and from nostalgic, softening Romantic inertia.

We want to color Italy with Futurist audacity and risks, and finally give Italians joyful and bellicose clothing.

Futurist clothing will therefore be:

1. Aggressive, able to increase the courage of the strong and to disrupt the sensitivity of cowards.

2. Nimble; that is, able to increase the flexibility of the body and to favor its surge to fight, to race or to charge.

3. Dynamic, with the dynamic colors and patterns of fabrics triangles, cones, spirals, ellipses, circles able to inspire the love of danger, of speed and assault, the hatred of peace and of immobility.

4. Simple and comfortable; that is, easy to put on and off, adapted for rifle shooting, for crossing rivers, and for swimming.

5. Hygienic; that is, cut in such a way that every pore of the skin can easily breathe during long marches and steep climbs.

6. Joyful. Fabrics with enthusiastic colors and iridescence. Use muscular colors, very vivid violets, the bloodred, the intense turquoise, the greenest of greens, vivid yellows, very colored oranges, and vermilions.

7. Illuminating. Phosphorescent fabrics that can ignite temerity in a timorous crowd, spread light when it rains, and lift the melancholic dullness of twilight in the streets and in the hearts.

8. Strong-willed. Violent, imperative, and impetuous colors and designs like the ranks on a battlefield.

9. Asymmetrical. For example, the tips of sleeves and fronts of jackets will be round on the left side and square on the right side. The same for waistcoats, trousers, and cardigans.

10. Short-lived, so that we may incessantly renew the pleasure and liveliness of our body and patronize the fabric industry.

11. Variable, by means of *modifier*s (appliqué pieces of cloth of differing size, thickness, and color) that can be attached at will to any part of the dress with pneumatic buttons. Thus, anyone can invent a new dress at any instant. The modifier could be arrogant, shocking, explosive, decisive, warlike, etc.

The Futurist hat will be asymmetrical and of joyful, aggressive colors. Futurist shoes will be dynamic, distinctive from one another in form and color, and cheerfully able to kick all neutralists.

The juxtaposition of black and yellow will be totally prohibited.

One thinks and acts as one dresses. Since neutrality is the synthesis of all passéismes today, we Futurists dress in these antineutral outfits as flags—that is, joyfully bellicose clothing.

Only the gouty ones will disapprove.

All the Italian youth will recognize in us, who wear them, the Futurist banners for our great, URGENT, necessary war.

If the government does not take off its passéist dress of fear and indecision, we will double, we WILL MULTIPLY BY TEN AND BY A HUNDRED the red of the tricolor flag, in which we dress.

Milan, 11 September 1914

Approved enthusiastically by the Directorate of the Futurist Movement and by all of the Italian Futurist groups.

VOLT (VINCENZO FANI) FUTURIST MANIFESTO OF WOMEN'S FASHION

"Manifesto della moda femminile futurista," *Roma Futurista* 3, no. 72 (29 February 1920)

Women's fashion has always been more or less Futurist. Fashion, female equivalent of Futurism. Speed, novelty, courage of creation. Greenish-yellow bile of professors against Futurism, beguines against fashion. For the moment, the last ones can rejoice! Fashion is going through a period of stagnation and boredom. Mediocrity and Meanness weave gray spider webs upon the colored flowerbeds of art and fashion.

Current fashion (the blouse and the shirtwaist dress) tries in vain to conceal its original poverty of conception under the false signs of distinction and sobriety. Chlorosis of fantasy. The imagination of the artist is relegated to details and nuances. The disgusting litanies of "saintly simplicity," "divine symmetry," and so-called good taste. A vague impulse of historical exhumation, "Let's return to the antique." Exhaustion. Softening of the brain. Senility.

We Futurists intend to react against this state of things with extreme brutality. We do not need to start a revolution. It will be enough to multiply by a hundred times the dynamic virtues of fashion, smashing all breaks that hinder them to run, flying over the dental vertigos of the Absurd.

A. GENIUS One must absolutely proclaim the dictatorship of the artistic Genius in female fashion against the parliamentary interfering of unintelligent speculation and the routine. A great poet or a great painter must assume the general directorship of all great firms of women's fashion. Fashion is an art, like architecture and music. A woman's dress brilliantly designed and worn well has the same value as a fresco by Michelangelo or a Madonna by Titian.

B. AUDACITY The Futurist woman must have the same courage in adopting the new trends of clothing as we did in declaiming our *parole-in-libertà* against the rebellious ignorance of Italian and foreign audiences. *Women's fashion can never be extravagant enough.* Here too we will begin by *abolishing symmetry.* We will design zigzag décolletage, sleeves that differ from one another, shoes of different forms, colors, and heights. We will create illusionistic, sarcastic, sonorous, noisy, deadly, and explosive garments; dress that hide surprises and are transformable, outfitted with springs, stingers, photographic lenses, electric currents, reflectors, perfume fountains, fireworks, chemical preparations, and thousands of mechanisms able to play the worst tricks and disconcerting pranks on clumsy suitors and sentimental lovers. *Let us idealize in woman the most fascinating conquests of modern life.* So we will have the machine-gun woman, the thanks-de-Somme woman [*sic*], the radiotelegraph antenna woman, the seaplane woman, the submarine woman, the motorboat woman. We will transform the elegant lady into a true living plastic complex. One should not fear that in doing so the female figure will lose its capricious and provocative grace. The new forms should not hide but accentuate, develop, and exaggerate the gulfs and promontories of the female peninsula. Art exaggeration. We will use the most aggressive lines and garish colors of our Futurist paintings upon the feminine profile. We will exalt the female flesh in a frenzy of spiral and triangles. We will succeed in sculpting the astral body of woman with the chisel of an exasperated geometry.

C. ECONOMY   The new fashions will be affordable for all the beautiful women, who are legion in Italy. It is the more or less precious cloth that makes the dress expensive, not its form and color, which we offer, free, to all Italian women. After three years of war and shortages of raw material, it is ridiculous to continue making leather shoes and silk garments. *The reign of silk in the history of female fashion must end,* just as the reign of marble is now declining in architectural constructions. One hundred new revolutionary materials noisily demonstrate in the square, seeking to be admitted into the manufacture of women's clothing. We open wide the doors of the fashion ateliers to paper, cardboard, glass, tinfoil, aluminum, majolica, rubber, fish skin, burlap, tow, hemp, gas, green plants, and living animals.

Every woman will be a walking synthesis of the universe.

You have the high honor of being loved by us, sappers-soldiers in the avant-garde of an army of lightnings.

F. T. MARINETTI, FRANCESCO MONARCHI, ENRICO PRAMPOLINI, AND MINO SOMENZI   THE FUTURIST MANIFESTO OF THE ITALIAN HAT

"Il manifesto futurista del cappello italiano," *Futurismo,* 5 March 1933

The indispensable and longed-for revolution in Italian men's clothing was initiated on 11 September 1914 with the celebrated manifesto "The Antineutral Dress," signed by the great Futurist painter Giacomo Balla.

This synthetic, dynamic, nimble suit with white, red, and green parts was worn by the Futurist *parolalibero* Francesco Cangiullo in the patriotic demonstrations, followed by violent riots and arrests, that the Roman Futurists, led by Marinetti, launched against the neutralist professors at the University of Rome (11–12 December 1914).

We Futurists take up once again the leadership of the clothing revolution, confident in our victory, guaranteed by the now proven creative power of our race. While we prepare a comprehensive manifesto, which will be signed by specially designated Futurists, today we launch one dedicated to the Italian hat.

The world preeminence of the Italian hat was absolute for a long time. Recently, because of xenophilia and a misunderstanding of hygiene, many young Italians have taken up the American and Teutonic way of the bare head. The decline of the hat, which impoverished its market and prevented possible improvements, has damaged the male look, amputating the silhouette and substituting for this removed part the most idiotic savagery of more or less aggressive, virile, or smart mops of hair.

The combatants who surpassed the heroism of the Romans at Vittorio Veneto, in the shock brigade actions in the Italian squares, and in the March on Rome must not, centuries after and in a changed climate, copy their cultural fashions. The young Italian sportsmen, victorious in Los Angeles, must now still overcome this barbaric habit that derived from a stupid historical sentimentalism.

Affirming, therefore, the aesthetic necessity of the hat:

1. We condemn the Nordic use of black and neutral hues that give the streets of wet, snowy, and foggy cities their stagnant muddy melancholy or a brown torrent full of tortoises and huge stony trunks.

2. We condemn the various passéist headgear that does not match the speed and the practicality of our great mechanical civilization, as, for example, the pretentious top hat hinders the running pace and distresses funerals. In August, in the Italian squares flooded by dazzling light and torrid silence, the black or gray hats of the passersby float sadly like excrement. Color! We need color to compete with the Italian sun.

3. We propose the Futurist functionality of the hat, which until now has done little or nothing for man; from now on it must illuminate him, signal to him, take care of him, defend him, speed him up, cheer him up, etc.

We will create the following types of hat, which through aesthetic, hygienic, and functional improvements will serve, complete, or correct the ideal Italian masculine figure, emphasizing the variety, pride, dynamic momentum, and lyricism that are generated by the Mussolinian atmosphere:

1. Speedy hat (for daily use); 2. Night hat (for evening); 3. Sumptuous hat (for parading); 4. Aerial-sportive hat; 5. Sun hat; 6. Rain hat; 7. Mountaineering hat; 8. Marine hat; 9. Defensive hat; 10. Poetic hat; 11. Publicity hat; 12. Simultaneous hat; 13. Plastic hat; 14. Tactile hat; 15. Light-signaling hat; 16. Phonohat; 17. Radio-telephone hat; 18. Therapeutic hat (resin, camphor, menthol, circle moderating the cosmic rays); 19. Auto-greeting hat (using a system of infrared rays); 20. "Genializing" hat for the imbeciles who will criticize this manifesto.

They will be made in velvet, straw, cork, light metals, glass, celluloid, particleboard, leather, sponge, fiber, neon tubes, etc., in materials combined or separate.

The polychromy of these hats will give to the sunny squares the flavor of immense fruit dishes and the luxury of huge jewelry stores. The night roads will be perfumed and lit by melodious currents, which will definitively kill the timeworn moonlight nostalgia.

So will emerge the ideal hat, an Italian work of art, at the same time cheering and multipurpose, which, while intensifying and propagating the beauty of the race, will once again impose one of our most important national industries upon the world.

Given that our beautiful peninsula is the place to visit for half of the tourists of every nation, they may come bareheaded if they like; we will welcome them with our usual gentility but we will keep on our heads the new Italian hat, to show them that there is no longer anything in common between the servility of the ciceroni a hundred years ago and proud inventive originality of the fascist Futurists today.

ERNESTO THAYAHT   THE AESTHETICS OF DRESS: SUNNY FASHION,
FUTURIST FASHION   "Estetica del vestine: Moda solare, moda futurista," *Oggi e domani:
Altoparlante del rionovamento spirituale italiano* 1, no. 10 (23 June 1930)

Summer fashion is a sunny fashion. It is highly probable that a Futurist style will develop
from this sunny fashion—a vivid and colorful style that is simpler and more practical than
present-day clothing.

Futurist fashion should have a spontaneous, almost explosive development in Italy.
If this is not the case, that is due mainly to the inert and stagnant mentality of those who, in
the fashion industry, speak a lot about renewal but do not have the courage to go beyond
the lead set by models from London or Paris. These gentlemen either do not know or do
not want to use the more adventurous, young, and revolutionary forces that alone would
be able to break up the closed group of these ridiculous and harmful "starched collars."

F. T. Marinetti, the illustrious Italian academic, said in one of his lectures glorify-
ing Italian artistic primacy: "The typical qualities of the Italian race are those of artistry, in-
ventiveness, and improvisation. These qualities produced the great poets, painters, and
architects of the past, and the great personalities of today."

*This truth should be meditated on deeply and, in the case that concerns us here,
especially by the leaders of those industries that may have some influence on the renewal
of clothing in Italy.* Fashion, especially for men, has come to a dead end and is based on
an aesthetic monotony that one can define as "tubular."

What is to be done to free us from this slavery? How can we renew fashion?

A first decisive step would be to *collectively* reject the sort of clothing created
under the sad, gray skies of some northern metropolis. These northern forms are based on
neutral colors derived from gray and brown—colors that are appropriate for hiding dust
and sweat, and therefore practical to a certain extent, but fundamentally antiluminous,
unhealthy, and antiyouth.

Happily, in Italy, even in industrial cities, the atmosphere is no longer full of soot,
as it is in so many great European cities. Consequently, we can have clothes with light, limpid
colors instead of dark, muddy ones. As an homage to the beautiful Italian climate, this orientation toward colorful clothing is appropriate not only in summer but also in winter.

As Italians of the Fascist era, we should have the courage to create a new type
of clothing that is intimately connected with our landscape, clothing that expresses maximum vitality and that is designed for joy rather than melancholy.

Speaking about the problem of Italian theater, Marinetti has said: "Our women
are all actresses, more or less, who admire the wonderful Mediterranean; our airy blue
cities are more or less ideal, pleasant, and noisy stages—and you should see our men!"

Is it not incredible nonsense that the delightful actors and the beautiful actresses
of our daily life are dressed in Anglo-Saxon cut suits, in American-type clothes, or in
French-style dresses?

Today, fashion is international, they proclaim, but now the time has come for a profound change! We should not miss this opportunity, which is clearly defined by historical facts.

One can sense a new orientation in the elegant world: in New York, in Berlin, in Madrid, in London there are people who prefer to dress as we do in Rome or Florence.

Some world-famous Parisian fashion houses have created special patterns for clients from Florence, Naples, or Milan! This means that Italian taste offers *something that cannot be found elsewhere.*

It is necessary to study this subtle "something" in order to define it, if possible, and to develop it on *the national market* and then, afterward, to launch it on the *world market.*

In my opinion, this mysterious "something" consists of precisely the simple and slightly crude aria of healthy youth, where typical Italian innovations can sometimes be found. Undoubtedly, an element of solar vividness and adventurous joy is an integral part of everything that emerges and flourishes on this peninsula.

Here, one should note a very important and significant fact: Italian Futurism (which generated so many polemics in Italy and abroad, only to then be appreciated and exploited by foreigners while it was rejected and misunderstood in its homeland) is now returning to Italy, imported in a thousand unexpected forms. A foreign label of origin makes acceptable what previously was criticized as unbearable extravagance.

A great deal of rectilinear decorative forms, all the ornamental projections of speed, the simplification of surfaces, and the juxtaposition of a few limpid colors are derived from the Italian Futurist movement, created in 1909 in Milan.

This artistic movement launched in the face of the world by a few typically Italian revolutionaries has, *unlike any other aesthetic movement of the modern era,* deeply penetrated the living mass of civilized mankind.

If you look around at a gathering of elegant people, at any fashionable occasion or sports event, you can see the truth of this assertion.

Can you see that little hat with its irregular felt and straw relief, with its light surface and that brilliant metallic arrow on one side? *That is a Futurist hat*! Even if it was designed in Paris. It could have been an Italian innovation and fetched a high price in Italy. Instead, it is an example of French manufacturing exploiting an idea that was originally Italian.

Look at this fabric with its linear pattern of rays intersected by a thousand dynamic angles! This is a Futurist fabric manufactured in Germany but based on an idea derived from Italian Futurism. If you go to a shop, you will have to pay dearly for fabric like this because it comes from abroad and is *a great novelty.*

Can you see these two-tone shoes—fresh, youthful, and speedy? *They are Futurist shoes!* They come from America, but the juxtaposition of leather of different grains and colors and the unusual shape, which seems to emphasize the lightness of the advancing step, everything you like about them and that really is elegant, that combination of tactile values (leather, canvas, rubber), is derived from Italian Futurism.

So why not launch our own truly Futurist style in Italy before a similar fashion is launched and exploited abroad?

After twenty years of existence, Futurism is still the avant-garde of world art. The time has come to recognize, among the many merits of this invigorating movement, that it has rejuvenated the way we dress, liberating the youth of the whole world from a pervasive and suffocating grayness, simplifying the clothing of men and women, making it lighter, healthier, and more comfortable.

In Italy, is it not the black shirt that is the symbol of this great saving liberation?

A *naked man* always stands more or less beyond time, and an Adam is an almost abstract shape.

A *dressed man* instantly indicates history, defining his time and the conditions of life that generated his dress.

The new Italian fashion will be courageously simplified, adventurous, and colorful—a solar fashion, a powerful weapon of commercial expansion, which for several years has already been using the ideas of Futurist artists *in a diluted form.*

It is the role of Italian tailors, of Italian milliners, of the great Italian fashion houses to enable avant-garde artists to develop and manufacture *in their homeland* some genial inventions that could create the new aesthetics of Italian clothing.

They want more color, more joy that is carefree, more dynamism; and less grayness, less stagnation, less prudent and intimidated dignity, less pessimistic skepticism concerning the problems of modern clothing.

Let us recapitulate: a great change is coming!

The old northern forms are *exhausted;* for northern people, southern [*sic*] and melancholic colors are becoming more boring and more unbearable by the day.

It is in Italy that a new, world fashion must be launched!

If we do not have the courage and the strength to take a decisive, innovative, and revolutionary step in the field of fashion, it is certain that others abroad will know how to exploit to their own advantage the huge artistic and commercial possibilities of a solar, Futurist fashion.

ERNESTO THAYAHT AND RUGGERO MICHAHELLES MANIFESTO FOR THE TRANSFORMATION OF MALE CLOTHING "Manifesto per la transformazione dell' abbigliamento maschile" (Tonfano, Fonte dei Marmi, 20 September 1932)

A long time ago, female fashion set itself free from aesthetic and hygienic principles, simplified clothes, and liberated the woman from passéist complications. Let us thus concentrate our attention on male clothing that needs radical transformation.

1. We claim the same freedom for male clothing that has been achieved for a long time by women's clothing.

2. In order to get this freedom, first of all we have to root out the passéist concept in accordance with which a well-dressed man should necessarily wear the following clothes:

Undershirt—underpants—socks and garters—shoes—shirt—collar—tie—cuffs with cuff links—four-pocket trousers—trouser cuffs—belt—adjustable loops and suspenders—waistcoat with four pockets—another adjustable loop—a jacket with inner and outer pockets—facing—a button row with false buttonholes on the cuffs—a felt or straw hat with its ribbon—silk and leather linings—raincoat or overcoat—gloves—scarf—umbrella or walking stick, according to season.

3. We have to ENCOURAGE the youthful, optimistic and sporting taste for a fresh, airy, and synthetic wardrobe, not only at the seaside or in the countryside but also in town and for daily life. SYNTHETIC CLOTHES are especially necessary for those who work in offices, shops, banks, and factories, in order to facilitate their movements, increase their physical fitness, and liberate them from the constraint of expensive, uncomfortable and antihygienic clothes.

4. We have to abolish the black-and-white typographic cliché of the evening dress and of all puritan and Anglo-Saxon, northern, and anti-Mediterranean cuts. We thus have to eliminate collars, cuffs, belts, adjustable loops, suspenders, garters, and all symbols of slavery that hinder blood circulation and freedom of movement (the often-ignored causes of lack of appetite, feelings of faintness, bad temper, and family quarrels or friction). We have to eliminate linings, useless pockets and irrational rows of buttons, trouser cuffs, berets, petticoats, half belts, collars, padding, and other similar antique, ridiculous, and antisporting remnants that are nothing other than dirt and sweat collectors.

5. For every season, we have to reduce to an indispensable minimum the number of items that are worn at the same time.

We have to reduce to an indispensable minimum the SPECIFIC WEIGHT OF EVERY PIECE OF CLOTHING, proportionally and in accordance with the climate. We have to reduce to a strict minimum sewings, hems, and buttonholes (that is to say, the bill) of every item in the wardrobe in order to facilitate manufacturing, washing, ironing, folding; thereby diminishing the cost of production and increasing sales and the likelihood that every city dweller can change his clothes more often.

6. The SYNTHETIC CLOTHING we want to design must be practical and aesthetic:

α) PRACTICAL: it has to follow every movement of the body, and instead of hindering it has to incite action and facilitate it. One ought to be able to put it on quickly, and it has to protect one from rain, cold, and wind, as well as from heat, dust, and sun.

b) AESTHETIC: it has to emphasize the most beautiful and the most characteristic lines of the male body, in contrast with the feminine lines. If possible, it should have an even more brilliant color than women's dress (an obvious law among animals).

7. We have to design new pieces of clothing for male attire, giving them new names, and transform the existing ones so that they will be better adapted to the requirements of contemporary life.

8. In 1918, we designed and launched the TUTA. In a very short time, we will launch, in a sensational show, a complete series of our designs, which we have named:

1. TORACO: A sleeveless, low-necked, and buttonless undershirt, with a rectilinear cut, in cotton, wool, or silk, worn as an undershirt in winter, a bathing suit or jersey in summer; white and washable colors.

2. CAMITO: A sort of antihinderance shirt, without pockets, cut almost skintight, in an elastic cotton or linen, only two buttons, white and very light, washable colors.

3. CORSANTE: A half-sleeve chest cover, two pockets, one button, wool, silk, leather, rubber according to the season, differently colored areas.

4. FEMORALI: A thigh cover that is not tight, knee-length, four pockets, three buttons, opaque wool, cotton linen, silk, intense colors, plain or with geometrical patterns.

5. CONICI: A foot cover with a conical cut, three buttons, two pockets, worsted or brilliant cloth, very light for summer, cool colors; in wool for winter, warm colors.

6. ANCALI: A short hip cover, with a sporting cut, closed with a buckle, two pockets, vivid colors in cotton, for the beach, for swimming or for training.

7. TUBARIA: An ample foot cover, tight at the level of the ankle, sturdy material, individually sewn, two pockets, self-fastening.

8. CALZARI and CALZALI: Differently cut foot covers, mesh, to be worn without garters, white or colored to match the conici or the femorali.

9. AEROSCARPA: A kind of very light and elastic shoe, built to air the foot, light and opaque colors for summer.

10. SCAFA: brilliant and waterproof shoes in leather, brass, or aluminum, self-fastening.

11. SPIOVA: Winter headgear, with an extendable rainguard for the shoulders.

12. ASOLE: A light summer cap, with an adjustable sun shade, in paper, canvas, straw, aluminum, celluloid, white, light green, and electric blue.

13. PARAVISTA: An eyeshade to add to the ASOLE to protect the eyes from the reflection of the street or of the sky.

14. RADIOTELFO: A kind of ultralight travel helmet with a miniature radio with separate headphones.

15. LUCA: A kind of winter coat, knee-length, one sleeve only, one pocket, buttonless, two seams, silky, light reversible and waterproof fabric, dark and strong colors.

16. TRIFERMO: An overjacket with tubular sleeves to the wrists, big reversible collar, three buttons, interior pockets, tight at the waist, pure thick cloth, neutral or varied colors.

All our products are patented and protected in accordance with the law to ensure the exclusivity of their manufacture and sale.

We expect the Italian dressmaking houses that understand the importance of our project, so rich in commercial opportunities, to join us in an intelligent and effective way for the large-scale manufacturing and launching of the new FUTURIST SYNTHETIC WARDROBE.

RENATO DI BOSSO AND IGNAZIO SCURTO THE FUTURIST MANIFESTO OF THE ITALIAN TIE *"Manifesto futurista sulla navatta italiana"* (Verona, March 1933)

Renewing the Italian male wardrobe means to prefer to the common xenophilia and to the anti-Italian Gallic or Anglo-Saxon imports the innovative pride of our race, which is more genial, more intuitive, more rapid than that of any other past, present, or future nations.

The volcanic genius of F. T. Marinetti released one more time the signal of the revolution, attacking the common, monotonous, and uniform daily-use hat.

The painter and sculptor RENATO DI BOSSO and the poet IGNAZIO SCURTO, with the collaboration of young and valorous Venetian Futurists, are aggressively, ferociously, and mercilessly campaigning against the slipknots of gray, black, or polychrome ties, real nooses that recall the infamous rope with which the enemies of yesterday strangled the apostles of Italianness.

Each man wears around his neck the black or colored desire of an inglorious end, a cloth or silk broad hint at his own social servility.

Italians, abolish knots, bow ties, tiepins, and clasps, all antirapid, antihygienic, and antioptimist trifles! Give them to your children to tie to the cats' and dogs' tails, the only place where they are not ridiculous!

Liberate yourselves from the burden of foreign fashion, from the daily fatality of tie peddlers, from the yellow fatality of the Chinese who try to have you stuck with a smile and a rag-passport of coarseness.

The tie he wears reveals a man's character. Today, a divine, motorized, simultaneous epoch, a man's character should be expressed not by a knot and a piece of cloth, but through the brilliance and purity of metal.

We thus invite all Italian males to boycott the ties used daily and use instead the Futurist tie, which we launched on 27 March in Verona.

The Futurist tie, ANTITIE IN VERY LIGHT, BRILLIANT, DURABLE METAL, denotes the elasticity, the force, the intelligence, the sobriety and firmness, the innovative and the Italian spirit of the wearer.

The antitie that we designed can be:

in tin with horizontal undulations;

in opaque aluminum with antitraditional decorative patterns;

in brilliant aluminum with modern incisions;

in simple chromed metal;

in aluminum with gradations of brilliance and opaqueness;

in precious metal;

in brass;

in copper.

The metals that are used should be two to four tenths of a millimeter thick, thus having a minimal weight, and the knot should be totally abolished. The length should be of a few centimeters.

Our practical demonstration in Verona, the enthusiasm with which our innovation was welcomed by both the people and the intellectuals, the demands from other cities for samples and advice—all these make us foresee that the antitie will soon replace with optimism, elegance, practicality, brilliance, resistance the antilyricism of cloth, silk, and canvas.

The antitie, held by a light elastic necklace, reflects all the sun and blue that we Italians have in plenty and removes the pessimistic and melancholic note from the chest of our men.

Young boys wearing a tie, like diplomats or some lazy solicitors, are ridiculous. Mothers, give your sons a very brilliant Futurist antitie, which will inspire their genial and optimistic ideas, their desires for light and flight.

With their antities, each of our men, teenagers, and youngsters will wear an aerial note to which each Italian is entitled.

It is better to be decorated by an airplane wing in the sun rather than by a ridiculous neutral and pacifist rag.

Futurists, boycott all loops and nooses!

Italians, do not dress as future hanged men, but dress instead in a manly way!

VARST (VARVARA STEPANOVA) PRESENT DAY DRESS—PRODUCTION
CLOTHING "Kostium segodniashnego dnia—prozodezhda," *LEF* 1, no. 2 (1923)

Fashion is a psychological reflection of the habits of daily life and aesthetic taste. As such, it is giving way to programmed clothing, suited to the wearer's work in different sectors or for a specific social activity. Similarly, fashion is replaced by clothes that can be worn everywhere, which have no independent value and are not an art product. Now, the most important thing is the processing of the material—that is, the actual production of clothing. It is not enough to have clever designs; they have to be produced in the factory and tested at work. Only then is it possible to clearly judge their qualities. Shop windows containing variously dressed wax dummies are just an aesthetic relic. Contemporary clothing must be seen "in action." It makes no sense out of its context, just as any machine looks absurd out of the context of its function. The following slogan abolishes every decorative detail: "The comfort and practical aspect of clothing must match a specific practical function." Not only must the type of clothes worn necessarily be submitted to mass control, but clothing also has to evolve from being the product of an artisan to that of industrial mass production. It thereby loses its ideological connotation and becomes one aspect of the cultural reality.

It is obvious that the evolution of clothing is linked to industrial development. Only today, thanks to the progress of industry and technology, is it possible to produce outfits for pilots and drivers, workers' overalls, football shoes, and military tunics and raincoats. One should supervise the manufacturing of contemporary clothing from the design stage to its material production; Its cut must be chosen in accordance with the specific nature of the work for which it is intended. The aesthetic elements should be replaced with the production process, so that identical clothes can be sewn. I will explain more clearly: this means that one cannot use appliqué decorations on a dress, as it is the stitching that will give it shape. All stitching, buttons, and so on should be made visible. The coarse stitchings of the artisan do not exist anymore: the sewing machine industrialized the tailor's work and deprived dressmakers of their manufacturing secrets, if not of the fascination of an individualized and personalized manual task. Today, the shape—that is, the "look"—of the clothing is no longer arbitrary, as far as it is designed in accordance with the requirements of the work for which it is intended and with the properties of the material it is made from.

Contemporary clothing is production dress (*prozodezhda*), which differs according to various working conditions. Thus, clothing becomes autonomous, at the same time that it puts on a particular nuance. For example, the cut of work clothes must obey general rules: the clothes have to protect the worker from injuries that could be caused by the machine he works with. Moreover, depending on different types of production, and whether the wearer is a typographer, the driver of a locomotive, or a metalworker, the choice of material and the way in which it is cut will include some individual details though the general design remains unchanged. The construction engineer's outfit will necessarily have plenty of pockets; their size and position are related to the type of instruments that he uses. Likewise, the size and position of pockets for woodworkers, weavers, airplane builders, or metalworkers will be determined by the nature of their specific work. Among these mass-produced clothes, the special dress (*spetsodezhda*) is a specialized garment designed for specific requirements. These type of garments include surgeons' clothes, pilots' outfits, protective clothes for workers who labor in acid environments, firemen's uniforms, and equipment for polar expeditions.

Sport clothes *(sportodezhda)* have the same requirements as any *prozodezhda:* they have to be adapted to the specific sport they are intended for—soccer, winter sports, rowing, boxing, or exercises. A specific requirement is the need to distinguish members of one team from another through the necessary inclusion of precise symbols (emblems, forms, color of the uniform, etc.). As the competitions take place in large spaces and in front of a large crowd, the color of the uniform is an essential element. From far away, one cannot distinguish the sportsmen by the cut of their jerseys. Moreover, players will find it much easier to recognize their teammates by the color of their attire. Sport clothes must be produced in a great variety of colors. The fundamental principle that determines their cut, which applies to all sports, is the following: maximum practicality, simplicity, and ease of wear. In this issue of *LEF,* three types of uniforms for football teams are illustrated: 1. a three-color uniform (red, black, and gray) with a red star on the chest; 2. a single-color uniform (red), in jersey, with a large badge on the chest; 3. a two-color striped uniform (red and white) without badges. All these uniforms are plain shirts with straight sleeves and shorts. The uniform of the women basketball players has a black stripe on the chest and a striped skirt, which makes it appear bell-shaped. A lot of attention has been given to the simplicity and vividness of the color combination. The characteristic element of sport garments is their simplicity, required for freedom of movement. In this particular case, there are no buttons or cuts that may hinder movement.

NADEZHDA LAMANOVA CONCERNING CONTEMPORARY DRESS

"O sovremenem kostiume," *Krasnaia niva,* no. 27 (1923)

Our modern Russian era can no longer accept the tyranny of fashion and recklessness in the field of dress. In this field, as in all other fields, we want to understand the meaning and the process of production. Already in Russian folk costumes, despite their dependence on customs and tradition, we notice a certain functionality; they are suited to the goal they were made for. There are everyday clothes and "Sunday" clothes.

The same principle of organizing clothing by their use is present in complex urban life; for a large number of occupations, the working clothes should be functional—that is, simple and comfortable—and should be suited to the wearer's type of work (for example, a tight garment is not acceptable for someone who needs to move when he works). For "Sunday" clothes, while respecting all the principles of simplicity and comfort, it is possible instead to take a more individual approach, related to the personality of the wearer; in other words, one might use more complex shapes and more vivid colors. The city has its own celebrations and amusements, so the festive clothes are divided into day and evening dress; the latter is also divided between normal evening dress and the stage costume, which necessarily requires more ornamentation and an emphasis on its shape.

Therefore, when designing a garment, one must not forget the goal for which it is created, in order to approach most appropriately its shape, color, and fabric. It is necessary to take into account the properties of the fabric because they resist being forced; opposing the nature of the material risks bed results. Every fabric, even the cheapest, can be the starting point for a beautiful shape, providing that one takes into account its properties, its width, its softness, and its coarseness. In exactly the same way, a clearly conceived shape requires "its own" fabric.

However, it is even more important to consider the person for whom the clothing is made—that is, to notice all physical particularities, everything that demands the garment's reshaping in order to achieve the most harmonious figure possible.

Here, we touch on the very essence of clothing design, the correct, modern conception that is not subject to fashion, because it levels people without taking into account the characteristics and shortcomings of their bodies (let us recall only crinolines, or the fashion of strait "bound up" skirts). Anyone, in spite of all congenital or other types of bodily faults, has the right to enjoy harmony. The present conception of dress tries to achieve this by consciously modifying the human figure using the creative construction of dress to achieve more appropriate proportions.

It was thought possible, for example, to fight a massive figure by lacing it tightly in a corset, or in narrow clothes; in fact, this had the opposite effect, emphasizing even more the lack of proportion between the parts. The fight against a corpulent body has to take a different direction; a silhouette cannot be slimmed except by hiding disproportions, breaking them into planes of a different shape. On the contrary, if we want to give more importance to a woman's frail, or even meager, body, it is indispensable to maintain her very lightness—not in the aesthetic sense, but the lightness of her mobility.

Our era rejects anything static, in life or in art. Therefore, dress should be constructed according to "the principle of contrast," in order to achieve the maximum dynamism and also decorative interest. This applies to wide as well as to narrow garments. Such a love for contrast can be noticed in folk costumes; think of the Ukrainian *plashta,* which is very tight at the hips, in contrast with the widening of its upper part. One can see diametrically opposed examples in many illustrations from last year's fashion magazines. Contrast is totally absent and stasis is everywhere. For example, a narrow dress has narrow sleeves. This absence of contrast and, consequently, of dynamism produces a dry and monotonous silhouette. The Japanese costume is an example of just the reverse: the width of the sleeves juxtaposed to the tightness of the lower part of the dress make a figure light, contrasted, and animated.

Thus, the garment has to be constructed before it is sewn. To achieve the best construction of clothing, one has to mentally divide the given body into geometric shapes, in order to have a clearer representation of the real silhouette. When visually translating the body into surfaces, we have to consider it as a series of planes. If these planes, because of the body's faults, are disproportionate, we can achieve more harmonious relationships among the parts and a corrected outline by breaking them up with other planes. By dividing the contemporary dress, we can hide a long waist, lengthen a petite figure, or shorten a tall one (splitting it in two).

Each piece of the dress is a part of the total geometric figure. This is why the sleeves or the collar should not be considered as isolated elements. It is obvious that the neckline cannot be a distinct element from the whole of the dress. For any given form, the choice of collar and neckline (round, triangular, square, closed, or open) cannot be isolated from the whole; on the contrary, the general shape of the dress requires this or that collar or neckline. We can choose here between two principles: a garment is constructed either in contrast to the general shape or in a strict logical relationship with it. The same applies to decoration. Just as for the collar or the sleeves, the finishing of an outfit with decorative embroidering, with appliqué leather or fur, must not oppose the general shape. The finishing touches of a garment using this or that color—what is commonly called trimming—are important for the whole construction: they can accentuate the rhythm of planes and emphasize the general shape, lightening or making it heavy, in accordance with the chosen color. Moreover, the choice of the shape and hang of its ornamentation will certainly influence the general shape of the garment: one decoration can emphasize it, another one can soften it, etc. Therefore, when working at a garment, one has to keep in mind the integrity of the general project: lack of precision and inconsistency can alter the initial idea, the fundamental purpose.

The emergence of an interest in the artistic-constructive aspects of dress is significant. If, as a result of this interest and of the research we do in the scientific laboratory of artistic dress from NKP, we gain comfortable, harmonious, and functional clothing, we will achieve at the same time an enrichment of our daily life, and we will wipe out the prejudice of fashion, this false idea that has, until now, forced working women to submit to bourgeois fashion instead of elaborating their own principles in the field of dress. The new dress will suit the new life—active, dynamic, and conscious.

Nadezhda Lamanova—Project for a
dress, 1923.

NADEZHDA LAMANOVA THE RUSSIAN FASHION "Russkaia moda," *Krasnaia
niva,* no. 30 (1923)

One of the most interesting concerns of modern clothing is the study of the folk costume
and of the possibility of adapting its form and character to our modern dress.

The functional character of the folk costume that has been developed out of the
collective creativity of the people, which is centuries old, could serve as ideological and
plastic material to be integrated in our urban clothing. The elementary forms of the folk
costume are always right. Take, for example, the costume of the Kievian province; it is
composed of a *jupak* (outer jacket), a *plashta* (skirt), and a shirt with embroidered borders
and sleeves. A folk costume like this is a sort of *prozodezhda* designed for physical work;
it is easily transformed from summer wear into winter wear, and from daily clothes into
festive clothes, by simply adding a necklace, a decorative headband, or a colored scarf.
Starting from this typical costume, linked to the conditions of work and life, elaborated in
a certain atmosphere based on the characteristic physical particularities of the Russian
body, it is easy to create town wear grounded in all the functions of the folk costume. By
using the picturesque aspects of the folk costume and by integrating them into the functional dress, according to a rhythmic logic, we achieve a type of clothing that is suited to
our contemporary life.

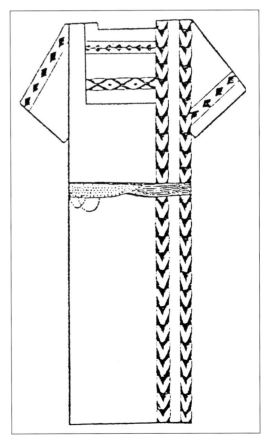

ALEKSANDRA EXTER THE CONSTRUCTIVIST DRESS "O konstruktivnoi odezhde," *Atel'e*, no. 1 (1923)

Every object is submitted to the laws imposed by its material. When choosing a fabric to cut, one has to consider its density, weight, width, and color. Coarse wool cloth requires a rectangular cut or, at least, a cut with straight angles, without any additional elements that are difficult to manufacture. This cut will prevent choices that are contrary to the nature of the material. When they are appropriately treated, soft and wide fabrics, such as wool or silk, make it possible to create a more complex and distinctive figure. This type of silhouette, which could be inscribed in a more complicated form, can be combined with the most varied rhythms. A thin fabric logically calls for a straight vertical and tight-fitting cut, which replaces width with space, using pleats or slits to increase bodily comfort. Combinations of thin fabrics produce a conciseness of expression and a clear construction of pleats. Because of their properties, elastic fabrics, such as some types of silk, could be used to design clothes for movement (dancing, for example) and to conceive more complicated shapes (circles, polygons). This type of garment, which is "constructed" according to the dynamics of the body's movements, must be composed out of mobile elements. A heavier material is suitable for a more peaceful form (square, polygon, etc.) and could be used for slower movements (walking or running).

Shape is indissolubly linked with color. When studying the properties of single-color garments, which have been designed in an elementary geometric shape, one notices that these shapes require the use of primary colors; in contrast, a more complicated form requires complementary colors or tones. If we compare two identical squares, one black and one white, the black square appears smaller and lighter than the other square (conforming to the theory of color weight). This is why, in order to balance two dresses in these colors, the cut of the black one should be made more complicated.

Research into a new way of clothing is the business of the day. Since the working class is the majority of the population, clothing should be adapted to laborers and their type of work. The cut of these clothes should not be too narrow, in order to avoid hindering movement, as happens with too large headgear or too tight-fitting garments. The cut of modern clothes should suit the requirements of our life, taking into account all possibilities. One should emphasize the intensity of color, a characteristic element of our Russian folk costume, without being influenced at all by the Western designs generated by a different ideology.

Working clothes have not yet been thoroughly studied. Their cut is the result of the conditions of life, of work and leisure. It is necessary to envision a rational and economic change, which has great hygienic and psychological importance.

Research concerning *prozodezhda* (production dress) or mass-produced clothes shows that they have to be constructed on the basis of simple geometric shapes and primary colors, including different rhythms. Clothes intended for physical work should be designed accordingly; they have to be related to the movements of the body and respect

Aleksandra Exter—Projects for
women's clothes, 1923.

Aleksandra Exter—Projects for
clothes, 1923.

the harmony of bodily proportions. The majority of mass-produced objects are ill-proportional; for that reason, they are not comfortable.

For manual or for office workers, the outer garment should be adapted to their working conditions. This is the theoretical approach for *prozodezhda* and all mass-produced clothes.

The design of the personal garment rests on a totally different ideological basis. In this case, it is essential to distinguish different human types and to design the character, the shape, and the color of the garment accordingly.

For its practical manufacture, it is necessary that the artist should collaborate with the technician. The artist's job is creating new shapes appropriate for today's people, finding new starting points for research into contemporary clothing, inventing new means of expression by modifying the preestablished proportions of different parts, choosing the right color for a given shape, selecting and contrasting figures and materials, defining new rhythms, and establishing a correspondence between the figure and the dynamics of the human body.

The technician that understands the artist's language well could transpose all this scientific work into reality; the technician's correct interpretation is the first and most important condition for producing clothing. Only the collaboration between the artist and the technician can solve the problem of clothing.

GUILLAUME APOLLINAIRE THE FORTNIGHT REVIEW: THE REFORMERS OF DRESS "Revue de la quinzaine: Les Réformateurs du costume," *Mercure de France,* no. 397 (1 January 1914)

One has to go to the Bullier on Thursday and Sunday to see Mr. and Mrs. Delaunay, painters, who are undertaking the reform of dress.

Simultaneous Orphism has produced new clothing that is not to be scorned. These would have provided Carlyle with a curious chapter in his *Sartor Resartus.*

Mr. and Mrs. Delaunay are innovators. They do not trouble themselves with the imitation of old fashions, and since they want to be of their own time, they did not try at all to innovate on the level of the form of the cut, following the fashion of the day, but they try to influence it by using new materials that are infinitely varied in color.

This is, for example, a suit of Mr. Robert Delaunay: a violet jacket, a beige waistcoat, and black trousers. And here is another: red overcoat with a blue collar, red socks, yellow and black shoes, black trousers, green jacket, and a minuscule red tie.

Here is a description of a simultaneous dress of Mrs. Sonia Delaunay Terck: a violet suit, a long green-and-violet sash, and, under her jacket, a bodice divided into areas of vivid, tender, and faded colors, in which there were mixed old pink, yellowish-orange, Nattier blue and scarlet, etc. appearing on different materials such as woolen cloth, taffeta, tulle, flannelette, moiré, and poult-de-soie juxtaposed.

So much variety cannot pass unnoticed. It puts fantasy in elegance.

And if, when going to the Bullier, you cannot immediately see them, do know that the reformers of dress are generally near the band, from where they can contemplate without contempt the monotone clothing of dancers.

BLAISE CENDRARS ON HER DRESS SHE HAS A BODY "Sur la robe elle a un corps" (February 1914)

The woman's body is as bumpy as my skull
Glorious
If you incarnate with spirit
Dressmakers do a stupid job
As much as phrenology
My eyes are kilos that measure women's sensuality

Everything that runs away protrude advance into the depths
The stars hollow the sky
The colors undress
On her dress she has a body
Under the heather arms hands half-moons and pistils
when the waters flow themselves into the back with the glaucous shoulder blades
Belly a moving disc
The double shell of the breasts goes under the bridge of rainbows
Belly
Disc
Sun
Colors' perpendicular cries fall upon the thighs
St. Michael's Sword

Hands that extend
In the dress's train the beast all eyes all bands all the habitués of the Bal Bullier
And on the hip

The poet's signature

SONIA DELAUNAY THE INFLUENCE OF PAINTING ON FASHION

"L'influence de la peinture sur la mode," *Bulletin d'Etudes Philosophiques et Scientifiques pour l'examen des tendances nouvelles* (Paris) (1927)

The question of painting's influence on fashion is closely linked to the craft, or technique, of painting, and this is the point of view from which I am writing this article. Besides, the theme is broad enough. I will, therefore, attempt to give a brief outline of the artistic evolution that interests us. Without wishing to work through the whole history of modern art, I have to start with Impressionism in order to emphasize the influences that are the subject of this talk.

The revolution brought about by the Impressionists was already foreshadowed, begun, and more or less formulated by Eugène Delacroix. He is the starting point for the new visual sensitivity. I can mention Eugène Delacroix's extraordinary genius only in passing and would like to move on to those who carried out what he had already foreseen. Tired of convention, the Impressionists placed themselves in Nature as if they were facing a new world. They allowed Nature to work on them. It is with them that Art and Life began to approach one another.

The Impressionists broke away from conventions and from the use of color surfaces in accordance with academic rules built up from the time of the Renaissance. The sensitivity of their eyes, which they focused on Nature, attempted to reproduce directly the multitude of elementary color tones that, when juxtaposed on the retina, give the impression of a unified color. A seemingly uniform tone is made up of a mass of different colors visible only to a trained eye. It is an atmospheric rather than a synthetic vision. It involves decomposing colors into their constitutive elements, derived from the spectrum of a prism and therefore formed by pure color. Their palette became simpler and clearer in order to achieve this effect, a process called optical mixing.

But this breaking up of color, though rich in new sensitivity, was carried out on the traditional basis of line and form in light and dark painting. Here is what Seurat said, the first of the Impressionists to try to define an inner, constructive order in painting:

Art is Harmony, the equivalence of opposites, the analogy of similar tones and colors; in other words, red and its complementary color, green; orange and its complementary color, blue; yellow and its complementary color, violet. . . . Its means of expression is the optical mixing of tones and colors and their interactions (aftershadows), according to strict laws.

Although he was the most consistent, meticulous, and visionary of the Impressionists, Seurat remained committed to the use of light and dark shading and was unable to free himself from this conventional limitation. This weakness became obvious with the neo-Impressionists, who tried to systematize the principles of color perception that the Impressionists had grasped intuitively. The mixing of optical sensations for the Impressionists was a way of ordering perception scientifically but not of systematizing it. And thus we came to define the mixing of optical sensations as the mixing of bright colors—for example, a cluster of distinct, bright color tones on the same spot of the canvas. In the same way that a physician can demonstrate the phenomenon of optical mixing by means of a quickly rotating disc made up of different colored segments, an artist can create a unified color by juxtaposing different colors next to one another. The eye will distinguish individually neither the segments of color nor the brushstrokes but will see only the end result—a single color.

Cézanne was linked with the Impressionists but he was not satisfied with analyzing the chromatic scale. For him the mosaic of colors of the pure Impressionists was not a goal but a point of departure for new research into composition. He felt that conventional drawing was no longer appropriate for this expression, and in his research he pursued the notion that color changes corresponded to the movement from one plane to another. It was these planes themselves that created mass and volume. In an attempt to create volume, he enlarged his strokes of color and destroyed the outline of the object, the drawing. He began to destroy outlines, just as that the Impressionists had begun to destroy color, and it is through him that dependence on academic rules finally disappeared. His work offered the possibility of overthrowing everything and the promise of a new sort of composition—the doors were wide open for future research.

After this dissolution of tradition had reached its culmination, over years of desperate striving to free itself from all its academic shackles in order to develop new forms, it was possible to begin again from the very beginning. Matisse took on the task that Cézanne had articulated and made more difficult, by emphasizing the relationship between colors. This emphasis distorted color and broke up line, thereby reinforcing the dissolution of tradition and, finally, attaining harmony. From his first paintings, he tried to free himself from the use of shading, attempting to achieve the effect of flat objects on a single plane, like the flat surface of a poster. On this path, Matisse sought inspiration in miniature painting, Persian ceramics, and certain elements of folk art, such as cloth and toys. After the research and the exhausting struggles of his predecessors, Matisse freed the sensibility, in a way that was perceptible to everyone, from the academic limitations that had imprisoned it. He had shown the path to a multitude of individual experiences of color. This was not an innovation, however, but the opening of a direction that allowed a new way of composing with light and color.

In the group around Matisse, Dufy stood out as an individual. He had brought together the influence of Persian ceramics and fifteenth-century wood engravings with the lessons of Cézanne. More forcefully than in his paintings and his wood prints, he expressed himself in designs for cloth with bold patterns of flowers and fruit that were composed like paintings. These painterly, fresh, and decorative patterns came at a time when for years, only variations (copies or more or less successful interpretations) of motifs drawn from the same periods of the past had been used. Dufy's designs were like a ray of sunshine on a gloomy day. They were picked up by fashion and gave the trade a surprising, joyful touch that until then had been unknown.

Another painter besides Dufy affected this period and to some extent even brought these two influences together. Bakst, who also was influenced by Matisse, developed an Oriental style that he modernized and introduced to the theater. His costumes and stage sets for the Ballets Russes were a revelation, as much for the theater as for clothing in general, which it influenced through their new color scheme and Oriental atmosphere. In fact, they gave rise to a mass of imitations, which from that time on were labeled the Ballets Russes style. The influence of Bakst, whose work was nowhere near as good as Dufy's, was of dubious taste and quality, and his style quickly became outdated—unlike the decorative work of Dufy that, although old, maintains its value.

In addition to the lively quality of both of these painters, there was another factor that contributed to the influence of their creations on clothing. At that time, fashion was going through a critical period that corresponded with a revolutionary period. Shortly before the war, it had begun to free itself from the academic rules of dress design. It had got rid of the corset, the high collar, and all the elements of female dress that fashionable aesthetics required but that were contrary to the health and freedom of movement of women. Above all, the changes in the way women lived brought about this revolution. Women became increasingly active. Not only for . . .

Fashion, clearly influenced as it now is by painting, has to become creative. The cut of a dress will be conceived at the same time as its decoration. This new attitude has logically led to an invention that R. Delaunay recently patented and that was last used by myself in collaboration with the Redfern Company. This is the fabric-pattern (*tissu-patron*). The dress pattern was conceived by its designer at the same time as the decoration. The pattern, together with decorative elements appropriate to the design, was then printed on the cloth. So this is a first step, from an artistic point of view, in the collaboration between the dress designer and the designer of the cloth. From the point of view of the standardization toward which all modern trends tend, the fabric-pattern will enable a dress to be precisely reproduced at the other end of the world at minimal cost and with minimum wastage of material. So when the fabric is sold, the design and the trimmings are sold simultaneously.

Those who believe that the present movement is a passing phase are wrong. They may very well announce that geometric patterns will soon be old-fashioned and will be replaced by innovations drawn from old motifs, but they are badly mistaken. Geometric patterns will never become old-fashioned, simply because they have never been fashionable. It was the mistaken interpretations of the mediocre designers making copies that determined the decoration. If geometric forms were used here, it was because these simple, practical elements seemed suitable for distributing the colors whose interactions were the real aim of our research. But these geometric shapes do not characterize our art, and the distribution of color could just as well be achieved using complex shapes such as flowers etc. . . . the way these shapes are used would just be a little more difficult.

At the moment, one movement is influencing fashion as it is influencing interior design, the cinema, and all the visual arts; anything that does not submit to these new principles that artists have been seeking over the past hundred years will be outdated. However, we are just at the beginning of the research into new relationships between colors (still so full of mysteries to be discovered) that is the basis of contemporary vision. It is possible to enrich and develop this research, it is possible that others will continue this work, but it is not possible to turn back.

SONIA DELAUNAY ARTISTS AND THE FUTURE OF FASHION "Les artistes et l'avenir de la mode" 1931

Fashion today does not reflect the artistic tendencies of our century. Present-day art has had the courage to undergo a complete revolution and to begin rebuilding on new foundations. The art of our times is visual and constructive. The fashion business is not yet constructive, offering nothing but an accumulation of refined details. Instead of adapting clothes to the needs of everyday life and the movement it requires, dress has become more complicated in the belief that in this way it will satisfy the tastes of buyers and exporters. That is why we have been forced to suffer dresses, for example, that are too tight, or too short, or too long. Rather than adapting dresses to the way we walk, we have had to adapt our gait to the dresses, which is absurd.

Fashion, nowadays, should be based on two principles: vitality, the unconscious, and visual appeal on the one hand; craft and design on the other. In other words, ideas shouldn't be taken from the past; the subject instead should be tackled afresh as if we were starting today from scratch.

I imagine the future of fashion in these terms: there will be design centers, research laboratories that will deal with practical applications, constantly adapting to the changing conditions of life. Research into the materials used and a simplification of aesthetic notions will become increasingly important. On such carefully considered and up-to-date foundations, vision and sensuality will find a wide field opening up before them. The cost of these improved creations will correspond to the value of the research put into them. They will be sold to industries that will themselves work out how to reduce prices by means of mass production and will see to distributing them on a large scale. In this way, fashion will become more democratic—a development for which one can only be grateful, since it will raise overall quality. It will also bring about an end to copying, which is the bane of contemporary fashion.

Liubov Popova—Actor's *prozodezhda,* 1921. Modern reconstruction, 1992.

Liubov Popova—Actor's *prozodezhda,* 1921. Modern reconstruction, 1992.

Liubov Popova—Actor's *prozodezhda,* 1921. Modern reconstruction, 1992.

Following page:

Varvara Stepanova—Sport clothing, 1924. Modern reconstruction, 1992.

Varvara Stepanova—Woman's *prozodezda,* 1924. Modern reconstruction, 1992.

Aleksandra Exter—Winter outfit, 1923. Modern reconstruction, 1992.

Kazimir Malevich—Suprematist dress. Modern reconstruction after a project, 1992.

Mrs. E. B. wearing a dress created by Henry van de Velde
From *Deutsche Kunst und Dekoration,* May 1902
Page 12

Henry van de Velde—Afternoon and street dresses
From *Deutsche Kunst und Dekoration,* May 1902
Page 12

Maria van de Velde in a dress by Henry van de Velde
From *Deutsche Kunst und Dekoration,* May 1902
Page 12

Henry van de Velde—Street dress
From *Deutsche Kunst und Dekoration,* May 1902
Page 12

Marie Beyers de Graaff—Reform dress 1900s
Wool
Nederlands Kostuummuseum, The Hague
Page 16

"Reform" dresses, about 1900
Dresses created by the Flöge sisters in their Vienna salon
Page 17

Alfred Mohrbutter—House dress
From Anna Muthesius, *Das Eigenkleid der Frau* (Krefeld, 1903)
Page 18

Alfred Mohrbutter—Silk dress
From Anna Muthesius, *Das Eigenkleid der Frau* (Krefeld, 1903)
Page 18

Wassily Kandinsky—Project for a dress, 1904
Pencil on paper, 22.2 × 28.3 cm
Städtische Galerie im Lenbachhaus, Munich
Page 19

Wassily Kandinsky—Project for a dress, 1904
Pencil on paper, 20.8 × 16.7 cm
Städtische Galerie im Lenbachhaus, Munich
Page 19

Peter Behrens—Visiting dress
From *Deutsche Kunst und Dekoration,* May 1902
Page 21

Peter Behrens—Visiting dress, back view
From *Deutsche Kunst und Dekoration,* May 1902
Page 21

Henry van de Velde—Evening dress
From *Deutsche Kunst und Dekoration,* May 1902
Page 21

Anna Muthesius—Green silk dress
From Anna Muthesius, *Das Eigenkleid der Frau* (Krefeld, 1903)
Page 21

Gustav Klimt in one of his dresses, 1914
Page 24

Gustav Klimt—Dress
Page 24

Gustav Klimt and Emilie Flöge
Photographed in the gardens of Klimt's atelier by Moriz Nähr, 1905–1910
Page 25

Emilie Flöge in a dress that was probably designed by Klimt
Photographed in the gardens of Klimt's atelier by Moriz Nähr, 1905–1910
Page 25

Josef Hoffmann—Summer dress
Archiv Photoban "Mode," 1911
Page 25

Koloman Moser—Project for a dress, 1902
Lithograph, 47.5 × 31.7 cm
Historisches Museum, Vienna
Page 27

Eduard Wimmer-Wisgrill—Project for a dress with "harem trousers," 1914
India ink on transparent paper, 30 × 18 cm
Hochschule für Angewandte Kunst, Vienna
Page 27

Giacomo Balla—Project for a scarf, 1925–1930; project for a dress, 1920s
Double-sided, oil on plywood, 30 × 43 cm
Collection of Laura Biagiotti, Guidonia
Page 31

Giacomo Balla—Male suit with modifiers, 1913–1914
From "Male Futurist Dress: A Manifesto"
Page 33

Giacomo Balla—Modifiers, 1914
From "Male Futurist Dress: A Manifesto"
Page 33

Giacomo Balla—Projects for Futurist ties, 1925–1930
Black pencil enhanced by watercolor, 26 × 35 cm
Collection of Laura Biagiotti, Guidonia
Page 34

Giacomo Balla—Projects for scarves, 1919
Watercolor on paper, 24 × 22 cm
Collection of Laura Biagiotti, Guidonia
Page 34

Giacomo Balla—Projects for Futurist jackets, 1914
Watercolor on paper, 34 × 104 cm
Collection of Laura Biagiotti, Guidonia
Page 34

Giacomo Balla—Projects for Futurist suits, 1913–1914
Pencil and india ink on paper, 32 × 53 cm
Collection of Laura Biagiotti, Guidonia
Pages 35–36

Giacomo Balla—Projects for Futurist shoes, 1928–1929
Pencil and india ink on paper, 32 × 53 cm
Collection of Laura Biagiotti, Guidonia
Page 38

Giacomo Balla—Futurist shoes, 1916–1918
Collection of Laura Biagiotti, Guidonia
Page 39

Giacomo Balla—Futurist shoes, 1929
Silk
Collection of Laura Biagiotti, Guidonia
Page 39

Giacomo Balla—Dress, 1930
Wool, 80 × 126 cm
Collection of Laura Biagiotti, Guidonia
Page 39

Tullio Crali—Synthetic jacket, 1932; jacket, worn by the artist, 1931
Photo, collection of the artist
Page 41

Mino delle Site—Projects for Futurist Ties, 1932
Page 43

Ernesto Thayaht (Michahelles)—Tuta, 1918–1919
Page 43

Ernesto Thayaht (Michahelles)—Woman's tuta
Page 43

Varvara Stepanova—Caricature of Alexei Gan, 1922
From *Zrelishcha,* 1923
Page 46

Vladimir Tatlin—Man's suit and overcoat, 1924
From *Krasnaia Panorama,* 1924
Page 49

Vladimir Tatlin—Project for a dress, 1924
Pencil on paper, 56.8 × 77 cm
Bakhrushin Theater Museum, Moscow
Page 50

Vladimir Tatlin—Project for an overcoat, 1924
Pencil on paper, 62 × 39.5 cm
Bakhrushin Theater Museum, Moscow
Page 50

Varvara Stepanova wearing a Constructivist dress, 1924
Page 51

Caricatures of Liubov Popova and Varvara Stepanova
From *Nach Gaz,* 1924
Page 51

Caricatures of Varvara Stepanova and Aleksandr Rodchenko
From *Nach Gaz,* 1924
Page 51

Aleksandr Rodchenko in his Constructivist attire, 1922
Page 52

Varvara Stepanova—Caricature of Aleksandr Rodchenko
From *Zrelishcha,* 1923
Page 52

Aleksandr Rodchenko in his Constructivist attire, 1922
Page 52

Nadezhda Lamanova—Pioneer's attire
From *Iskusstvo bytu* (Moscow), 1925
Page 57

Nadezhda Lamanova—Projects for sport clothes
From *Iskusstvo bytu* (Moscow), 1925
Page 57

Nadezhda Lamanova—Projects for dresses
From *Iskusstvo bytu* (Moscow), 1925
Page 58

Nadezhda Lamanova—Projects for dresses
From *Krasnaia Niva,* 1923
Page 58

Sofia Beliaeva-Ekzempliiarskaia—Studies of visual perception laws applied to dress design
From Sofia Beliaeva-Ekzempliiarskaia, *Modelirovanie odezdy po znakom zritel'nogo vospriiatia*
(Moscow, 1924)
Page 59

Aleksandra Exter—Project for a dress
From *Atel'e,* 1923
Page 60

Aleksandra Exter—Project for an overcoat
From *Atel'e,* 1923
Page 60

Ilia Chashnik—Project for a young girl's dress, 1924
Pencil and watercolor on graph paper, 19.7 × 16.7 cm
Collection of Lev Nussberg, Orange, Calif.
Page 61

Ilia Chashnik—Project for a Suprematist dress, 1924
Pencil and watercolor on graph paper, 16.6 × 19.8 cm
Collection of Lev Nussberg, Orange, Calif.
Page 61

Peake, "Why not let the Cubists and Futurists design the spring fashions?"
From *Punch,* 1913
Page 64

Advertisement for Mandel Brothers
From *Chicago Tribune,* 1914
Page 66

Henry van de Velde—Street dress
From *Deutsche Kunst and Dekoration,* May 1902
Page 134

Henry van de Velde—Afternoon dress
From *Deutsche Kunst and Dekoration,* May 1902
Page 135

Alfred Mohrbutter—Town dress
From Anna Muthesius, *Das Eigenkleid der Frau* (Krefeld, 1903)
Page 136

Giacomo Balla—Manuscript of the "Futurist Manifesto of Male Dress," 1913–1914
40 × 93 cm
Collection of Laura Biagiotti, Guidonia
Page 154

Nadezhda Lamanova (and Vera Mukhina?)—Dress inspired by the Russian folk costume, 1923
Page 175

Nadezhda Lamanova—Project for a dress, 1923
From *Krasnaia Niva,* 1923
Page 177

Aleksandra Exter—Projects for women's clothes, 1923
From *Krasnaia Niva,* 1923
Page 179

Aleksandra Exter—Projects for clothes, 1923
From *Krasnaia Niva,* 1923
Page 179

Liubov Popova—Actor's *prozodezhda,* 1921; modern reconstruction by Sylvia Krenz, 1992

Liubov Popova—Actor's *prozodezhda,* 1921; modern reconstruction by Sylvia Krenz, 1992

Liubov Popova—Actor's *prozodezhda,* 1921; modern reconstruction by Sylvia Krenz, 1992

Varvara Stepanova—Sport clothing, 1924; modern reconstruction by Sylvia Krenz, 1992

Varvara Stepanova—Woman's *prozodezda,* 1924; modern reconstruction by Sylvia Krenz, 1992

Aleksandra Exter—Winter outfit, 1923; modern reconstruction after a project by Sylvia Krenz, 1992

Kazimir Malevich—Suprematist dress; modern reconstruction after a project by Sylvia Krenz, 1992
Pages 187–188

Henry van de Velde—Ornament for a dress, 1896–1898
Black velvet, 44/57.5 × 18.5 cm
Museum Bellerive, Zurich
Plate 1

Wiener Werkstätte—Women's shoes, 1914
Silk and leather
Historisches, Museum, Vienna
Plate 2

Koloman Moser—Visiting dress, 1905
131 cm
Historisches Museum, Vienna
Plate 3

Dagobert Peche—Project for a dress, 1914
Pencil, gouache, and watercolor on graph paper
Österreichisches Museum für Angewandte Kunst, Vienna
Plate 4

Eduard Wimmer-Wisgrill—Project for the Norne dress, 1922
Pencil and colored pencil on paper, 33.7 × 25.4 cm
Österreichisches Museum für Angewandte Kunst, Vienna
Plate 5

Eduard Wimmer-Wisgrill—Project for sport clothing in wool, 1921
Pencil and colored pencil on paper
Österreichisches Museum für Angewandte Kunst, Vienna
Plate 6

Eduard Wimmer-Wisgrill—Project for the Bubi outfit, 1912
Pencil and watercolor on paper, 29.5 × 17.8 cm
Österreichisches Museum für Angewandte Kunst, Vienna
Plate 7

Eduard Wimmer-Wisgrill—Project for a summer dress, 1911
Pencil and watercolor on graph paper, 29.5 × 18.5 cm
Österreichisches Museum für Angewandte Kunst, Vienna
Plate 8

Eduard Wimmer-Wisgrill—Project for the Ethel overcoat, 1913
Pencil and watercolor on paper, 30 × 18 cm
Österreichisches Museum für Angewandte Kunst, Vienna
Plate 9

Max Snischek—Project for an evening dress, 1918
Pencil and colored pencil on paper, 34 × 22 cm
Österreichisches Museum für Angewandte Kunst, Vienna
Plate 10

Max Snischek—Project for a coat, 1914
Pencil and watercolor on paper, 38.5 × 30.7 cm
Österreichisches Museum für Angewandte Kunst, Vienna
Plate 11

Piet Zwart—Projects for clothing, 1916–1917
Gemeentenmuseum, The Hague
Plate 12

Kazimir Malevich—Projects for Suprematist clothing, 1923
Gouache on paper, 18.9 × 16.9 cm; pencil and watercolor, 19 × 17 cm
Russian Museum, St. Petersburg
Plate 13

Varvara Stepanova—Projects for sport clothing, 1924
From *LEF,* 1924
Plate 14

Nadezhda Lamanova—Project for a caftan
From *Iskousstvo bytu* (Moscow), 1925
Plate 15

Nadezhda Lamanova—Project for a dress
From *Iskousstvo bytu* (Moscow), 1925
Plate 16

Giacomo Balla—Projects for blouses and sweaters, ca. 1930
Watercolor on paper, 19 × 13.5 cm
Collection of Laura Biagiotti, Guidonia
Plate 17

Giacomo Balla—Three projects for Futurist suits: morning, afternoon, and evening, 1914
Watercolor on cardboard, 29 × 21 cm
Collection of Laura Biagiotti, Guidonia
Plate 18

Giacomo Balla—Three projects for Futurist fabrics, 1913
Watercolor on cardboard, 13 × 19 cm
Collection of Laura Biagiotti, Guidonia
Plate 19

Giacomo Balla—Project for a scarf, 1922
Watercolor on paper, 57 × 185 cm
Collection of Laura Biagiotti, Guidonia
Plate 20

Giacomo Balla—Project for a sweater, 1920
Pencil and watercolor on paper, 21 × 13 cm
Collection of Laura Biagiotti, Guidonia
Plate 21

Giacomo Balla—Two projects for a sweater, 1929
Tempera and pencil on paper, 21 × 31.5 cm
Collection of Laura Biagiotti, Guidonia
Plate 22

Giacomo Balla—Three Futurist ties, 1914
Collection of Laura Biagiotti, Guidonia
Plate 23

Giacomo Balla—Project for a Futurist tie, 1916
Pencil and watercolor on paper, 20 × 45 cm
Collection of Laura Biagiotti, Guidonia
Plate 24

Giacomo Balla—House dress worn by the artist, 1925
Various fabrics
Private collection, Rome
Plate 25

Giacomo Balla—Embroidered waistcoat worn by the artist, 1924
Height 55 cm
Collection of Laura Biagiotti, Guidonia
Plate 26

Giacomo Balla—Project for a bag, 1916
Watercolor on paper, 28.5 × 22.5 cm
Collection of Laura Biagiotti, Guidonia
Plate 27

Giacomo Balla—Eight modifiers, 1914
56 × 56 cm
Collection of Laura Biagiotti, Guidonia
Plate 28

Giacomo Balla—Project for a fan, 1918
Lacquer on paper, 39 × 50 cm
Collection of Laura Biagiotti, Guidonia
Plate 29

Giacomo Balla—Study for a modifier, 1914
Tempera on paper, 11 × 33 cm
Collection of Laura Biagiotti, Guidonia
Plate 30

Giacomo Balla—Project for a dress, 1928–1929
Tempera and india ink on paper, 22.2 × 15.7 cm
Collection of Laura Biagiotti, Guidonia
Plate 31

Giacomo Balla—Project for a swimming suit, ca. 1930
Watercolor on paper, 19 × 13.5 cm
Collection of Laura Biagiotti, Guidonia
Plate 32

Giacomo Balla—*The Conversation,* 1934
Oil on canvas, 92 × 106 cm
Collection of Laura Biagiotti, Guidonia
Plate 33

Giacomo Balla—Project for scarves, 1918–1925
Tempera on paper, 68 × 27 cm, 38 × 18.5 cm, 38 × 19.5 cm, 38 × 19 cm, 254 × 67 cm, 114 × 61 cm
Collection of Laura Biagiotti, Guidonia
Plate 34

Tullio Crali—Projects for men's clothes, 1932
Pencil, india ink, and watercolor on paper, 29 × 34 cm
Collection of the artist, Milan
Plate 35

Tullio Crali—Projects for men's suit and shirt, 1932
Watercolor and india ink on paper, 33 × 25 cm
Collection of the artist, Milan
Plate 36

Tullio Crali—Project for a dress, 1932
Watercolor on paper, 28 × 19 cm
Collection of the artist, Milan
Plate 37

Tullio Crali—Project for men's suits, 1932
Watercolor on paper, 29 × 34 cm
Collection of the artist, Milan
Plate 38

Tullio Crali—Project for a dress, 1932
Tempera on paper, 31 × 32 cm
Collection of the artist, Milan
Plate 39

Tullio Crali—Projects for dresses, 1932–1933
Tempera on paper, 31 × 22 cm, 32 × 23 cm, 32 × 23 cm, 31 × 23 cm
Collection of the artist, Milan
Plate 40

Tullio Crali—Projects for dresses, 1932–1933
Tempera on paper, 31 × 23 cm, 29 × 19 cm, 30 × 20 cm, 30 × 20 cm
Collection of the artist, Milan
Plate 41

Sonia Delaunay—Jacket, 1923
Wool and silk, 69 × 50 cm
Union française des Arts et du Costume, Paris
Plate 42

Sonia Delaunay—Coat "Autumn Leaves," later transformed into a curtain
Union française des Arts et du Costume, Paris
Plate 43

Sonia Delaunay wearing her jacket, 1923
Wool and silk
Union française des Arts et du Costume, Paris
Plate 44

Sonia Delaunay—Projects for dresses, 1924–1925
Stencils, 56 × 38 cm
Drawn for *Sonia Delaunay: Ses peintures, ses objets, ses tissus simultanés, ses modes* (Paris, [1925])
Museum für Gestaltung, Zurich, Graphics, Collection
Plate 45

Sonia Delaunay—Project for a swimming suit, 1928
Watercolor, 27 × 20 cm
Collection of Eric and Jean-Louis Delaunay, Paris
Plate 46

Adaskina, Natalia. "Constructivist Fabrics and Dress Design." *Journal of Decorative and Propaganda Arts,* no. 5 (summer 1987): 144–159.

Anderson, Mark M. *Kafka's Clothes: Ornament and Aestheticism in the Habsburg Fin de Siècle.* Oxford, 1992.

Aubry, Françoise. "Henry van de Velde ou la négation de la mode." *Revue de l'Institut de Sociologie* (Brussels) 1, no. 2 (1977): 293–306.

Bell, Quentin. *On Human Finery.* London, 1947.

Benhamou, Viviana. "Ernesto Thayaht (1893–1959): Nouvelles perspectives." In *Europe 1910–1939: Quand l'art habillait le vêtement.* Paris, 1997.

Blanc, Charles. *L'art dans la parure et le vêtement.* Paris, 1875.

Boehn, Max von. *Bekleidungkunst und Mode.* Munich, 1918.

Bourdieu, Pierre. *Distinction: A Social Critique of the Judgement of Taste.* Translated by Richard Nice. Cambridge, Mass., 1987. Originally published as *La distinction: Critique sociale du jugement* (Paris, 1979).

Bowlt, John E. "Constructivism and Early Soviet Fashion Design." In *Bolshevik Culture,* edited by Abbott Gleason, Peter Kenez, and Richard Stites. Bloomington, Ind., 1985.

———. "From Pictures to Textile Prints." *Print Collector Newsletter* 7, no. 1 (March–April 1976): 16–29.

Bowman, Sara. *A Fashion for Extravagance: Art Deco Fabrics and Fashions.* New York, 1985.

Brauer, Gerda. "Der Künstler ist seiner innersten Essenz nach glühende Individualist: Henry van de Veldes Beiträge zur Reformierung des Krefelden Industrie Grenzen einer Geverbeförderung durch Kunst." In *Henry van de Velde Henry: Ein europaischer Künstler seiner Zeit,* edited by Klaus-Jürgen Sembach and Birgit Schulte. Cologne, 1992.

Braun, Emily. "Futurist Fashion: Three Manifestoes." *Art Journal* 54, no. 1 (spring 1995): 34–41.

Breward, Christopher. "Manliness, Modernity, and the Shaping of Male Clothing." In *Body Dressing,* edited by Joanne Entwistle and Elizabeth Wilson. Oxford, 2001.

Buck, Anne. "John Ruskin and Dress, 1882." *Costume* 32 (1998): 80–81.

Buckberrough, Sherry A. *Sonia Delaunay: A Retrospective.* Buffalo, N.Y., 1980.

Buckley, Cheryl, and Hilary Fawcett. *Fashioning the Feminine: Representation and Women's Fashion from the Fin de Siècle to the Present.* London, 2002.

Carlano, Marianne. "Wild and Waxy: Dutch Art Nouveau Artistic Dress." *Art Journal* 54, no. 1 (spring 1995).

Cohen, Arthur A. *Sonia Delaunay.* New York, 1975.

Crispolti, Enrico. "Balla beyond Painting: The 'Futurist Reconstruction' of Fashion." In *Balla: Futurismo tra arte e moda: Opere della Fondazione Biagiotti Cigna,* edited by Fabio Benzi. Milan, 1998.

———. *Il Futurismo e la moda: Balla e gli altri.* Venice, 1986.

———. "The 'Futurist Reconstruction' of Fashion." In *Art/Fashion,* edited by Germano Celant, Ingrid Sischy, and Pandora Tabatai Asbachi. New York, 1997.

Cunningham, Patricia A. "Classical Revivals in Dress." In *Fashioning the Future: Our Future from the Past.* Columbus, Ohio, 1996.

———. *Reforming Fashion, 1850–1914: Politics, Health, and Art.* Columbus, Ohio, 2000.

Damase, Jacques. *Sonia Delaunay: Rythmes et couleurs.* Paris, 1971.

Davis, Fred. *Fashion, Culture, and Identity.* Chicago, 1992.

Doherty, Brigid. "Fashionable Ladies, Dada Dandies." *Art Journal* 54, no. 1 (spring 1995): 46–50.

Douglas, Charlotte. "Suprematist Embroidered Ornament." *Art Journal* 54, no. 1 (spring 1995): 42–45.

Eisler, Max. *Dagobert Peche.* 1925. Reprint, Vienna, 1992.

Ewing, Elizabeth. *History of Twentieth Century Fashion.* London, 1974.

Fagiolo dell'Arco, Maurizio. "'Fiat Modes Pereat Ars' or Surrealism and Fashion." In *Art/Fashion,* edited by Germano Celant,

Ingrid Sischy, and Pandora Tabatai Asbaghi. New York, 1997.

Filin-Yeh, Susan, ed. *Dandies: Fashion and Finesse in Art and Culture.* New York, 2001.

Fischer, Gayle V. *Pantaloons and Power: A Nineteenth-Century Dress Reform in the United States.* Kent, Ohio, 2001.

Fischer, Wolfgang Georg. *Gustav Klimt and Emilie Flöge: The Artist and His Muse.* Translated by Michael Robinson, New York, 1982.

Fontanel, Beatrice. *Support and Seduction: The History of Corsets and Bras.* New York, 2001.

Fortassier, Rose. *Les écrivains français et la mode: De Balzac à nos jours.* Paris, 1988.

Friedl, Bettina. "Fashion and/as Art: Dress as Artistic Expression in Modernism." In Transatlantic Modernism, edited by Martin Klepper and Joseph C. Schöpp. Heidelberg, 2001.

Gautier, Theophilus. *Fashion.* Paris, 1858. Originally published as Théophile Gautier, *De la mode* (Paris, 1858).

Guillaume, Valérie. "Les artistes russes à Paris et la Mode." In *Europe 1910–1939: Quand l'art habillait le vêtement.* Paris, 1997.

Hansen, Traude. *Wiener Werkstätte: Mode, Stoffe, Schmuck, Accessoires.* Vienna, 1984.

Hollander, Anne. *Seeing through Clothes.* New York, 1975.

———. *Sex and Suits: The Evolution of Modern Dress.* New York, 1995.

Hüter, Karl Heinz. *Henry van de Velde: Sein Werk zum Ende seiner Tätigkeit in Deutschland.* Berlin, 1967.

Kallir, Jane. *Viennese Design and the Wiener Werkstätte.* New York, 1986.

Kiaer, Christina. "Les objets quotidiens du constructivisme russe." *Les Cahiers du Musée National d'art moderne,* no. 64 (summer 1998): 31–69.

———. "The Russian Constructivist Flapper Dress." *Critical Inquiry* 28, no. 1 (autumn 2001): 185–243.

Krabbe, Wolfgang. *Gesellschafts-Veränderung durch Lebensreform: Merkmale einer Sozialreformatorischen Bewegung in Deutschland der Industrialisierung-Période.* Göttingen, 1974.

Kunzle, David. *Fashion and Fetishism: A Social History of the Corset and Other Forms of Body-Sculpture in the West.* Totowa, N.J., 1982.

Lapini, Lia, Carlo V. Menichi, and Silvia Porto, eds. *Abiti e costumi futuristi.* Pistoia, 1985.

Laver, James. *Modesty in Dress: An Inquiry into the Fundamentals of Fashion.* London, 1969.

Lavrentiev, Alexandre. "Minimalisme et création textile ou l'origine de la mode constructiviste." In *Europe 1910–1939: Quand l'art habillait le vêtement.* Paris, 1997.

———. *Varvara Stepanova: A Constructivist Life.* Edited and introduced by John E. Bowlt. London, 1988.

Lehmann, Ulrich. *Tigersprung: Fashion in Modernity.* Cambridge, Mass., 2000.

Lemaire, Claude. "Abandon, grâce, souplesse." In *Art Nouveau Belgique.* Brussels, 1980.

Lipovetsky, Gilles. *The Empire of Fashion: Dressing modern democracy.* Translated by Catherine Porter. Princeton, 1994. Originally published as *L'empire de l'éphémère: La mode et son destin dans les sociétés modernes* (Paris, 1987).

Lista, Giovanni. "La mode futuriste." In *Europe 1910–1939: Quand l'art habillait le vêtement.* Paris, 1997.

Magron, Louis. *Le Romantisme et la mode: D'après des documents inédits.* Paris, 1911.

Mahn, Gabriele. "Autour de Sophie Tauber et Johannes Itten." In *Europe 1910–1939: Quand l'art habillait le vêtement.* Paris, 1997.

Marly, Diana de. *The History of Haute Couture, 1850–1950.* London, 1980.

Martin, Richard. *Cubism and Fashion.* New York, 1998.

———. "Dress and Dream: The Utopian Idealism of Clothing." *Arts Magazine* 62, no. 2 (October 1987): 58–60.

———. *Fashion and Surrealism.* New York, 1987.

McLeod, Mary. "Undressing Architecture: Fashion, Gender, and Modernity." In *Architecture: In Fashion,* edited by Deborah Fausch, Paulette Singley, Rudolphe El Khoury, and Zvi Efrat. New York, 1994.

Moers, Ellen. *The Dandy: Brummell to Beerbohm.* London, 1960.

Mohrbutter, Alfred. *Das Kleid der Frau.* Darmstadt, 1903.

———. *Das künstlerische Kleid der Frau.* Leipzig, 1904.

Montague, Ken. "The Aesthetics of Hygiene: Aesthetic Dress, Modernity, and the Body as Sign." *Journal of Design History* 7, no. 2 (summer 1994): 91–112.

Morano, Elizabeth. *Sonia Delaunay: Art into Fashion.* Foreword by Diana Vreeland. New York, 1986.

Muthesius, Anna. *Das Eigenkleid der Frau.* Krefeld, 1903.

Newton, Stella Mary. *Health, Art, and Reason: Dress Reformers of the Nineteenth Century.* London, 1974.

Noever, Peter, ed. *Dagobert Peche und die Wiener Werkstätte: Die Überwindlung der Utilität.* Stuttgart, 1998.

Ormond, Leonée. "Dress in the Painting of Dante Gabriel Rossetti." *Costume* 8 (1974): 26–29.

———. "Female Costume in the Aesthetic Movement of the 1870's and 1880's." *Costume,* Vol. 1 and 2 (1967–1968): 47–52; 33–38.

Partsch, Susanna. *Gustav Klimt: Painter of Women.* Munich, 1994.

Pudor, Heinrich. *Die Reformkleidung.* Leipzig, 1904.

Quattordio, Alessandra. "Moda e aerogioielli." In *Crali aeropittore futurista.* Milan, 1987.

Radford, Robert. "Art and Fashion, a Love Affair or a Shoot Out? An Application of Lipovetsky's Cultural Theory of the Ephemeral." *Issues in Architecture, Art, and Design* 3, no. 2 (1994): 82–94.

———. "Dangerous Liaisons: Art, Fashion, and Individualism." *Fashion Theory: The Journal of Dress, Body, and Culture* 2, no. 2 (1998): 151–164.

Recklies, Karen Adele. "Fashion behind the Footlights: The Influence of Stage Costumes on Women's Fashion in England from 1878–1914." Ph.D. diss., Ohio State University, 1982.

Risselin, Marie. "La mode et l'art textile." In *Henry van de Velde, 1863–1957.* Brussels, 1963.

Rücker, Elisabeth. *Wiener Charme: Mode 1914/15. Graphiken und Accessoires.* Nuremberg, 1984.

Schaffer, Talia. *The Forgotten Female Aesthetics: Literary Culture in Late-Victorian England.* Charlottesville, Va., 2000.

Schneider Maunoury, Monique. "Sonia Delaunay: The Clothing of Modernity." In *Art/Fashion,* edited by Germano Celant, Ingrid Sischy, and Pandora Tabatai Asbaghi. New York, 1997.

Schulte, Birgit. "Ich bin diese Frau, die um jeden Preis Ihr Glück will . . . Maria Sèthe und H. van de Velde—eine biographischen Studie." In *Henry van de Velde: Ein europaischer Künstler seiner Zeit,* edited by Klaus-Jürgen Sembach and Birgit Schulte. Cologne, 1992.

Schultze-Naumburg, Paul. *Die Kultur des weiblichen Körpers als Grundlage der Frauenkleidung.* Leipzig, 1903.

Schweiger, Werner J. *Wiener Werkstätte: Kunst und Handwerk 1903–1932.* Vienna, 1982.

Simmons, Sherwin. "Expressionism in the Discourse of Fashion." *Fashion Theory: The Journal of Dress, Body, and Culture* 4, no. 1 (2000): 49–87.

Sonia Delaunay: ses peintures, ses objets, ses tissus simultanés, ses modes. Introduction by André Lhote. Paris [1925].

Stamm, Birgit. "Auf dem Werk zum Reformkleid—Die Kritik des Korsetts und der diktierend Mode." In *Kunst und Alltag,* edited by Ekkard Siepmann. Giessen, 1978.

Steele, Valerie. *The Corset: A Social History.* New Haven, 2001.

———. *Fashion and Eroticism: Ideals of Feminine Beauty from the Victorian Era to the Jazz Age.* New York, 1985.

———. *Paris Fashion: A Cultural History.* Oxford, 1988.

Steiner, Ulrike. "Die Frau im modernen Kleid: Emilie Flöge und die Lebensreform-Bewegung."

In *Gegenwelten: Gustav Klimt-Künstlerleben im Fin de Siècle.* Munich, 1996.

Stern, Radu. *Gegen den Strich: Kleider von Künstlern/A Contre-Courant: Vêtements d'artistes, 1900–1940.* Bern, 1992.

———. "'Ni vers le nouveau, ni vers l'ancien, mais vers ce qui est nécessaire': Tatline et le problème du vêtement." In *Europe 1910–1939: Quand l'art habillait le vêtement.* Paris, 1997.

Thiel, Erika. *Künstler und Mode.* Berlin, 1979.

Thönnissen. "Bauhaus-Tracht-Mythos oder Realität." In *Künstler ziehen an: Avantgarde-Mode in Europa 1910–1939,* edited by Gisela Framke. Dortmund, 1998.

Troy, Nancy J. "The Logic of Fashion." *Journal of the Decorative Arts Society,* no. 19 (1995): 1–7.

Veblen, Thorstein. *The Theory of the Leisure Class.* 1899. Reprint, New York, 2001.

Velde, Henry van de. *Aperçus en vue d'une Synthèse d'Art,* Brussels, 1895.

———. *Les Mémoires inachevés d'un artiste européen,* Edited by Léon Ploegaerts. Brussels, 1999.

———. "Première prédication de l'Art." *L'Art Moderne* 13, no. 53 (December 1893).

Velde, Marie van de. *Album moderner, nach Künstler-Entwürfen ausgeführter Damenkleider.* Düsseldorf, 1900.

———. "Sonderausstellung moderner Damenkostüme." *Die Kunst* 4, no. 1 (1901).

Völcker, Angela. "Kleiderkunst und Reformmode im Wien der Jahrhudertwende." In *Ornament und Askese,* edited by Alfred Pfabigan. Vienna, 1986.

———. "Kleiderreform, Künstlerkleid und Mode." In *Drüber und Drunter: Wiender Damenmode von 1900–1914.* Vienna, 1987.

———. *Wiener Mode und Modephotographie: Die Mode-abteilung der Wiener Werkstätte 1911–1932.* Munich, 1984.

Welsch, Sabine. *Ein Austieg dem Korsett: Reformkleidung um 1900.* Darmstadt, 1996.

Wigley, Mark. *White Walls, Designer Dresses: The Fashioning of Modern Architecture.* Cambridge, Mass., 1995.

Wilckens, Leonie von. "Künstlerkleid und Reformkleid. Textilkunst in Nürnberg." In *Peter Behrens und Nürnberg.* Munich, 1988.

Wilson, Elizabeth. *Adorned in Dreams: Fashion and Modernity.* Berkeley, 1987.

Wollen, Peter, ed. *Addressing the Century: 100 Years of Art and Fashion.* London, 1999.

Zalambani, Maria. "L'art dans la production: Le débat sur le productivisme en Russie soviétique pendant les années vingt." *Annales* 52, no. 1 (January–February 1997): 41–61.

Zaletova, Lidya, Fabio Ciofi degli Atti and Franco Panzini, eds., *Costume Revolution: Textiles, Clothing, and Costume of the Soviet Union in the Twenties.* London, 1989.

INDEX

Aestheticism, 5, 8, 9
Aesthetic Movement, 9
Aglaia, 7, 105
Americanism, 53
Antifashion, 3, 4, 5, 8, 9, 14, 15, 22, 29, 30, 32, 48, 51, 65, 124–125, 128, 136, 138, 172, 174
Antineutral, 32, 37, 157–159, 162
Apollinaire, Guillaume, 65, 66, 181
Armstrong, Thomas, 7
Art, 45, 183
  and clothing, 6, 178–179
  and fashion, 2, 3
Artistic dress, 19, 20, 22, 40, 137
Arts and Crafts, 5, 11, 14, 15
Arts décoratifs, 148–149
Arvatov, Boris, 53
Ashbee, Charles Robert, 24

Bahr, Hermann, 23
Bakst, Léon, 184–185
Bal Boullier, 63, 65, 68
Balla, Elica, 30
Balla, Giacomo, 29–40, 41, 155, 162
Balla, Luce, 39
Ballets Russes, 184, 185
Baranoff-Rossiné, Vladimir, 64
Baudelaire, Charles, 2, 3, 120
Beauty, 2, 3, 5, 9, 11, 19, 20, 26, 49, 115, 118, 120, 121, 133, 139, 140, 144
Behrens, Peter, 19, 23, 140
Beliaeva-Ekzempliiarskaia, Sofia, 58
Bell, Vanessa, 10
Bernhardt, Sarah, 112
Bloemenwerf, 11, 20
Bloomer, Amelia, 5, 26, 82, 119
Bloomerism, 14
Bloomsbury, 10
Blount, Godfrey and Ethel, 5
Boccioni, Umberto, 29, 37
Bogdanov, Aleksandr, 48
Bosso, Renato di, 40, 170
Botticelli, Sandro, 26
Bourdieu, Pierre, 2
Bourke-White, Margaret, 56
Brauchitsch, Margarete von, 17, 137
Braun, Emily, 30
Brauner, Victor, 67
Breus, C., 142
Brik, Osip, 45
Brinkmann, Justus, 15
Burne-Jones, Edward, 106

Cangiullo, Francesco, 37
Carlyle, Thomas, 181
Carpenter, Edward, 5
Carrà, Carlo, 29, 37, 42
Cendrars, Blaise, 63, 64, 65, 67, 182
Century Guild, 24
Cézanne, Paul, 184
Chashnik, Ilia, 62
Clothing, 47, 172
  as art, 4
  and the body, 8
Constructivist, 22, 37, 45, 48, 56, 178
Corpechot, Lucien, 37
Corra, Bruno, 30
Corset, 7, 111, 128, 142, 144, 146, 149
Crali, Tulio, 40–42
Crane, Walter, 25, 105
Cravan, Arthur, 64
Crevel, René, 67
Crinoline, 4, 5, 7, 84, 93, 113
Crispolti, Enrico, 29, 37, 42
Cubist, 10, 37, 59, 63, 65
Cunard, Nancy, 68

Darwin, Charles, 129–130
Darwin, George, 20, 96, 129–130
Delacroix, Eugène, 183
Delaunay, Robert, 63–68, 181, 185
Delaunay, Sonia, 55, 63–68, 181, 183
Delteil, Jacques, 67
Deneken, Friedrich, 15, 137, 143
Depero, Fortunato, 32, 40
Deutsche Werkbund, 22
Devéria, Eugéne, 4
Diaghilev, Aleksei, 67
Distinction, 2
Doucet, Jacques, 63
Dress
  as art, 4, 7, 9, 17, 19, 29, 82–83, 106, 125–126, 138–139, 150, 184
  ideal, 115
  reform of, 8, 15, 19, 22, 25, 26, 56, 57, 63, 80, 82, 138, 142, 144, 146
Dufy, Raoul, 184, 185
Du Maurier, George, 9
Dürer, Albert, 9

Eckmann, Otto, 144
Eigenkleid, 20, 23, 25, 57, 122–124, 132–133, 143, 145
Eisenstein, Sergei, 52
Eurocentrism, 2
Exter, Aleksandra, 56, 58, 178

Fashion, 2, 3, 5, 6, 7, 8, 15, 19, 22, 29, 48, 80,
  82, 126, 150, 151, 152, 164–165
  and art, 5, 29, 84, 87, 88, 89, 94, 96, 99, 100,
  111, 119, 125, 127, 186
  and change, 2, 3, 5, 6, 7, 29, 92, 126–127,
  136, 185
  immorality of, 13–14, 132
  influence of painting on, 183–185
  mercantile nature of, 6, 126
Fedorov-Davydov, Aleksei, 53, 54
Feminists, 5, 14, 19
Filippov, Aleksei, 46
Flöge, Emilie, 23
Foà, Giacomo, 37
Fon-Meck, Vladimir, 55
Fry, Roger, 10
Functional, 5, 7, 174, 177, 178
Functionalism, 22
Futurism, 29–44, 63, 155–166

G (Constructivist magazine), 22
Gan, Aleksei, 45
Gauthier, Théophile, 4
Germany, 11, 13, 22, 138–139, 145–147,
  151
Gesamtkunstwerk, 13, 20, 23, 24, 26
Gestalt, 58
Gilbert and Sullivan, 9
GINKhUK, 48
Ginna, Arnaldo, 30
Godwin, E. W., 6, 9, 83, 113, 115, 117
Gómez de la Serna, Ramón, 67
Greek, 8, 87, 106, 113, 117, 120, 129, 146
Grosvenor Gallery, 9
Guild of Handicraft, 24

Haas-Heye, Otto Ludwig, 22
Hamnett, Nina, 10
Harberton, Florence, 7
Harris, Frank, 8
Haslemere Peasant Industries, 5
Hausmann, Raoul, 22
Haweis, Mary Elisa, 5, 8, 20
Healthy and Artistic Dress Society, 7
Heim, Jacques, 68
Hermann, Curt, 17, 137
Hitler, Adolf, 53, 54
Hoffmann, Josef, 23
Holiday, Henry, 7
Hunt, William Holman, 7
Huyshe, Wentworth, 113, 114, 115–119
Hygienic, 50, 51
Hygienists, 5, 8, 14, 19, 113

Impressionists, 183
INKhUK, 45
Iribe, Paul, 63

Jugendstil, 22

Kandinsky, Wassily, 19, 23, 58, 67
Kerzhentsev, Platon, 47
King, Emily M., 7
Klimt, Gustav, 23
Koch, Alexander, 137
Koenig, Helena, 40
Kraft-Ebbing, Richard, 142
Kropotkin, Pyotr, 47
Kruger, Franz August Otto, 17, 137, 144
Künstlerkleid, 19, 20, 22, 23, 26, 133,
  138, 143

Lamanova, Nadezhda, 56, 58, 174, 177
Lambourne, Lionel, 7
Lang, Marie, 142
Lavrentiev, Aleksandr, 52
Le Corbusier, 30
LEF, 45, 48, 173
Lenin, Vladimir, 53
Lepape, Georges, 63
Liberty, Arthur Lasenby, 9
Lipovetsky, Gilles, 2, 30
Loos, Alfred, 13, 24
Löwenstein, Grethel, 30
Luther, Martin, 8

Mackmurdo, Arthur, 24
Magron, Louis, 4
Malevich, Kazimir, 59–62
Marinetti, Benedetta, 41
Marinetti, Filippo, 29, 32, 34, 37, 40, 66, 157,
  162, 164
Martin, Darwin D., 13
Martin, Isabella, 13
Marx, Karl, 46
Matisse, Henri, 184
Merrifield, Mary, 5
Meyerhold, Vsevolod, 52
Michahelles, Ruggero, 44, 167
Michelangelo, 29
Middle Ages, 155
Miklashevski, Konstantin, 51
Mode-abteilung, 24, 25–26
Modehaus Alfred-Marie, 22
Modernity, 2, 29, 120
Modifiers, 32, 37, 155, 158
Moholy-Nagy, László, 42

Mohrbutter, Alfred, 20, 22, 137, 143, 144, 145
Monarchi, Francesco, 162
Montaigne, 111
More, Thomas, 48
Morris, Jane, 5, 7
Morris, William, 5, 8, 11, 13, 106, 125
Moser, Koloman, 23
Münter, Gabrielle, 19
Mussolini, Benito, 53
Muthesius, Anna, 22, 145, 146
Muthesius, Hermann, 22

Oliphant, Margaret, 5
Omega Workshops, 10
Original, 122–123
Orphism, 181
Orphist, 65
Orwell, George, 48, 53
Osthaus, Karl Heinz, 13

Pal, Siddy, 142
Pankok, Bernhard, 17, 137, 144
Peche, Dagobert, 27
Pictopetry, 67
Poiret, Paul, 56, 63,
Popova, Liubov, 51, 52, 55, 56
Prampolini, Enrico, 162
Pre-Raphaelites, 5, 14, 106, 129
Productivists, 45–46, 48–49, 54, 55, 56, 59
Prozodezhda, 51, 52, 53, 57, 59, 172, 177,
    178–179
Punch, 9

Rational Dress Society, 7, 15
Rauecker, Bruno, 22
Red House, 11
Reich, Lilly, 22, 151
Rembrandt, 120
Renaissance, 7, 155, 183
Reynolds, Joshua, 120
Riemerschmid, Richard, 17, 137, 144
Robe-poème, 67
Robe simultanée, 65, 68
Rodchenko, Aleksandr, 42, 45
Roller, Alfred, 141
Romantic, 155
Romanticism, 4, 5
Rossetti, Dante Gabriel, 7, 106
Royal Academy, 9
Rozanova, Olga, 60
Rücker, Elisabeth, 23
Ruskin, John, 5, 7, 8, 11, 125
Russolo, Luigi, 29, 37

Sallon des XX, 11
Sartor Resartus, 181
Scavini, Ettore, 40
Schauta, Friedrich, 142
Schultze-Naumburg, Paul, 137, 138, 144
Scurto, Ignazio, 40, 170
Secession, 23
Sèthe, Maria (van de Velde), 13, 137
Severini, Gino, 29, 65
Siddal, Elisabeth, 7
Simultaneism, 63, 66
Sitte, Mino delle, 40, 44
Snischek, Max, 27
Somenzi, Mino, 162
Soupault, Philippe, 67
Spetsodezhda, 51, 52, 53, 172
Sport, 53–54
Sportodezhda, 51, 172
Stalin, Josef, 53
Stanton, Elizabeth Cady, 80
Stepanova, Varvara, 45, 51–55, 56, 57, 172
Stites, Richard, 47, 51
Sukhovo-Kobylin, Aleksandr, 52
Suprematism, 59–62
Swanson, Gloria, 68
Synthetic clothes, 40, 167–169

Tarabukin, Nikolai, 45
Tatlin, Vladimir, 48–51, 58
Taylorism, 50, 51
Terry, Ellen, 7
Thayaht, Ernesto, 42, 164, 167
Tissu-patron, 68, 185
Titian, 29
Toulouse-Lautrec, Henri, 13
Tretiakov, Sergei, 48
Trotsky, Leon, 55
Tugenkhold, Iakov, 59
Tuta, 42–44
Tzara, Tristan, 67

Ugliness, 7, 8, 84, 94, 118, 133
Urkleid, 23

Van der Velde, Henry, 6, 11, 13, 17–20, 23, 24,
    125, 137, 140, 145
Van der Woude, Hugo, 17, 137, 144
Veblein, Thorstein, 2
La Veillée des anges, 11
Verein für die Ver-besserung der Frauenklei-
    dung, 15
Vionnet, Madeleine, 44
Volt, 30, 40, 160

Walden, Herwarth, 22
Watts, George Frederic, 7, 8
Webb, Philip, 11
Whistler, James, 9, 120–121
Wiener Werkstätte, 23–28
Wilde, Oscar, 7–9, 111, 113, 115
Wimmer-Wisgrill, Eduard, 24, 26–27, 148
Wright, Frank Lloyd, 13

Zamiatin, Yevgeny, 48
Zell, Marianne, 27
Zuckerkandl, Bertha, 26